AMY SYMINGTON

THE
LONG TABLE
COOKBOOK

**Plant-based Recipes
for Optimal Health**

Douglas & McIntyre

Douglas and McIntyre (2013) Ltd.
P.O. Box 219, Madeira Park, BC, V0N 2H0
www.douglas-mcintyre.com

Recipe development by Amy Symington, Christine
    Song, Kelly-Anne Kerrigan, Bronwyn Cawker,
    Tamara Saslove
Nutritional information compiled by Amy
    Symington and the cookbook team
Research consulting by Jaime Slavin, RD
Recipe styling by Nancy Midwicki and Heather
    Shaw, photography by Darren Kemper
Edited by Nicola Goshulak
Indexed by Nicola Goshulak
Cover and text design by Setarah Ashrafologhalai

Printed and bound in Canada

Douglas and McIntyre (2013) Ltd. acknowledges
the support of the Canada Council for the Arts,
which last year invested $153 million to bring the
arts to Canadians throughout the country.

*Nous remercions le Conseil des arts du Canada de
son soutien. L'an dernier, le Conseil a investi 153
millions de dollars pour mettre de l'art dans la vie des
Canadiennes et des Canadiens de tout le pays.*

We also gratefully acknowledge financial support
from the Government of Canada and from the
Province of British Columbia through the BC Arts
Council and the Book Publishing Tax Credit.

LIBRARY AND ARCHIVES CANADA
CATALOGUING IN PUBLICATION

Title: The long table cookbook : plant-based
recipes for optimal health / Amy Symington.

Names: Symington, Amy, 1982- author.

Description: Includes bibliographical
references and index.

Identifiers: Canadiana (print) 20190127767 |
Canadiana (ebook) 20190127775 |
ISBN 9781771622271

(softcover) | ISBN 9781771622288 (HTML)

Subjects: LCSH: Vegetarian cooking. |
LCSH: Cooking (Natural foods) |
LCSH: Entertaining. | LCGFT: Cookbooks.

Classification: LCC TX837 .S96 2019 | DDC
641.5/636—dc23

For Sharon Helps-Symington

Contents

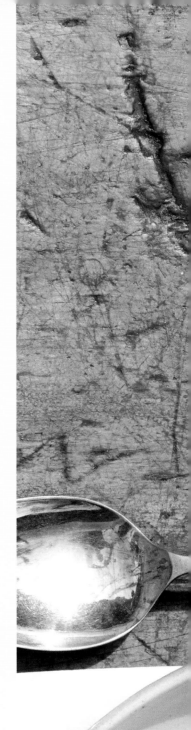

Preface

CHEF AMY SYMINGTON demonstrates perfectly that eating nutritiously is not about eliminating the dishes we love, but adapting them with subtle changes, using healthy fresh local ingredients. The theme that forms the core of this cookbook resonates with me; the idea of taking the time to eat and share homemade, nutritious meals with friends and family is something I believe in. This guide reinforces and teaches us all that the simple act of sharing and breaking bread together not only improves the family bond but can create significant benefits for your health.

CHEF LYNN CRAWFORD

Introduction

AM SITTING NOW at my childhood dining table—an antique oak table that came from my family farm in southwestern Ontario, and the place where my eating and food career began. The table was always packed with fluffy pancakes, goods from the garden, Mom's meatloaf, the local church ladies' pot pies and Grandma Symington's butter tarts, and surrounded by family. This table was the centre of our family life, including all of our important meals—from our weekly Sunday breakfast spread (compliments of my baloney-frying, pancake-flipping father) to family celebrations—as well as difficult conversations and celebrations of loved ones lost.

We were a busy household, between my mom's school and community work, my dad's farm chores and my brother's hockey practices, but we always made time to sit, eat and share together. As for me, I lived for cooking shows and baking with my grandmother, and from the age of 15 worked my legs off in kitchens, diners and dining halls to fund my education.

For me, the family table was an early introduction to the benefits of eating together. These days, the idea of long table eating, or sharing a communal meal with a large and varied group of people, is experiencing a resurgence, as restaurateurs and community event planners begin to recognize the many ways this longstanding tradition is good for us.

My family's table could always stretch to accommodate more family members, friends and new acquaintances, and after my mother was diagnosed with cancer it often welcomed nurses, volunteer nurses, personal support workers and ministers, as well as friends and family members. This to me is the essence of what a long-table meal means: people coming together who may or may not know one another, sitting down and sharing a wholesome, slow-cooked meal.

After losing my mother to breast cancer, I was inspired to learn more about cancer nutrition, so after completing my culinary nutrition studies I pursued a master's degree in applied human nutrition. I am now a plant-based chef, nutrition professor and research associate at a George Brown College. I also work with a not-for-profit cancer organization called Gilda's Club Greater Toronto, running their culinary nutrition programming, including nutrition workshops to support members in following a healthy anti-cancer diet. Growing up I excelled at math, science and the arts, and was always interested in baking, cooking and nutrition, so perhaps I would've ended up where I am today anyway, but there is no question that my mother's death sped up this outcome exponentially. I was determined to learn more, share my knowledge far and wide, and help others in similarly life-changing scenarios. And perhaps even spread a little of the heartwarming joy and sense of belonging that my mother often left people with.

In all of my work, my mission is to share with others how they can improve their diets to prevent or manage chronic disease, particularly cancer. I also appreciate how important social and emotional support can be in optimizing health and managing disease. In particular, social relationships and interactions, like preparing and eating meals together, with loved ones or even new friends, in a family-style setting not only provides health benefits, but promotes mental well-being as well. These types of support networks are not necessarily available to all; unfortunately my mother did not have access to such social, emotional and nutritional support resources. But I now know first-hand how much positive impact they can have, and that is why I advocate for them.

At Gilda's Club, I run a supper club program twice a week with a team of wonderful volunteers. The program feeds a delicious, four-course health-promoting meal to people who have been touched by cancer. We're talking creamy oyster mushroom chowders, crunchy rainbow coleslaws and satisfying stick-to-your-ribs mains like lentil bourguignon pot pies with herbed mushroom gravy, finished with double chocolate black bean brownies topped with coconut cream. Members come, sit and eat together at long tables and share their sometimes difficult, but mostly inspirational, stories. It's a very beautiful thing. The best part for me is that the food is often used as the opening line to deeper conversations.

I came up with idea for *The Long Table Cookbook* as a way to extend this supper club tradition to a wider circle, and make it easier for anyone who is supporting their own health or the health of a loved one to share in delicious and health-promoting community meals. Each recipe is designed to be easy to prepare, focused on simple, whole ingredients and wonderful to eat in the company of family and community.

Since the long table spirit underlies my approach to nutrition, the organization of the recipes is designed to inspire various occasions for a celebratory communal meal. Each themed section comes equipped with suggested four-course menus, or you can mix and match recipes according to your tastes. For each recipe, I've provided directions to cook enough for either a feast or a smaller family gathering, and they are all best served family style at a long table of your choosing.

You will also find that all of the recipes in this book are plant-based: scientific evidence shows that consuming more whole plant-based foods is an integral part of a healthy, disease-preventing diet. To make this easier, I've included some nutritional guidelines describing the advantages of functional, plant-based foods, and show you how to easily incorporate more of these foods into your daily routine. Luckily, plant-based cuisine need not be boring or tasteless—enter my Spicy Chocolate-Dipped Oranges (page 161), Kung Pao Chickpeas over Sesame-Fried Millet (page 151) and Caramelized Fennel, Sweet Potato and Pine Nut Cheese Pizza (page 175).

I like to think of this book as a stress-free guide that translates science-based nutritional information into practical guidelines that anyone can use, even if cooking from scratch or plant-based eating are new to you. In particular, my Foods to Eat table (page 6) and Cooking Fundamentals and Culinary Terminology section (page 25) are designed to make it easier to find and prepare the healthiest foods available to you.

I must also mention that I have been beyond lucky in the creation of this book. The recipe development team and my advisors and supporters have put their hearts and souls into turning my vision into a reality. From the culinary nutrition chefs (including my past students) to dietitians, doctors, editors, food stylists, food prop stylists and photographers, tons of expert knowledge has been poured into this book, for which I am incredibly grateful.

So this is a short version of how you and I ended up here, together at my childhood dining table. I welcome you to learn more about how to feel better through whole plant-based foods, prepared and eaten with those you love. I also want you to know that, while you gain a new repertoire of healthy and delicious meals, you are giving to charity too. I will be donating all of my royalties from this book to Gilda's Club Greater Toronto, to fund their much-needed culinary nutrition programming.

So whether you are a health-conscious foodie hoping to improve your eating habits for disease prevention, someone dealing with or recovering from health issues, or a big-hearted caregiver who wants to make show-stopping, freezable meals, come, sit, eat and share a long table meal with me.

CHEF AMY SYMINGTON

Harnessing Nutrition for Optimal Health

The Benefits of Plant-Based Eating

Nutrition can be a confusing topic that often people find difficult to navigate, and understandably so. We have easy access to a great amount of nutrition information, which is wonderful, but with that information comes a great amount of misinformation regarding lifestyle and diet. This can be quite confusing and frustrating to those serious about improving their health. However, all nutrition experts agree that there are staples in the nutrition and lifestyle advice world that should never vary: drink plenty of water, get enough sleep, exercise regularly and eat plenty of plants.

As people become more aware of the benefits of adopting a healthy diet, plant-based whole food diets and plant-forward eating have steadily increased in popularity. Many now recognize the value of packing more fruits, vegetables, nuts, seeds, legumes, whole grains and good-quality protein into their daily meals and snacks, in an attempt to reduce their risk of developing non-communicable diseases (NCDs).

According to the World Health Organization, NCDs are responsible for 41 million deaths each year, or 71 percent of all deaths worldwide. Cardiovascular diseases account for the majority of NCD deaths, followed by cancers, respiratory diseases and diabetes.[1] However, it may be possible to prevent many of these deaths by changing the lifestyle factors that can lead to them, like inactivity, smoking, alcohol consumption and poor diet. Diet, in particular, has a great influence over decreasing chronic disease risk, increasing longevity and improving quality of life in general.

Since plant-based foods offer a host of nutritional benefits, consuming more of them will increase your intake of beneficial antioxidants, fibre, unsaturated fats, vitamins and minerals and significantly reduce potentially disease-causing inflammation in the body.[2] The advantages of increasing your plant intake range from an increase in energy, clear skin, and ease in weight loss and weight maintenance to more significant long-term effects, including a decrease in your overall risk of high cholesterol, hypertension, stroke, heart disease in general, type 2 diabetes, obesity, hypothyroidism and cancer.[3]

Most whole plant-based foods are what are known as "functional foods"— foods that provide vital health benefits in addition to nutrients. Many contain phytochemicals, which are chemical compounds that help fight off chronic disease. Whole plant-based foods also help maintain stable blood sugar levels, which significantly reduces disease-promoting inflammation in the body.[4] If that wasn't enough, consuming fibre, which is present in fruits, vegetables, nuts, seeds, legumes and whole grains, has been shown to significantly reduce premature death.[5] With all of these factors, the health benefits that emerge from a plant-centric diet are seen time and time again, and have been shown to help prevent and manage the top chronic diseases. And in addition to making you feel better, adopting a plant-based diet will make you feel good about your impact on the environment.

When focusing on fibre-rich foods, your carbon footprint is cut in half by decreasing global greenhouse gas emissions, pollution and deforestation, and less overuse of fossil fuels and water.[6] Once adopted on a broad scale, such changes will significantly aid in decreasing climate change and increase the demand for efficient use of land for feeding the world's population.[7]

The Essential Guide to Eating for Optimal Health

When determining what's for dinner, the focus needs to be on eating more nutrient-dense, high-fibre and phytochemical-filled foods so that the not-so-good-for-us empty-calorie foods are pushed out. Once this focus is in place, you'll increase your chance of obtaining optimal health while reducing your chances of chronic disease, without going hungry or feeling unsatisfied. However, the first step to achieving this focus is knowing what foods should be consumed and why, so you're able to consistently get the good food into your body.

To help make these nutrition guidelines as easy to follow as possible, I've compiled a list of the healthiest foods you can eat, along with information about what makes them so good for you, and suggestions for how they can be incorporated into delicious recipes. The best news is that these foods are both delicious to eat and good for you, so you'll feel great eating them while enjoying the health benefits they offer.

FOODS TO EAT	HEALTH BENEFITS	HOW TO EAT THEM
Allium vegetables: chive, garlic, leek, onion, scallion, shallot	While eating lots of allium vegetables may repel anyone within a close distance, they may also repel bacteria and disease. The pungent smell comes from organosulfur compounds, which have proven favourable as a dietary chemopreventive and tumour inhibitor, with garlic being the strongest. Garlic contains allicin, which is responsible for its odour and antibacterial properties. Garlic has also been studied for its role in managing hypertension, cardiovascular disease and type 2 diabetes. Onions are an abundant source of quercetin, which has been studied for its anti-cancer properties. Allium vegetables also contain inulin, a prebiotic fibre that has been studied for its role in gastric health.	Garlic is best eaten raw to preserve the allicin that is generated when crushing and chopping it. Incorporate it into dips, salsas and salad dressings. Alternatively, roasting garlic gives it a caramelized flavour that is a nice addition to savoury dishes. Onions can be eaten raw in salads or sandwiches and provide an incomparable base of flavour for cooked dishes like stews and soups. Try them out in the following recipes: Watermelon, Mint, Feta and Arugula Salad (page 96) and Traditional Greek Salad with Tofu Feta (page 72).

FOODS TO EAT	HEALTH BENEFITS	HOW TO EAT THEM
Citrus fruits: grapefruit, lemon, lime, orange, pomelo, tangerine	Both the juice and zest of citrus fruits are flavourful additions to your plate. While known for their high vitamin C content, citrus fruits are also a primary source of soluble fibre. They contain nutrients like potassium, folate and calcium and phytochemicals like carotenoids, alkaloids and flavonoids. Grapefruit contains the carotenoid lycopene, which has been studied for its chemopreventive properties. Citrus fruits contain more than sixty kinds of flavonoids that have been studied for their antioxidant and chemopreventive activity. Dietary intake of flavonoids has also been associated with decreased risk of cardiovascular disease, coronary heart disease and total mortality. Grapefruit has been associated with a lower risk of mortality from coronary heart disease. Citrus contains the bioflavonoid hesperidin, which has been studied as a potential anti-inflammatory. The peel of citrus fruits contains the oil d-limonene, which has been studied for its potential role in breast cancer and squamous cell carcinoma prevention.	Citrus is versatile. You can add brightness and acidity to dishes, make a tangy salad dressing, infuse it into drinks and incorporate it into delicious desserts. Yet citrus fruits are best eaten whole to reap the benefits of the soluble fibre they contain. Be sure to wash your citrus fruits before you consume them to minimize pesticide consumption; as for the peels, you can store citrus zest in the freezer to use in future dishes! Try them out in the following recipes: Spicy Chocolate-Dipped Oranges (page 161) and Lavender Lemonade (page 222).
Coconut and coconut oil	The consumption of coconut oil has been called into question in recent times—is it healthy or unhealthy? While the evidence is inconclusive, the fat in coconut oil has a unique composition of medium-chain triglycerides (MCTs). MCTs undergo fast absorption in the intestine, providing easily accessible energy and promoting fullness, which aids in healthy weight maintenance. While MCTs do contain saturated fat, they have been shown to boost HDL cholesterol levels, in addition to LDL and total cholesterol. Coconut oil also contains antibacterial properties, is rich in antioxidants like vitamin E and is stable to cook with at higher temperatures. Raw coconut and coconut flour are also excellent sources of insoluble fibre.	You can use coconut oil as an alternative to butter in baked goods, or as a cooking oil for high-heat temperatures. Use coconut flour as a high-fibre, grain-free flour replacement, and use coconut milk to add creaminess to soups or stews. Try them out in the following recipes: Cinnamon Bun Cookies (page 60) and Creamy Cauliflower and Potato Soup (page 116).
Cruciferous vegetables: arugula, bok choy, broccoli, Brussels sprout, cabbage, cauliflower, collard greens, daikon, horseradish, kale, mustard greens, radish, rapini, wasabi, watercress	Cruciferous vegetables are a powerhouse for disease prevention. Their characteristic bitter taste and aroma comes from sulfur-containing compounds called glucosinolates, which when eaten are broken down into compounds that are believed to contain their health-promoting properties. They also contain carotenoids, fibre and vitamins C, E and K. A high intake of cruciferous vegetables has been associated with reduced risk of cancer, type 2 diabetes, atherosclerosis and total cardiovascular disease mortality.	Eat a variety of raw cruciferous vegetables or use gentle cooking techniques like steaming or stir-frying to preserve their beneficial compounds. When in doubt, load them up in a big salad or serve them on a crudité platter with a tangy dip or dressing. Try them out in the following recipes: Moroccan Quinoa Power Bowl (page 198) and Waldorf Salad with Pomegranate and Pistachio (page 46).
Herbs: basil, bay leaf, cilantro, dill, fennel, lavender, mint, oregano, parsley, rosemary, sage, thyme	Herbs add a punch of flavour to your plate without added salt and contribute antioxidants and flavonoids to the diet. Dietary intake of flavonoids has been associated with decreased risk of cardiovascular disease, coronary heart disease, total mortality, bladder cancer and strokes.	You can buy herbs at the grocery store, or you can easily grow them at home year-round. Finely chop raw herbs to add flavour to any dish or incorporate them into a dip, dressing or pesto. Use dry herbs to increase flavour in cooked dishes without adding unnecessary salt, unhealthy fat or sugar. Try them in the following recipes: Falafel Sliders with Kale Tabbouleh, Spicy Tahini Sauce and Papaya Chutney (page 124) and Creamy Dill and Cannellini Bean Dip (page 172).

FOODS TO EAT	HEALTH BENEFITS	HOW TO EAT THEM
Mushrooms: cremini, king oyster, maitake, portobello, shiitake	Functional mushrooms like chaga, reishi and lion's mane are definitely trendy right now. However, varieties like cremini, king oyster, portobello and shiitake that can be found in your local grocery store are also beneficial to your health. Beta-glucans, glucose polymers found in the cell walls of mushrooms (and also cereal grains and seaweed), have been shown to have anti-carcinogenic properties, and to be a protectant against obesity and metabolic syndrome. Mushrooms also contain fibre, protein, antioxidants, B vitamins, vitamin D, potassium and selenium. Mushrooms have been studied as a potential anti-cancer agent and a protectant from dementia and inflammation.	Mushrooms are great for adding body to dishes and are excellent in soups, stocks, salads, stir-fries and gravies and on the BBQ. Locate them in the produce aisle of your grocery store, or head down to the farmers' market for unique local varieties. Try them out in the following recipes: Okra and Oyster Mushroom Gumbo with Red and White Beans (page 66) and Mushroom and Lentil Shepherd's Pie (page 79).
Nuts: almond, Brazil nut, cashew, hazelnut, macadamia nut, peanut, pecan, pine nut, pistachio, walnut	Nuts are rich in omega-3 fatty acids (particularly found in walnuts), dietary fibre, antioxidants, polyphenols, vitamin E, magnesium and amino acids like L-arginine. L-arginine changes into nitric oxide in the body, which is responsible for helping the blood vessels relax. Plant-derived L-arginine has also been shown to have a cardioprotective effect. Incorporating nuts into your diet has been shown to be beneficial for all-cause mortality, including cardiovascular disease, all cancers, diabetes and respiratory disease. A study found that women who ate three or more servings of nuts per week had a 51 percent lower risk of death, and men had a 16 percent lower risk.	Nuts can be bought at grocery stores and bulk grocers, and are best stored in the freezer to extend their shelf life. They are extremely versatile and can be incorporated into nut-based milks, cheeses, granola, salads and sweets, or eaten raw as a satiating snack. Try them in the following recipes: Lentil and Walnut Tacos with Mango Avocado Salsa (page 213) and Veggie Cannelloni with Cashew Ricotta, Basil Pesto and Parmesan (page 179).
Oils: avocado, grapeseed, olive, safflower, sesame, walnut	When cooking, reach for oils like avocado, grapeseed or sesame, which have higher smoke points and are excellent sources of mono- and polyunsaturated fatty acids, oleic acid and polyphenols. Extra-virgin olive oil is rich in oleic acid, polyphenols and antioxidants. Polyphenols have been shown to reduce morbidity, neurodegenerative disease, cancer, diabetes and cardiovascular disease. A higher intake of olive oil has been associated with lowered risk of all-cause mortality, cardiovascular events and stroke. In another study, those who ate a Mediterranean-style diet supplemented with nuts and extra-virgin olive oil had a lower incidence of cardiovascular disease than those who ate a lower-fat diet. Olive oil intake has also been shown to lower cancer prevalence. Replacing saturated fats with polyunsaturated fats found in vegetable oils reduces the risk of cardiovascular disease. A 2010 review determined that replacing saturated fat with polyunsaturated fat would significantly reduce rates of coronary heart disease. And consumption of polyunsaturated fat and vegetable fat is associated with lower gastric cancer risk.	Olive oil and walnut oil are best eaten in their cold states—salad dressings, a raw drizzle—to preserve their beneficial compounds, and because they have low smoke points. Be on the lookout for extra-virgin olive oil: it is the highest grade because it is processed without the use of chemicals or high heat. Look for oil that is stored in a dark glass bottle, which prevents light from spoiling it, and store it in a cool, dark place. Avocado, grapeseed and safflower oils can withstand higher cooking temperatures without smoking, becoming carcinogenic and consequently introducing free radicals into the body. Store these oils in a cool, dark place to extend their shelf life. Try them in the following recipes: Apple, Fennel and Beet Salad with Orange-Ginger Cider Vinaigrette (page 171) and Warm Farro Salad with Spicy Citrus Dressing (page 129).
Orange vegetables and fruits: apricot, cantaloupe, carrot, grapefruit, mango, nectarine, orange, orange pepper, peach, persimmon, pumpkin, sweet potato, winter squash	The vibrant hue of carrots, squash and sweet potatoes comes from plant pigments called carotenoids. They contain alpha- and beta-carotene, which can be converted into vitamin A in the body. They also contain lutein, fibre and vitamin C. Vitamin A is essential for healthy growth and development, maintaining the immune system, skin health and eye health. A high intake of vitamin A has been associated with a reduced risk of bladder cancer, cervical cancer, lung cancer and cataracts. A diet high in carotenoids has been associated with a reduced risk of oral, pharyngeal and laryngeal cancer, HPV and non-Hodgkin's lymphoma.	Orange vegetables and fruits can be incorporated into a variety of sweet and savoury dishes. Carrots can be eaten raw on a crudité platter, or roasted as a side dish to accompany a meal. Sweet potatoes and squash can be baked, boiled or roasted. Try it out in the following recipes: Butterscotch Squash Coffee Cake (page 57) and Yam and Coconut Curry Soup (page 142).

FOODS TO EAT	HEALTH BENEFITS	HOW TO EAT THEM
Pulses: beans, chickpeas, lentils, peas	Pulses are an incredibly affordable plant-based protein option that is high in fibre, low in saturated fat, cholesterol free and low on the glycemic index. They also contain beneficial nutrients like iron, copper, magnesium, manganese, zinc, phosphorus and B vitamins. Studies have shown that regular consumption of pulses has preventive effects for heart disease through aiding cholesterol management. It has also been shown to reduce the risk of colorectal cancer, prostate cancer and metabolic syndrome.	Cooking pulses from scratch can be time-consuming, but with the popularity of electric pressure cookers, you can cut the cooking time in half! Dried pulses can be bought at grocery stores and at bulk grocers, and are best stored in glass jars in a cool, dark place. If time doesn't permit, look for prepared pulses (in BPA-free cans) that are low in sodium, and rinse them thoroughly before cooking. Incorporate into stews, soups, sandwiches, falafel and burritos. Try them out in the following recipes: Tex-Mex Black Bean Burgers (page 208) and Curried Chickpea Salad Sandwiches with Turmeric Garlic Parsnip Fries (page 99).
Red vegetables and fruits: beet, radish, raspberry, red cabbage, red lettuce, red onion, red pepper, rhubarb, strawberry, tomato, watermelon	The red hue in tomatoes and berries comes from the pigments lycopene and anthocyanin. Lycopene is a red-hued carotenoid and antioxidant that has shown chemopreventive properties. Frequent consumption of tomatoes and tomato products (like sauces and pastes) is associated with a lower risk of prostate cancer, cervical cancer and gastrointestinal cancer. Lycopene has also been shown to lower LDL cholesterol, which is good for cardiovascular disease prevention. Anthocyanin is a flavonoid that lends its red-purple hue to berries, red cabbage and red onions. A high intake of anthocyanin has been associated with a lower risk of type 2 diabetes, heart attack and all-cause mortality.	Eat berries raw as a snack or in a smoothie, place them on top of oatmeal or bake them in a crisp or crumble. Tomatoes can be eaten raw in sandwiches or salads, or cooked in soups and sauces. A 2002 study showed that cooked tomatoes have a higher lycopene content than their raw counterparts. Try them out in the following recipes: Strawberry and Hazelnut Streusel Cake with a Maple Vanilla Glaze (page 133) and Roasted Tomato and Garlic Soup (page 168).
Seeds: chia, flaxseed, hemp, pumpkin, sesame, sunflower	Seeds are an excellent source of fibre, antioxidants, omega-3 fatty acids and protein. Chia seeds have a high proportion of fibre. They are also a great source of omega-3 fatty acids, iron, calcium and magnesium. Flaxseed is a potent source of soluble fibre, omega-3 fatty acids, lignans and protein. Flaxseed contains nearly 100 times more lignans than other foods, and these polyphenols have shown promise in cardiovascular disease and breast cancer prevention. Omega-3 fatty acids have been associated with the prevention of cardiovascular and cognitive disease. While benefits are commonly attributed to marine sources of omega-3, flaxseed is also a potent source of alpha-linolenic acid, which is potentially beneficial for cardiovascular health. A diet high in fibre is associated with a reduced risk of cardiovascular disease, cancer, type 2 diabetes, obesity and mortality from all causes. This makes seeds an excellent option when you are looking to meet your fibre needs.	Buy seeds at grocery stores or bulk grocers and store in the fridge or freezer for a longer shelf life. Ground flaxseed is preferable to whole because its nutrients are easier to digest and absorb when it is ground. Add seeds to desserts, breads, puddings and oatmeal for an extra boost of fibre. Ground flaxseed and chia seeds are particularly great to use in baked goods in place of eggs. Try them out in the following recipes: Vanilla Chai Chia Seed Pudding (page 162) and The Ultimate Chocolate Protein Powder (page 63).
Soy	Soy is a plant-based source of complete protein and lacks the saturated fat present in meats. Higher in polyunsaturated fatty acids and protein, and lower in carbohydrates, soy protein is said to be higher in quality than that of other legumes. Soy contains phytochemicals like isoflavones, saponins, potassium, iron, fibre (in whole soybeans) and calcium. Fermented soy products like tempeh and miso contain bacteria that are beneficial in maintaining a healthy gut microbiome. The isoflavones in soy have been shown to improve risk factors for cardiovascular disease such as high blood pressure, cholesterol, obesity and inflammation. Soy has also been studied for reducing the severity of hot flashes in postmenopausal women, as a chemopreventive and in osteoporosis prevention.	Eating soy in its whole form is preferable, and will add extra fibre to your diet. Incorporating fermented soy products like natto, miso and tempeh is beneficial in introducing gut-friendly bacteria into your diet. Try soy out in the following recipes: Miso, Mushroom and Edamame Pot Pie (page 52) and Creamy Corn Chowder with Tempeh Chorizo (page 192).

FOODS TO EAT	HEALTH BENEFITS	HOW TO EAT THEM
Spices: allspice, cardamom, cayenne, cinnamon, cloves, cumin, fennel, ginger, nutmeg, pepper, star anise, turmeric	These warm, fragrant spices are excellent for adding flavour and antioxidants to your dishes. A USDA study found that the top five antioxidant-containing foods were dried spices: ground cloves, oregano, ground cinnamon, ground ginger and ground turmeric. Ginger has been studied as a chemopreventive agent, and for its anti-nausea properties when consumed during pregnancy and cancer treatment. Turmeric contains anti-inflammatory properties that may be beneficial in managing conditions like arthritis, metabolic syndrome and hyperlipidemia, and is potentially chemopreventive. Cinnamon has been studied for its potential role in managing type 2 diabetes, and for its properties as an anti-inflammatory, anti-microbial, potential chemopreventive and potential protectant against cardiovascular disease. A 2003 study suggests that the inclusion of cinnamon in the diet has potential to mitigate risk factors for cardiovascular disease and type 2 diabetes.	Use dry spices to add flavour to both savoury and sweet dishes without added salt, sugar or unhealthy fat. Buy them at grocery stores or bulk grocers and keep in glass jars in a cool, dry area, replacing every two to three years. Whole spices tend to keep their potency longer, although they are not as convenient to use. Try them in the following recipes: Turmeric Ginger Latte (page 89) and Vanilla Chai Chia Seed Pudding (page 162).
Sweeteners: blackstrap molasses, dates, honey, maple syrup	While even natural sweeteners can have an effect on your blood sugar, raw honey, pure maple syrup and dates are lower on the glycemic index and contain minerals and antioxidants that are not present in white sugar. According to a 2009 study, replacing your daily average intake of refined sugars with alternative sweeteners like maple syrup, honey and blackstrap molasses can increase your daily antioxidant intake in an amount that is comparable to a serving of nuts or berries each day. Dates are high in fibre, iron and antioxidants like flavonoids, carotenoids and phenolic acid. Among dried fruits, they contain the highest concentration of polyphenols. Maple syrup contains trace minerals like manganese, riboflavin and phenolic compounds. Honey in particular has been studied for its potential in disease prevention due to its antioxidant, antibacterial and anti-inflammatory properties from polyphenols and flavonoids. Sufficient evidence exists to recommend the use of honey in the management of disease.	When choosing alternative sweeteners, go for raw, unprocessed honey, Medjool dates, blackstrap molasses and pure maple syrup. Use sparingly as a sweetener or in dressings. Note: Some who follow strictly plant-based diets avoid honey, but due to its health benefits, I have included it in some of the recipes in this book. However, it can always be replaced with maple syrup. Try them out in the following recipes: Maple Caramel Sauce with Granny Smith Apples and Toasted Walnuts (page 83) and Chocolate Avocado Pie (page 218).
Whole grains: amaranth, barley, brown rice, buckwheat, farro (wheat berry), kamut, millet, oat, quinoa, rye, spelt, triticale, wild rice	Unlike processed grains, whole grains are high in insoluble dietary fibre, which is beneficial for digestion and blood sugar control. They also are an excellent source of soluble fibre, which aids in cholesterol and blood pressure management. Inulin is a type of soluble fibre that is found in grains like oats, barley and rye and has prebiotic qualities. Inulin stimulates the growth of diverse bacteria like bifidobacterium and lactobacilli in the gut. Prebiotics like inulin and probiotics are associated with improved immunity, improved risk factors for cardiovascular disease and type 2 diabetes, brain health and absorption of minerals (enhancing bone density). Whole grains contain antioxidants and phenolic compounds, vitamin E, B vitamins, beta-glucans, protein and trace minerals like iron, magnesium and zinc. A diet high in whole grains and high in fibre is associated with a reduced risk of cardiovascular disease, cancer, type 2 diabetes, obesity and mortality from all causes.	Buy whole grains from grocery stores or bulk grocers and store in glass jars in a cool, dark place. Replace refined, starchy grains with whole grains like brown rice, barley, farro and quinoa. In baking, replace white flour with kamut, spelt or quinoa flour. Try them out in the following recipes: Caramelized Fennel, Sweet Potato and Pine Nut Cheese Pizza (page 175) and Warm Farro Salad with Spicy Citrus Dressing (page 129).

Grocery Reference List

Refer to this list when you plan meals and grocery shop to help incorporate more health-promoting ingredients into your regular meal and snack rotation.

Please note that this is general nutritional advice and not all of it will apply to every individual. Some of these ingredients can cause allergic reactions in those allergic or interfere with medication, so follow the advice of your healthcare providers in deciding which of these foods are right for you.

INGREDIENTS TO REDUCE

- Alcohol
- Artificial sweeteners
- Dairy
- Fried foods

- Highly processed foods, e.g., canned soups, boxed macaroni and cheese, instant noodles, breakfast cereals, cake mixes, diet shakes, frozen meals, protein bars

- Processed meats, e.g., bacon, salami, sausage, pâté
- Red meat
- Refined white sugar
- Simple, refined carbohydrates, e.g., white pasta, white flour, white bread, soda crackers

- Sodium (500 mg or less per entrée is ideal)
- Trans fats and foods containing trans fatty acids, e.g., baked goods, fried foods, stick margarine, shortening

INGREDIENTS TO INCREASE

- ☐ Citrus fruits, e.g., oranges, grapefruit, lemons, limes
- ☐ Colourful fruits and vegetables—a rainbow of them!
- ☐ Cooked and raw orange vegetables, e.g., carrots, orange peppers, sweet potatoes, winter squash, pumpkins
- ☐ Cooked and raw red fruits and vegetables, e.g., strawberries, tomatoes, beets, raspberries, rhubarb, red onions

- ☐ Cruciferous vegetables, e.g., bok choy, broccoli, cauliflower, Brussels sprouts, cabbage
- ☐ Dark leafy greens, e.g., mustard greens, Swiss chard, collards, kale
- ☐ Fermented foods, e.g., miso, sauerkraut, kimchi, tempeh (consume low-sodium varieties when possible)
- ☐ Fresh and dried herbs and spices, e.g., turmeric, black pepper, cinnamon, cumin, coriander, paprika, basil, oregano, chili flakes

- ☐ Healthy fats, e.g., avocados, nuts, seeds, olive oil, grapeseed oil
- ☐ Healthy/good-quality protein, e.g., edamame, tempeh, tofu, nuts, seeds, legumes
- ☐ Beans and legumes, e.g., chickpeas, black beans, kidney beans, cannellini beans, adzuki beans, pinto beans, black-eyed peas, lima beans, lentils

- ☐ Nuts and nut butters, e.g., walnuts, almonds, pecans, pistachios, hazelnuts, cashews
- ☐ Seeds and seed butters, e.g., sesame seeds/tahini, pumpkin seeds, chia seeds, hemp seeds, flaxseed
- ☐ Whole grains, e.g., quinoa, brown rice, millet, spelt, kamut, freekeh, barley, whole rolled oats, whole grain flours

GENERAL TIPS FOR HEALTHY EATING

- ☐ Eat healthy fats from whole foods, e.g., avocados, walnuts, almonds, chia seeds, hemp seeds, flaxseed, pumpkin seeds, sunflower seeds

- ☐ Eat more beans and legumes. Use them in soups, stews, chilis, dressings, dips, desserts
- ☐ Eat more fibre-rich foods than not. Plant-based foods contain fibre and animal-based foods contain no fibre

- ☐ Eat whole grains, not refined. Add them to your salads, soups, stews and entrées, or serve them under your favourite chili or curry

- ☐ Focus on a whole food diet that is mainly based on fruits, vegetables, whole grains, nuts, seeds, beans, legumes and good-quality plant-based proteins (proteins that contain close to or all of the essential amino acids)

Plant-Based Diets and Chronic Disease

Here we move into the foundation of the cookbook. This section discusses the top four major chronic diseases that our society faces and the research related to the benefits of plant-based eating for prevention and management of each disease. This vital information was the basis for developing all of the recipes in this book, to make it easy to apply this nutritional knowledge to your own diet.

Plant-Based Diets and Cardiovascular Disease

Cardiovascular disease (CVD), which includes atherosclerosis, heart attacks and stroke, is the leading cause of death around the world.[8] However, it may be possible to reduce these deaths by as much as 54 percent for men and 49.6 percent for women by managing risks like high cholesterol, diabetes, hypertension, obesity and smoking.[9]

Current research suggests that CVD can be prevented in part through diet, including phytochemical, fibre, sodium, alcohol, saturated fat and functional food consumption—all of which can be addressed when focusing on whole, unprocessed, plant-based foods.[10] For example, vegetarians have been shown to have 29 percent lower heart disease mortality than non-vegetarians.[11] Vegetarians, and vegans especially, are also associated with having a lower blood pressure than meat eaters, partial vegetarians and fish eaters.[12] And maintaining a healthy plant-based diet has also been associated with a 25 percent lower risk of developing CVD in the first place.[13]

As further good news for the prevention of atherosclerosis, levels of LDL (the "bad cholesterol" responsible for clogging arteries) have been found to be lower in vegans compared to meat eaters, fish eaters and vegetarians.[14] For example, in a review of 27 randomized, controlled trials and observational studies in *The American Journal of Cardiology*, plant-based diets were found to decrease plasma cholesterol levels.[15] In addition to lowering blood pressure and promoting healthy cholesterol levels, an increased consumption of plant-based, fibre-rich foods has been shown to reduce the risk of stroke as well.[16]

Specific foods to consume for CVD prevention and management include:[17]

- Allium-rich foods (garlic, onions, leeks)

- Fibre-filled legumes

- Polyphenol-rich fruits like blueberries, raspberries and strawberries

- Leafy greens

- Carotenoid-rich foods like orange vegetables

- Nuts containing healthy fats (walnuts, almonds)

- Seeds, including phytoestrogen-rich flaxseed

- Whole grains, including beta-glucan-rich barley and oats

- LDL-cholesterol-lowering soy protein

- Foods containing organosulfur compounds, like cruciferous vegetables (cauliflower, kale, broccoli, Brussels sprouts, cabbage)

- Fibre-rich, antioxidant-laden, anti-inflammatory, whole plant-based foods in general

Ways you can reduce CVD risk and manage CVD:

- Follow a balanced diet rich in plant-based foods

- Reduce saturated and trans fat intake

- Eliminate or limit refined starches and added sugar

- Focus on eating whole fruits, whole vegetables and whole grains

- Consume a diet rich in omega-3 poly-unsaturated fatty acids (e.g., flaxseed, walnuts, hemp or chia seeds), soy protein and cruciferous vegetables

- Ensure sufficient folate intake (e.g., nuts, beans, lentils, leafy greens, whole grains)

- Consume foods rich in plant stanols and sterols (e.g., nuts, seeds, whole grains, legumes)

- Maintain or increase physical activity (30 to 60 minutes per day of moderate to vigorous activity is recommended for most people)

- Maintain or work towards a healthy weight

- Eat a low-sodium diet (in particular, avoid processed foods)

- Eliminate exposure to tobacco smoke

- Keep alcohol consumption to a minimum

Plant-Based Diets and Cancer

In 2017, it was calculated that nearly 50 percent of Canadians will be diagnosed with cancer in their lifetime and about 25 percent are expected to die from cancer. In spite of those overwhelming statistics, though, significant progress has been made in cancer control through prevention, screening, early detection and treatment. Dietary and lifestyle interventions have been part of that progress too.[18] As with the CVD recommendations, it is important to turn to the evidence related to dietary and lifestyle patterns and their link to disease prevention and management.

Authoritative reviews on the subject have estimated that approximately one-third of cancer diagnoses could be attributable to lifestyle factors including nutrition, dietary patterns and physical activity.[19] Following healthful, evidence-based recommendations for cancer prevention and management has been shown to affect cancer risk significantly,

may help during and following cancer treatment, can improve rates of cancer survival and can also reduce the risk of cancer recurrence.[20]

The following dietary recommendations for cancer prevention and management were developed by the World Cancer Research Fund (WCRF) and American Institute for Cancer Research (AICR).[21] In their discussion of the guidelines, Gonzales et al. determined that the evidence they are based on is "sufficiently compelling."[22]

1. Limiting or avoiding dairy products to reduce the risk of prostate cancer;

2. Limiting or avoiding alcohol to reduce the risk of cancers of the mouth, pharynx, larynx, esophagus, colon, rectum and breast;

3. Avoiding red and processed meat to reduce the risk of cancers of the colon and rectum;

4. Avoiding grilled, fried and broiled meats to reduce the risk of cancers of the colon, rectum, breast, prostate, kidney and pancreas;

5. Consuming soy products during adolescence to reduce the risk of breast cancer in adulthood and to reduce the risk of recurrence and mortality for women previously treated for breast cancer; and

6. Emphasizing fruits and vegetables to reduce the risk of several common forms of cancer.

Most important for our purposes is the discussion of what foods to consume for cancer prevention and management. For those who focus on eating foods from the plant kingdom, foods that are rich in fibre and phytonutrients, and functional foods, the evidence suggests that the overall incidence of cancer is lower.[23]

Eating a plant-based diet has been clinically shown to positively affect DNA modifications, which reduces gene expression related to cancer and overall cancer risk.[24] As a result, when reviewing the dietary patterns of those following a plant-focused diet, a review by Huang et al. showed that vegetarians had an 18 percent lower cancer mortality risk than non-vegetarians.[25] And a meta-analysis of observational studies of vegetarian and vegan diets by Dinu et al. revealed that a vegetarian diet may be protective and reduce cancer risk by 8 percent and a vegan diet by 15 percent.[26]

Moreover, in some cases with site-specific cancers, plant-based diets may be even more protective. For example, a vegan diet seems to confer lower risk for both overall and female-specific cancers in comparison to other dietary patterns, and vegetarians have an overall reduced risk of cancers related to the gastrointestinal tract.[27]

In a California Teachers Study cohort, including data from 91,779 women, a 15 percent reduced risk of breast cancer was found when following a plant-based diet.[28] Tantamango-Bartley et al. found 35 percent less prostate cancer among those following a vegan diet than men in the other dietary groups.[29] Researchers suspect that higher intakes of fibre, soy and anti-inflammatory antioxidants from fruits and vegetables and lower intakes of saturated fat, animal protein and dairy products in a vegan diet contribute to this lower cancer risk.[30] According to a study by Donaldson, adopting a nutritionally balanced cancer-fighting diet could produce "at least a 60–70 percent decrease in breast, colorectal, and prostate cancers, and even a 40–50 percent decrease in lung cancer, along with similar reductions in cancers at other sites. Such a diet would be conducive to preventing cancer and would favor recovery from cancer as well."[31]

Overall, including following a plant-focused diet, 30 to 40 percent of all cancers can be prevented by lifestyle and dietary measures, and those who do have cancer can follow similar recommendations to manage the disease and help prevent recurrence.[32] The following lists describe some lifestyle and dietary measures you can take to prevent or manage cancer.

Foods to consume for cancer prevention and management:

- Eat mostly foods of plant origin

- Eat a high-fibre diet, including ample fruits and vegetables (all plant-based foods contain fibre, while animal-based foods do not contain fibre)

- Maintain a balanced consumption of omega-3 and omega-6 fatty acids. Consuming fewer omega-6 than omega-3 fatty acids is more desirable in reducing the risk of many chronic diseases[33]

- Minimize your consumption of fast foods and include more omega-3-rich foods in your diet, like hemp seeds, chia seeds, flaxseed and walnuts

- Consume healthy fats and minimize the consumption of less-healthy fats. Focus on unsaturated fats (such as in nuts, seeds and avocados), eliminate trans fats, use cooking oils with a higher smoke point (like grapeseed, sesame and coconut) and focus on healthier cooking methods such as steaming, roasting, poaching and sautéing, rather than frying or grilling

- Regularly consume functional and phytochemical-rich foods, which include foods containing antioxidants, dietary fibre, unsaturated fatty acids, phytoestrogens, plant stanols and sterols, prebiotics and probiotics, soy proteins and sulphuric compounds. For more information, see The Essential Guide to Eating for Optimal Health (page 6)

- Consume allium and cruciferous vegetables as they are especially beneficial

- Consume protective elements such as selenium, folic acid, vitamin B12 and vitamin D[34]

Foods to reduce or avoid for cancer prevention and management:

- Reduce consumption of concentrated sugars and refined flour products, which contribute to insensitivity to the effects of insulin, making it more difficult to control blood glucose levels (which may lead to type 2 diabetes)

- Eliminate or limit the consumption of red and processed meat

- Eliminate or limit alcohol consumption to no more than one serving (12 oz beer, 1.5 oz spirits, 5 oz wine) per day for women and two servings per day for men

- Keep sodium intake to less than 2,400 mg (or 6 g of salt) per day

Other lifestyle measures for cancer prevention and management:

- Aim to meet nutritional needs through your diet, not supplements

- Have a sufficient, but not excessive, energy intake

- Maintain a healthy body weight

- Maintain or increase physical activity (30 to 60 minutes per day of moderate to vigorous activity is recommended for most people)

- Eliminate exposure to cigarette smoke

For those going through cancer treatment or those who have finished cancer treatment and want to avoid recurrence, the research and recommendations remain the same.[35] Similar to the cancer prevention dietary guidelines, the data overwhelmingly indicate that exercise, a high-quality diet focusing on plants and management of stress can improve the likelihood of cancer survival and prevent recurrence.[36] Maintaining a healthy dietary pattern has been associated with lower mortality among cancer survivors, whereas a Western dietary pattern (a diet high in alcohol, animal products and processed foods), is associated with higher mortality among cancer survivors.[37] In particular, consumption of vegetables is associated with lower mortality amongst cancer survivors, while alcohol is associated with higher mortality.[38]

Focusing on the lifestyle and dietary guidelines discussed here will provide a reduced risk of cancer along with a sense of empowerment to those wishing to prevent, manage or prevent recurrence of cancer, and they will help to reduce the risk of other chronic diseases as well.

For those looking for a more detailed discussion of cancer nutrition, including additional research, resources and food recommendations, see the *Community Guide for Cancer Nutrition* prepared by George Brown College and Gilda's Club of Greater Toronto, which I worked on as principal investigator.

Plant-Based Diets and Type 2 Diabetes

Diabetes is the fourth most common non-communicable disease world-wide. From 1980 to 2014 the incidence of diabetes rose from 108 million to 422 million and the global prevalence (age-standardized) of diabetes nearly doubled.[39] Type 2 diabetes (T2D; once referred to as non-insulin-dependent diabetes) is the type of diabetes that the majority of these numbers represent and includes adults and, most recently in our history, children. If left untreated it may lead to serious health complications, including heart attack, stroke, kidney failure, blindness or death.[40]

Type 2, unlike type 1, can be prevented, delayed or managed through proper exercise, eliminating cigarette smoke exposure, regulating blood glucose levels and adopting a healthy diet, including adhering to a plant-focused diet.[41] For dietary recommendations, once again we look to the research on eating patterns and chronic disease prevention and management, as well as recognized dietary guidelines.

The biggest risk factors for type 2 diabetes include obesity, impaired glucose tolerance or unstable blood glucose levels, high blood pressure and high cholesterol, all of which can be prevented or managed through lifestyle and diet.[42] Plant-based diets have been shown to help with losing weight, maintaining a healthy body mass index (BMI), promoting a healthy blood pressure, improving cholesterol and triglyceride levels and improving glycemia (excess insulin in the blood).[43] A healthy BMI, which is typically a characteristic of those who follow a vegan diet, can also decrease the likelihood of the other major risk factors.[44]

Satija et al. conducted a study related to healthy plant-based diets and type 2 diabetes that included 69,949 women from the Nurses' Health Study (1984–2012), 90,239 women from the Nurses' Health Study 2 (1991–2011) and 40,539 men from the Health Professionals Follow-Up Study (1986–2010). They found that "a diet that emphasizes healthful plant foods leads to higher intakes of fibre, antioxidants, unsaturated fat, and micronutrients, and lower intakes of saturated fat, heme iron and sugar. These intakes improve cholesterol profiles and insulin regulation, decrease inflammation, reduce blood pressure, and favor a healthier gut microbiome—all factors that may lower the risk for chronic disease," including type 2 diabetes.[45] Focusing specifically on plants in the diet and eliminating or limiting animal-based foods will consequently help to control or eliminate the risk factors related to T2D as well as significantly reduce the risk of insulin resistance, prediabetes and T2D overall.[46]

The study by Satija et al. also states that even after adjusting for weight, people who closely followed plant-based diets over animal-based diets had about a 20 percent reduced risk for diabetes in comparison to those who followed them less closely. And the risk continued to drop when they mainly consumed whole, unsweetened and minimally processed plant foods, lowering the odds of diabetes by about 34 percent in total.[47]

In a study made up of 22,434 men and 38,469 women conducted from 2002 to 2006, Tonstad et al.[48] found a similar outcome after controlling for weight in relation to prevalence of T2D in vegans. Further to that, in their 6,798-participant analysis of the Rotterdam Study, Chen et al.[49] found that those eating a plant-centric diet will lower insulin resistance, the risk of prediabetes and the risk of T2D.

Prevention of chronic disease is the ideal scenario, but for those who have been diagnosed with T2D, diet can help to minimize or eliminate symptoms of the illness. A whole foods, plant-based diet will help you to lose excess weight or maintain a healthy weight, control blood glucose levels, maintain good blood pressure and obtain or maintain healthy lipid levels.[50] Adhering to a healthy dietary plan that focuses on plants will also reduce the risk of life-threatening T2D complications, including heart attacks, strokes and kidney failure.[51]

Foods and drinks to consume to help you prevent or manage T2D:[52]

- Eat nutrient-dense, lower-calorie, plant-based foods

- Ensure an intake of high-fibre foods (equal to or higher than 25 g per day)

- Keep hydrated with water, rather than other beverages

- Consume foods appearing lower on the glycemic index to control blood glucose

- Consume more fruits and vegetables

- Consume more whole grains, nuts, seeds and legumes

- Focus on healthy fats (like mono- and polyunsaturated fats) and replace saturated and trans fats

Foods and drinks to reduce or avoid to help you prevent or manage T2D:

- Eliminate or limit red and processed meat

- Avoid added sugars and processed grains

- Keep sodium levels below 2,400 mg per day (or 6 g of salt)

- Eliminate exposure to tobacco smoke

- Limit or eliminate use of alcohol

- Avoid juices from concentrate and high-sugar sodas

Plant-Based Diets and Obesity

Globally, obesity is becoming more widespread each year; it has tripled in prevalence since 1979.[53] In 2016, more than 1.9 billion adults were overweight and of that number over 650 million were obese.[54] The highest rates of obesity are usually found where the standard American diet (SAD) is eaten. The SAD is mainly composed of meals rich in red meat, dairy products, processed and artificially sweetened foods and salt, and contains minimal portions of fruits, vegetables, beans, legumes, nuts, seeds and whole grains. As a result of increasing obesity rates, chronic diseases that are influenced by obesity, and mortality related to these chronic diseases, is rising worldwide.

Aside from having a higher intake of fibre, magnesium, potassium, beta carotene and nutrients in general, vegetarians and vegans have lower weights and body mass indexes (BMIs) in comparison to non-vegetarians.[55] As plant-based diets are high in fibre and more nutrient dense, they tend to increase satiation, filling us up rather than out. This is the reason Sabaté et al. recommend that American food policies should promote a plant-based diet to aid in the reduction of obesity.[56]

In comparison to non-vegan diets (vegetarian, semi-vegetarian, pescatarian and omnivorous), those following vegan diets have been shown to have better weight loss results, in addition to having a lower average annual weight gain, suggesting that it is easier to maintain a healthy weight when focusing on plant-based foods.[57] These findings are particularly important because each one of the major chronic diseases discussed here has obesity as a major risk factor—particularly T2D.[58]

Here are a few dietary tips for what to consume and what not to consume to reduce the risk of obesity, as well as how to maintain a healthy weight.

Foods and drinks to consume to reduce the risk of obesity:

- Minimally processed, whole plant-based foods

- Whole grains (whole wheat, steel cut oats, brown rice, quinoa)

- A wide, colourful variety of whole vegetables and fruits

- Nuts, seeds, beans and legumes

- Plant-based mono- and poly-unsaturated fats like avocados, olive oil and nuts

- Water in place of sugary or caffeinated beverages

Foods and drinks to reduce or avoid to lower the risk of obesity:

- Sugar-sweetened beverages (soda, fruit drinks, sports drinks)

- Fruit juice (keep consumption to ½ cup/ 125 mL per day if consumed at all and avoid fruit juice from concentrate)

- Refined grains (white bread, white rice, white pasta) and processed sweets

- Fried potatoes

- Red meat (beef, pork, lamb) and processed meats (salami, ham, bacon, sausage)

- Other highly processed foods, such as fast food

Other tips for maintaining a healthy weight:[59]

- Eat a healthy, balanced breakfast every day

- Get adequate sleep

- Make your own food and limit eating out

- Limit screen time

- Exercise daily and include muscle- and bone-strengthening activities at least three days a week

- Manage stress through exercise, breathing techniques and meditation

Prevention of excess weight gain through diet, exercise and lifestyle choices is of course extremely crucial and a good place to start to minimize the burden of chronic diseases and their negative side effects. National guidelines are a great source of information, as they are moving towards providing evidence-based advice concerning healthy behaviours like focusing on dietary quality, eating together and creating nutritionally sound food environments for all, with an emphasis on health-promoting dietary patterns.

You may, however, need some help translating these guidelines into an action plan that works for you. So if you are serious about healthy weight loss and weight management, it is recommended that you consult a nutrition expert such as a registered dietitian. With that said, focusing on whole plant-based foods and how they make you feel is a more sustainable and satiating step towards optimal health than drastic fad diets, going hungry or relying solely on the scale for feedback. Eating and eating well should be enjoyable and not something that conjures up feelings of fear or guilt.[60]

Vitamin and Mineral Intake with a Plant-Based Diet

Although focusing on healthy dietary patterns, like plant-based diets, may be the answer to chronic disease prevention and management, there are also vitamins and minerals that need special attention in order to maintain optimal health. In any dietary pattern, certain vitamins and minerals can become deficient if not consciously consumed, which could have a negative effect on health. Below are the macro- and micronutrients to be particularly aware of when following a plant-based diet, plus examples of plant-based foods in which they can be found.

- PROTEIN: found in tofu, edamame, tempeh, lentils, chickpeas, beans, nuts (almonds, walnuts, hazelnuts, cashews, Brazil nuts), seeds (chia seeds, hemp seeds, pumpkin seeds, sunflower seeds) and whole grains (quinoa, buckwheat, millet, oats, sorghum, teff, amaranth, wild rice)

- B12: found in fortified milk alternatives, nutritional yeast, or B12 supplements

- CALCIUM: found in kale, collard greens, spinach, broccoli, bok choy, cauliflower, tofu, tahini and mineral water

- IRON: found in lentils, chickpeas, beans, tofu, tempeh, edamame, leafy greens and dried fruit; combine these foods with vitamin-C-rich food sources to increase your body's ability to absorb the iron

- OMEGA-3 POLYUNSATURATED FATTY ACIDS: found in walnuts, flaxseed, chia seeds, hemp seeds and algae supplements

- VITAMIN D: found in sunshine, fortified milk alternatives, irradiated mushrooms and vitamin D supplements (recommended for anyone who doesn't receive sufficient sunlight; the recommended amount is 15 to 20 minutes for lighter-skinned people and 20 to 25 minutes for those with darker complexions)

Eat Well, and Eat Together

When selecting what food to eat, we should not only think of our physical health, but our emotional health as well. Preparing and eating meals together with loved ones or friends has the power to promote overall well-being, as well as deliver potential health benefits that are still being discovered.[61]

Current research related to social isolation suggests that socially isolated individuals, those who have a small or decreasing social network and reduced social interaction, are at an increased risk of cardiovascular disease,[62] cognitive decline,[63] heightened inflammation as a result of stress,[64] minimal exposure to relationships that could improve their health and overall well-being[65] and decreased longevity in general.[66] At some point we have strayed from the knowledge that interactions, meaningful relationships and face-to-face connections are human necessities, and it is potentially harming our health.

Dietary guidelines, like those outlined by Brazil and Canada, emphasize the sentiment of coming together and the sharing of a fresh, homemade and well-balanced meal—like the once mandatory family-style meals we may remember—for not just the good of physical health and disease prevention/management, but for mental and emotional well-being.[67] The Western diet and our food practices need to revisit these important and health-influencing priorities. We need to eat together more often and share more meaningful moments, in order to significantly and positively influence our overall physical and mental health.

Please enjoy the recipes in this book, and other nutritionally balanced plant-based meals, by preparing and sharing among family and friends, new and old.

Glossary of Nutrition Terms

ALLIUM refers to a pungent-smelling family of flowering plants that includes leeks, onions, garlic and chives. They have been studied for their cancer-preventing properties and contain organosulfur compounds, which have been shown to provide a number of health benefits. (For more information, see the entry for organosulfur compounds.)

ANTHOCYANIN is a flavonoid with a red-purple hue that is found in a variety of berries, red cabbage and red onions. It has been associated with decreased risk factors for type 2 diabetes.

ANTI-INFLAMMATORY FOODS reduce levels of inflammation in the body; inflammation is an immune system response provoked by injury, illness or the introduction of foreign substances. Chronic inflammation is a precursor for disease, so it is important to incorporate anti-inflammatory foods like leafy greens, vitamin-E-rich nuts, vitamin-C-rich fruits and high-quality oils.

ANTIOXIDANTS are chemicals that interact with and neutralize free radicals, preventing these chemicals from causing damage that can lead to inflammation and chronic disease. Examples of antioxidants include selenium, carotenoids, flavonoids and vitamins A, C and E.

BETA-CAROTENE is an antioxidant that neutralizes free radicals, improves cellular defences and creates vitamin A in the body. It is found in carrots, pumpkin, squash and sweet potatoes.

BETA-GLUCAN is a type of soluble fibre that is found in the cell walls of fungi (mushrooms), yeasts and cereal grains like oats and barley. They have been associated with cancer cell prevention and protection against type 2 diabetes, heart disease, stroke and obesity.

CAROTENOIDS are responsible for yellow, red and orange tones in fruits and vegetables. Beta-carotene, lutein and lycopene are all types of carotenoids. There are also two main categories of carotenoids: provitamin A, which can be converted into vitamin A in the body, and non-provitamin A, which cannot be converted. Carotenoids have been associated with cancer cell prevention and are beneficial for eye health.

CHEMOPREVENTIVE is used in reference to natural or synthetic compounds that interfere with the development of cancer cells.

CHOLESTEROL is an oily, waxy substance found in fat in the bloodstream. Cholesterol can be produced by the body or taken in through the diet. The two main categories of cholesterol are the "good" HDL (high-density lipoprotein), which transports excess cholesterol to the liver, and the "bad" LDL (low-density lipoprotein), which builds up in arteries and causes heart diseases like atherosclerosis. The body needs cholesterol to function properly, but the body can produce all that it needs and consuming excess LDL cholesterol in the diet is a major risk factor for cardiovascular disease.

CRUCIFEROUS vegetables are vegetables that belong to the brassica family, including cabbage, cauliflower, broccoli, Brussels sprouts and kale. Studies have shown that increased consumption of cruciferous vegetables can produce significant health benefits relating to the prevention of cancer and cardiovascular disease.

DANGER ZONE refers to the temperatures that harmful pathogens best grow in. Bacteria will grow most rapidly in the range of temperatures between 40F and 140F (4C and 60C) and can double in number in as little as 20 minutes.

DIETARY FIBRE is indigestible plant material that is found in all varieties of plant-based foods. This includes the indigestible (or non-starch) polysaccharides, which are not absorbed by the body but are required for a healthy digestive system. Examples include cellulose, dextrins, pectins, lignans and beta-glucans (like oats and barley). Fibre provides a wide range of health benefits, including improved blood sugar levels, improvements in gastrointestinal health, increased beneficial bacteria in the gut, reduced risk of cardiovascular disease, reduced risk of certain types of cancer and increased satiety, aiding in weight loss and maintenance.

FLAVONOIDS are a sub-class of plant pigments that act as an antioxidant. Over 5,000 naturally occurring flavonoids have been classified in numerous plants. Flavonol, flavone isoflavones and anthocyanins are sub-classes of flavonoids. Anthocyanins in particular have a deep blue colour that may appear red, blue or purple and, in addition to containing antioxidant properties, provide anti-inflammatory, antiviral and anti-cancer benefits.

FREE RADICALS are highly reactive chemicals with the potential to cause damage. They are formed naturally within the body and play an important role in normal cellular processes. However, at high concentrations they can be hazardous: they increase oxidative stress within the body and cause damage to cells as a result, which may play a role in cancer development, cardiovascular disease, diabetes, Alzheimer's disease and arthritis. Common sources of free radicals include cigarette smoke, UV rays, intense exercise and pollution. Antioxidants are able to neutralize unstable free radicals, so it is important that a balance between free radicals and antioxidants is present to encourage proper physiological function in the body.

FUNCTIONAL FOODS are foods or food ingredients that may provide health benefits beyond the nutrients that they contain.

LUTEIN is an antioxidant that helps maintain healthy vision. It is found in spinach, corn and citrus fruits.

LYCOPENE is an antioxidant found in red and pink vegetables and fruits that contributes to maintaining good prostate health. It can be found in tomatoes, watermelons and pink grapefruit.

MONOUNSATURATED FAT is a type of dietary fat that is considered to be "healthy fat" due to its role in promoting cardiovascular health and cholesterol management. Food sources include avocados, seeds, nuts and minimally refined oils, like extra-virgin olive oil.

ORGANOSULFUR COMPOUNDS are organic compounds that contain sulfur. They have anti-inflammatory, antibacterial and antiviral properties and have been shown to aid in reducing oxidative stress and minimize the risk of cardiovascular diseases, cancer, neurodegenerative disorders and diabetes. Organosulfur compounds are often found in allium vegetables like onions and garlic, and cruciferous vegetables such as cabbage, bok choy and cauliflower. For example, allicin, which is present in garlic, is what gives crushed garlic its pungent aroma.

OXIDATIVE STRESS is an imbalance of damaging free radicals and antioxidants in the body that may lead to inflammation and potentially to chronic disease. Oxidative damage is a result of the body's inability to keep up with the production of harmful free radicals. Antioxidants help the body's natural defences to neutralize unstable and damaging free radicals and avoid oxidative damage.

PHYTOCHEMICALS are chemical compounds that are often produced by plants and provide potential health benefits. Antioxidants are often found in phytochemical/phytonutrient-rich foods.

PHYTOESTROGEN is a compound that is found in plant foods and has a similar chemical structure to the estrogen found in animal and human bodies. Phytoestrogen has been shown to have health benefits related to heart health and cancer prevention. It is often found in flaxseed, soybeans and soy products.

PLANT-BASED FOODS are foods that are derived from plant sources and contain no animal products. They include fruits, vegetables, whole grains, nuts, seeds, legumes and oils.

PLANT STANOLS AND STEROLS are substances that are chemically similar to cholesterol and may help to reduce the risk of cardiovascular disease by decreasing the uptake of LDL cholesterol and increasing the excretion of cholesterol through the intestine. Food sources include nuts, seeds, whole grains, corn and soy.

POLYPHENOLS are a type of phytochemical and antioxidant and give plants their colour and flavour. They may provide health benefits relating to heart health, cancer and chronic inflammation in general. They contain several sub-groups, including anthocyanins, flavonoids, lignans and phenolic acids.

POLYUNSATURATED FAT is a type of dietary fat that is considered to be a "healthy fat" due to its role in cholesterol management and promising properties that may alter cancer cell growth.

Sources of polyunsaturated fat include walnuts, chia seeds, hemp seeds and flaxseed.

PREBIOTICS are indigestible food ingredients. When eaten they help the beneficial bacteria (probiotics) already present in the gut to grow. Food sources include garlic, onions, leeks, asparagus and whole grains.

PROBIOTICS are live beneficial bacteria that have the potential to provide health benefits when consumed. Probiotics live in the gut and can be increased by the consumption of probiotic-rich foods such as yogurt, tempeh, miso, kimchi and sauerkraut. In addition to helping with gut health and improved immunity, they may play a role in protecting DNA from oxidative stress, which may aid in cancer prevention.

SATURATED FAT is mostly found in animal food sources and is often referred to as unhealthy fat as it tends to increase your "bad" LDL cholesterol, which links it to an increased risk of chronic diseases such as cancer, heart disease and type 2 diabetes.

TRANS FAT is unhealthy hydrogenated fat and has been banned in some countries as it significantly increases your "bad" LDL cholesterol and lowers your "good" HDL cholesterol, which can increase the risk of chronic disease—particularly heart disease and type 2 diabetes.

TRIGLYCERIDE is a type of fat found in the blood of humans and animals. High triglyceride levels can lead to high cholesterol, metabolic syndrome and cardiovascular disease.

Cooking Fundamentals and Culinary Terminology

TO PRACTICALLY APPLY your nutrition knowledge, it is helpful to know the basics when it comes to culinary terms and approaches. I've collected some fundamental information about kitchen safety precautions, necessary tools and techniques, and commonly used culinary terms, to help on your path to eating for optimal health.

Food Safety Precautions

When cooking for anyone, but especially for those with health issues, it is important that food is not only prepared with love, but also with great care in both selecting the ingredients and handling them in the kitchen. Preventing food-borne illness is the name of the game, particularly when cooking for people who have compromised immune systems, which can often be the case for those going through cancer treatments or in hospitals and long-term care facilities.

The three main sources of food-borne illness are biological sources, where harmful pathogens like the *E. coli* Shiga toxin or the *Clostridium botulinum* toxin are consumed in food; chemical sources, where poisons like lead, cyanide or copper are introduced through cross-contamination; and physical sources, like pieces of glass, metal or other debris that make their way into food. Be aware of these hazards as well as how to prevent them from compromising the food you prepare.

Tips to reduce food-borne illness:

1. Wash hands frequently and appropriately whenever preparing or touching food. Get a good lather going with soap and warm water and rub your hands together for at least 20 seconds, ensuring that you also wash your wrists and forearms. Thoroughly rinse with hot water and dry with a clean paper towel or hot air dryer.

2. Avoid cross-contamination by practicing safe food handling and cleaning methods. Switch or thorough clean cutting boards between each task, wash produce before preparation, wash your hands thoroughly, store chemicals away from food, and follow other general guidelines for food safety. Although this book uses low-risk foods in terms of food-borne illness, if you do use higher

risk foods like eggs, dairy, fish and meat, be certain to educate yourself about safe practices using and properly storing these ingredients.

3. If using gloves, wash your hands prior to use and replace when changing jobs or if gloves are torn or soiled beyond cleaning. Thoroughly clean or replace gloves if working on the same task for longer than two hours.

4. Keep foods out of the temperature danger zone as much as possible, since harmful food pathogens can grow exponentially in this range. See the chart "Important Temperatures in Sanitation and Food Protection" (below) for a list of safe and unsafe temperatures.

5. When storing food just prior to service, ensure that you are keeping hot foods hot and cold foods cold. See the chart "Important Temperatures in Sanitation and Food Protection" for appropriate holding, cooking and cooling temperatures.

6. Cool foods as quickly and safely as possible, particularly for large quantities, since there is less surface area for cooling and the food may remain in the danger zone for a longer period of time as a result. See "Guidelines for Cooling Foods" (page 28) for more information.

7. Store foods at appropriate temperatures. See the chart "Important Temperatures in Sanitation and Food Protection" for more information.

8. Keep nuts and seeds in the freezer and flours and whole grains in a dry, dark place.

9. Ensure that any chemicals are safely stored far away from food preparation and storage areas.

Basic safety and sanitation tips:

1. Wear non-slip, closed-toed shoes.

2. Hair should be securely tied back and out of your face.

3. When walking with a knife, carry it at your side with the blade facing behind you while making sure others are aware that you are carrying a sharp object. Dirty knives should be left beside the sink in a visible place and never placed in the sink, to avoid injuries.

4. Indicate to others if you are carrying hot items or if something has been removed from the oven that is hot. Store hot items on an appropriate surface and place an oven mitt or dry towel on or beside the item to indicate that it is hot. If the hot item is a piece of equipment, it can be cooled down immediately with cool water. Never try to pick up a hot item with a wet cloth.

Important Temperatures in Sanitation and Food Protection[68]

TEMPERATURE RANGE	DESCRIPTION	EFFECT ON BACTERIA
165F (74C) to 212F (100C)	Cooking temperatures	Most disease-causing organisms killed in a few minutes.
140F (60C) to 165F (74C)	Hot food holding	Bacteria do not multiply, but most are not killed.
40F (4C) to 140F (60C)	Food danger zone	Bacteria multiply rapidly.
32F (0C) to 40F (4C)	Cold food storage (refrigeration)	Food safe for short periods. Little bacterial growth.
0F (-18C) to 32F (0C)	Subfreezing	Bacteria do not grow, but most are not killed.
Below 0F (-18C)	Freezer storage	Bacteria do not grow, but most are not killed. Best temperatures for frozen food storage.

▸ Culinary cuts, clockwise from top left: dice; grate; brunoise; zest; mince; julienne; slice; chiffonade.

1. Never put hot foods directly into the refrigerator or cooler. Not only will they cool too slowly but they will raise the temperature of other foods in the fridge.

2. If they are available, use quick-chill units or blast chillers to cool foods quickly before transferring them to cold storage.

3. Use ice water baths to bring down temperatures of hot foods quickly.

4. Divide large batches into smaller batches. This increases the amount of surface area for the volume of food and helps it cool more quickly. Pouring foods into flat, shallow pans also increases surface area and cooling speed.

Culinary Terminology[70]

Common Cuts

Many recipes, in this book and elsewhere, use different words for specific types of cuts. Here is an easy-to-navigate glossary of terms to ensure that your cuts are the right ones for each recipe.

BRUNOISE: Cut food into very small ⅛-inch (0.32-cm) dice.

CHIFFONADE: Stack, roll and thinly cut leafy vegetables and herbs into fine shreds.

CUBE: Cut food into symmetrical square shapes.

DICE: Cut food into small ¼-inch (0.6-cm) cubes.

JULIENNE: Cut food into small, thin strips that are about ⅛ inch (0.32 cm) wide and 1 to 2 inches (2.5 to 5 cm) long.

MINCE: Chop food into very fine pieces.

PAYSANNE: Cut food into similarly sized shapes, like rectangles, circles or squares, and roughly measure ½ × ½ × ⅛ inches (0.5 × 0.5 × 0.32 cm).

SLICE: Cut a piece of food by placing a knife at a sharp angle with the tip of the knife on the cutting board and then moving the knife simultaneously forward and down to cut through the food.

Healthier Cooking Methods

Choose the following cooking methods as often as possible to retain the food's nutritional benefits without adding excess fats:

BAKE: Cook food in dry heat, usually in an oven.

BOIL: Cook food in water or another liquid that is bubbling rapidly at 212F (100C).

BROIL: Cook food with heat radiating on one side, usually from above.

POACH: Simmer food in a small amount of water or another liquid. Poaching liquid should be at 140 to 180F (60 to 82C) and is usually discarded after use or utilized in a sauce.

ROAST: Cook food in an oven or on a spit over a grill or open fire by surrounding it with hot, dry air.

SAUTÉ: Cook food quickly in a small amount of fat.

SIMMER: Cook food in water or another liquid that is bubbling gently at 185 to 200F (85 to 95C).

STEAM: Cook food by placing it in the hot steam above boiling water (do not place directly in the water).

BEAT: Use a whisk, hand blender or stand mixer to thoroughly combine ingredients while incorporating air into them.

CARAMELIZE: Cook food slowly in fat until it turns brown and sweetens.

CREAM: Mix ingredients together to form a thick, even mixture.

FOLD IN: Carefully use a rubber spatula to gently combine ingredients without overmixing.

GARNISH: Use an edible item or key recipe ingredient as decoration to enhance the beauty of a dish.

GRATE: Break food down into small pieces by rubbing it on a grater.

MARINATE: Soak food in a flavourful liquid to allow it to absorb the flavour and sometimes to change the texture of the food.

PEEL: Remove the outer skin of a fruit or vegetable with a peeler or knife.

PREHEAT: Set an oven to reach the correct cooking temperature before cooking food in it.

PUREE: Use a blender or food processor to process food into a smooth paste.

WHISK: Use a whisk to stir or whip a mixture.

ZEST: The outside, coloured part of the peel of a citrus fruit that can be removed with a zester, microplane or grater and used to flavour food.

▲ The prep times listed in most cookbooks (including this one!) only include the time it takes to follow the actual steps in the method, not the time to wash, chop and measure ingredients. So to avoid stress in the kitchen, it's a good idea to prep ingredients ahead of meal time—and if you're truly strapped for time, many grocery stores offer common veggies precut in the produce section or salad bar.

```
Nutrition Facts
Valeur nutritive
Per 1 cup (250 mL)
par 1 tasse (250 mL)
─────────────────────────────────────────────
Calories  150              % Daily Value*
                           % valeur quotidienne*
─────────────────────────────────────────────
Fat / Lipides 8 g                      11 %
   Saturated / saturés 0.5 g
   + Trans / trans 0 g                  3 %
   Omega-3 / oméga-3 0 g
─────────────────────────────────────────────
Carbohydrate / Glucides 15 g
   Fibre / Fibres 4 g                  14 %
   Sugars / Sucres 9 g                  9 %
─────────────────────────────────────────────
Protein / Protéines 4 g
─────────────────────────────────────────────
Cholesterol / Cholestérol 0 mg
─────────────────────────────────────────────
Sodium 90 mg                            4 %
─────────────────────────────────────────────
Potassium 200 mg                        4 %
─────────────────────────────────────────────
Calcium 125 mg                         10 %
─────────────────────────────────────────────
Iron / Fer 1.25 mg                      7 %
─────────────────────────────────────────────
Vitamin A / Vitamine A 20 mcg           2 %
─────────────────────────────────────────────
Vitamin C / Vitamine C 5 mg             6 %
─────────────────────────────────────────────
Vitamin E / Vitamine E 5 mg            33 %
─────────────────────────────────────────────
*5% or less is a little, 15% or more is a lot
*5% ou moins c'est peu, 15% ou plus c'est beaucoup
```

EXAMPLE: Almond Apricot Blueberry
Smoothie (page 111)

A nutrition facts table
gives you information about:

- Serving size
- Calories
- Percentage (%) daily value, based on the
  recommended dietary allowance (RDA)
  for that specific nutrient

It also gives you information
about core nutrients, including:

- Fat
- Saturated fat
- Trans fat
- Carbohydrates
- Fibre
- Sugars

- Protein
- Cholesterol
- Sodium
- Potassium
- Calcium
- Iron

Other vitamins and minerals may be
included if the product producer would
like to include them. In the smoothie
example above, omega-3 fatty acids and
vitamins A, C and E have been added.

Nutrition facts tables are based on
a defined serving size of the food, so
compare this portion size to the amount
that you eat.

The serving size is:
- Listed under the nutrition facts title: "Per
  1 cup (250 mL)" in the smoothie example

- Listed in common measures you use at
  home and a metric unit: "cup" and "mL"
  in the smoothie example

- Used to determine the nutrition information provided by the percentage
  daily value

The percentage (%)
daily value is:[71]
- Used to determine whether there is a
  little (5% or less) or a lot (15% or more)
  of a nutrient in a serving size of the food

- A benchmark to evaluate the nutrient
  content of foods based on recommended
  dietary allowances (RDAs) established
  by the Dietary Reference Intake (DRI)
  committee, with guidance from the
  National Academy of Medicine of the
  National Academies in the United States

- Used to help you make healthier dietary
  choices (to show you which foods are
  high in fibre, vitamins, minerals and
  other nutrients)

Reading Nutrition
Facts Tables
When reading nutrition facts tables,
focus on the items that will benefit
your health the most, like fibre, protein,
vitamins, minerals and mono- and poly-
unsaturated fats. If you are following a
mostly whole plant-based foods diet, the
remaining items (calories, saturated fat
and cholesterol) may not necessarily
need as much attention. Calories in
particular can be misleading: sometimes
the calories listed may be high, but the
item may be high in nutrients as well,
making the food a nutrient-dense and
health-promoting option. Whereas a

processed food product could contain fewer calories but no nutritional value, which would not be a health-promoting option.

When in doubt, review the ingredient list to ensure that the ingredients are minimal and tend to consist of whole foods like fruits, vegetables, nuts, seeds, beans, legumes and whole grains, with minimal salt and no added sugar. However, if you are following the guidelines and suggestions set out in this cookbook and nutrition guide, your diet should be mostly made up of whole, unprocessed and minimally packaged foods, so you should encounter fewer nutrition facts tables and ingredient lists in general.

Note on Cooking Oils

Use oils that have a high smoke point to decrease the presence of harmful carcinogens (when consumed, these substances increase the oxidative stress and inflammation in our bodies). Good cooking oils include grapeseed, sunflower, avocado, coconut, peanut and sesame oil. Minimally refined extra-virgin olive oil can be cooked with at low temperatures or enjoyed on salads or with whole grain bread.

Note on Fruit and Vegetable Peels

The majority of the fruits and vegetables used in the recipes do not require peeling. This is because great amounts of fibre, nutrients and antioxidants can be found in their peels. If a recipe does not indicate the ingredients need to be peeled, assume that the peels should be left on. This is of course after the fruit or vegetable has been thoroughly washed or, in the case of root vegetables like potatoes, scrubbed.

I also highly encourage the use of peels that usually wouldn't be utilized. The peels of citrus fruits, in particular, including oranges, grapefruit, limes and lemons, are rich in beneficial phytochemicals and can provide a flavour boost to any muffin, cake, cookie, sauce, dip, dressing or smoothie without added salt, sugar or unhealthy fat. An easy way to incorporate the peels is by zesting all citrus fruits and either utilizing the zest in your current recipe or freezing it for future use.

Stocking Up on Whole Foods

Bring these lists to the grocery, bulk or general store to help stock your pantry with whole, unprocessed goods!

For your pantry

- Baking ingredients (baking powder, baking soda, pure vanilla extract, yeast, fair trade cacao or cocoa powder)

- Dried fruits (cranberries, currants, apricots, raisins, dates)

- Dried herbs (basil, rosemary, sage, oregano, thyme)

- Dried sea vegetables (kelp, agar-agar, dulse, wakame)

- Flour (spelt, gluten free, whole wheat)

- Garlic

- Green tea

- Legumes (dry and canned chickpeas, lentils, beans of all types)

- Maple syrup

- Nut butters (without added sugar, salt or fat)

- Nutritional yeast

- Oils (extra-virgin coconut, extra-virgin olive, grapeseed, sesame; see Note on Cooking Oils, page 31)

- Onions

- Salt

- Seed butters (sunflower, pumpkin, tahini, without added sugar, salt or fat)

- Spices (cinnamon, paprika, turmeric, cumin, ginger)

- Sweet potatoes

- Vinegars (balsamic, red wine, apple cider, rice)

- Whole grain pasta

- Whole grains (quinoa, brown rice, barley, millet, whole rolled oats)

For your fridge

- Apples

- Carrots

- Citrus fruits (lemons, limes, oranges, grapefruit)

- Cruciferous vegetables (broccoli, kale, cabbage, arugula, cauliflower)

- Dijon mustard

- Greens (collard greens, kale, spinach, watercress, arugula)

- Miso paste

- Mushrooms (button, shiitake, cremini, oyster)

- Pomegranates

- Soy (tofu, edamame, tempeh)

For your freezer

- Fruits (bananas, cherries, raspberries, strawberries, blackberries, blueberries)

- Nuts (walnuts, almonds, cashews, hazelnuts, pistachios)

- Seeds (hemp, chia, flaxseed, pumpkin, sunflower)

- Soy (edamame)

Kitchen Equipment to Have On Hand

This list contains all the basic equipment you'll need for nearly all of the recipes in this book, and most general recipes. Sometimes it is possible to substitute one item for another—for instance, while food processors, blenders, stand mixers and hand blenders all have different advantages, they can often be used interchangeably. (And much can be accomplished with a knife or a whisk, if you're patient and want a good workout!)

- Baking sheets
- Blender
- Box grater
- Bus bins (for community kitchens or those who often cook for large groups)
- Cake pans (bundt, 8-inch, 9-inch, 9 × 13-inch)
- Cast iron pan
- Chef's knife
- Colander and fine-mesh strainer
- Cutting boards
- Digital thermometer
- Food processor
- Hand blender
- Honing steel
- Mason jars of all sizes
- Measuring cups and spoons
- Microplane/rasp/zester
- Mixing bowls (large, medium and small)
- Muffin tin
- Parchment paper
- Paring knife
- Pots/saucepans of all sizes, with lids
- Pie plates (5-inch and 9-inch)
- Reamer
- Rolling pin
- Rubber spatulas
- Sauté/frying pans or skillets of all sizes
- Stand mixer
- Steaming basket
- Vegetable peeler
- Whisk
- Wooden spoons (long)

Easy and Nutritious Vegetable Stock

One easy way to cut down on food costs, increase nutritional value and minimize food waste is to make your own home-made stock from vegetable scraps that would otherwise be discarded. This is such a simple practice to incorporate in your home or community kitchen. Below are some tips and tricks about what to include and how to store your scraps and stock.

1. Save washed scraps from garlic, onions, celery, carrots, leeks and shallots, as well as stems from parsley, kale, mush-rooms, thyme, cilantro and basil. Ensure that none of the scraps are bruised, dirty or rotten. Do not include dark leafy greens, beets or cruciferous vegetables (kale leaves, broccoli, Brussels sprouts, cabbage, cauliflower) as they will make the stock bitter and sulfurous in flavour.

2. If you are not going to make the stock that day, freeze the scraps in a resealable bag. Continue to collect and add to the scraps kept from food preparation over the course of the week so that you have enough scraps to make a flavourful stock.

3. When ready to make stock, put all the scraps into a large stockpot with 2 to 3 bay leaves and 10 whole black pepper-corns and fill with cold water until covered (use about 1 cup/250 mL of water for each cup of scraps). Bring to a boil over medium-high heat, cover with a lid, then reduce heat and simmer for 1 hour.

4. When ready, strain the stock of all solids, including the bay leaves and pepper-corns. Use in soups, stews or sauces immediately or cool quickly and store in the freezer for future use. (Tip: if you're careful, you can use large heavy-duty freezer bags to store frozen stock and save space!)

How to Run a Community Supper Club

This list of tips and tricks about how to run your own community meals is based on the nutrition-focused supper club programming that I run at Gilda's Club Greater Toronto. It is one of the more popular programs as it brings together those in need of social, emotional and nutrition support with simple, nutrient-dense meals. With that said, eating together, particularly in larger groups, does take planning and effort—along with a good group of focused helpers.

Host To-Do List

1. Assign a chef or kitchen-savvy person to lead the supper club preparations. It is best if they have some knowledge related to food safety or have taken a food safety course like Hazard Analysis and Critical Control Point (HACCP). If you are this person, then well done on checking off the first to-do item!

2. Find eager and happy volunteers to help you execute the meal.

3. Find a venue to host the dinner! It could be out of someone's home, outdoors if the weather permits, or in a local healthcare institution, comm-unity centre or church.

4. The head chef or group should prepare a nutritionally sound menu for guests. A good guideline is to include a salad, a hearty side dish like soup, a main course and a dessert. If there will be children present, a kid-friendly option may be a good addition to the menu. Menus must take into consideration the dietary needs or restrictions of the guests as much as possible (such as lactose intolerance, plant-based diets, allergies and spice tolerance) and focus on disease preven-tion and management through proper nutrition.

5. Use the supper club menu to create a detailed grocery list, including exact amounts needed, in order to make grocery shopping easier. When making the list, consider including enough food to feed a few additional people in case guests bring a friend or would like seconds. Using a grocery delivery service may be helpful and save time for the host/chef if one is available and affordable.

6. On the night of the dinner, delegate work to volunteers appropriately. Determine the tasks that will need to be handled, including food preparation, service, dishwashing and general clean-up.

7. Make sure the whole team is aware of the menu for the evening, the ingredients used and any health benefits the ingredients provide so they are also able to relay this information to attendees during service.

8. Set an appropriate time for service and ensure that anyone who is helping is aware of the timeline and when each item should be prepared.

9. Know your volunteers' strengths. For example, if a volunteer is particularly skilled in the kitchen, have them take responsibility for the execution of an entire recipe.

10. Consistently maintain a clean and tidy work environment, with an eye to food safety. This is extremely important in order to avoid cross-contamination and food-borne illnesses. Hosts/chefs should maintain and encourage this rule.

11. Lead a positive and calm work environment for fellow volunteers as well as for guests. No one wants to attend a supper club where the host/chef and their volunteers are negative or stressed! To avoid unnecessary stress it is important to be organized and ensure that the menu you have selected is realistic for you and your volunteers to manage.

12. Lastly, and most importantly, remember not only to have fun, but make it fun for your volunteers and guests! Then watch the social and emotional support unfold in the form of a delicious and nutritious meal.

Recipes

During holidays, it is important to not only share in the celebration of the season, whatever that may mean for you, but also the coming together of friends and family, new and old. Mealtime is often the catalyst for these celebratory moments and memory-making opportunities. Holidays give us a good reason to sit together in one place, pass the potatoes and be thankful for good food, good health and good company! This section offers some fresh inspiration for family get-together dishes, plus tempting sweets and make-ahead recipes perfect for busy hosts.

**SUGGESTED MENU FOR
A HOLIDAY FEAST**

SOUP

*Artichoke and Oyster Mushroom
Chowder with Sweet Potato*

SIDE

*Brussels Sprouts with Roasted
Apples and Shiitake Bacon*

MAIN

Lentil, Spinach and Onion Pot Pie

DESSERT

Butterscotch Squash Coffee Cake

Feasts for Holiday Gatherings

Artichoke and Oyster Mushroom Chowder with Sweet Potato

PREPARATION TIME 30 minutes
COOKING TIME 35 minutes

This hearty chowder will be your new favourite quick but impressive recipe to share for fun and festive gatherings. Not only is it rich and satiating, it's also full of fibre and phytochemicals like flavonoid-rich artichokes, carotenoid-rich orange vegetables and leafy green herbs, as well as lemons loaded with vitamin C.

Per 1½ cups/375 mL serving: 250 calories; 16 g total fat; 25 g total carbs; 7 g fibre; 6 g sugar; 7 g protein; 440 mg sodium.

6 SERVINGS	24 SERVINGS	INGREDIENTS
2 tsp (10 mL)	3 Tbsp (45 mL)	grapeseed oil
¾ cup (180 mL)	3 cups (750 mL)	diced onions
3 (about 2 cups/ 500 mL)	12 (about 8 cups/ 2 L)	king oyster mushrooms, torn
⅔ cup (160 mL) (about 2 stalks)	2½ cups (625 mL) (about 9 stalks)	diced celery
⅔ cup (160 mL)	2½ cups (625 mL)	diced carrots
1 Tbsp (15 mL)	¼ cup (60 mL)	minced garlic
2 tsp (10 mL)	3 Tbsp (45 mL)	dried thyme
2 cups (500 mL)	8 cups (2 L)	low-sodium vegetable stock
1¼ cups (310 mL) (about ½ large)	7 cups (1.75 L) (about 2 large)	diced sweet potatoes
⅔ cup (160 mL)	2½ cups (625 mL)	diced white potatoes
1 (400 mL) can	4 (400 mL) cans	coconut milk
1¼ cups (310 mL)	5 cups (1.25 L)	unsweetened milk alternative
1 (398 mL) can	5 (398 mL) cans	artichoke hearts stored in water, drained, rinsed and sliced
2 tsp (10 mL)	3 Tbsp (45 mL)	dulse flakes (optional)
1 tsp (5 mL)	4 tsp (20 mL)	sea salt
2 tsp (10 mL) (about ½ lemon)	3 Tbsp (45 mL) (about 1–2 lemons)	fresh lemon juice
¼ tsp (1 mL)	1 tsp (5 mL)	lemon zest
¼ bunch	1 bunch	parsley, chopped

TIP

The oyster mushroom are easily torn by hand in lieu of chopping. This also gives them a seafood-like texture.

1. Heat oil in a large stockpot over medium heat. Add onions and sauté until soft and translucent, about 3 minutes.

2. Add oyster mushrooms and sauté for 5 minutes (or 10 to 12 minutes for 24 servings) until slightly brown.

3. Add celery, carrots, garlic and thyme, sautéing until celery is tender, about 5 minutes (or 10 to 12 minutes for 24 servings).

4. Add stock, increase heat to high, bring to a boil and then reduce to a simmer.

5. Add potatoes and allow to simmer until potatoes are tender, about 12 minutes (or 20 minutes for 24 servings).

6. Add coconut milk, milk alternative, artichoke hearts, dulse flakes (if using) and salt. Bring back to a simmer. Allow to simmer for 5 minutes (or 10 to 12 minutes for 24 servings).

7. Remove pot from heat. Stir in lemon juice and zest. Garnish with parsley and serve with crusty whole grain bread or top with homemade croutons.

Sweet Potato and Tahini Soup

PREPARATION TIME 20 minutes

COOKING TIME 40 minutes

Creamy and dreamy, sweet and spicy, this is a conversation-starting soup that will warm your heart and those you share it with. Make it ahead and enjoy its high protein and fibre content and anti-inflammatory properties for weeks in freezer batches, or share it immediately with some new—soon to be very good—friends!

Per 2 cups/500 mL serving with sesame brittle and pesto: 520 calories; 35 g total fat; 47 g total carbs; 9 g fibre; 14 g sugar; 11 g protein; 480 mg sodium.

6 SERVINGS	24 SERVINGS	INGREDIENTS
Soup		
1 tsp (5 mL)	4 tsp (20 mL)	grapeseed oil
1¼ cups (310 mL)	3 cups (750 mL)	diced onions
4 cloves	12 cloves	garlic, minced
1	4	small red chili pepper, minced
1 Tbsp (15 mL)	¼ cup (60 mL)	ground coriander
1 Tbsp (15 mL)	¼ cup (60 mL)	ground cumin
1 Tbsp (15 mL)	¼ cup (60 mL)	paprika
5 cups (1.25 L)	20 cups (5 L)	peeled and diced sweet potatoes
4 cups (1 L)	4 L	vegetable stock
1 (400 mL) can	4 (400 mL) cans	light coconut milk
½ cup (125 mL)	2 cups (500 mL)	tahini
1½ tsp (7.5 mL)	¼ cup (60 mL)	lime zest
¼ cup (60 mL)	¾ cup (180 mL)	fresh lime juice
½ tsp (2.5 mL)	2 tsp (10 mL)	salt
Garnish		
—	—	Sriracha Sesame Brittle (see recipe on following page)
—	—	Cilantro Pesto (see recipe on page 45)

1. Heat oil in a medium stockpot over medium-high heat. Add onions and sauté until translucent and fragrant, about 3 to 5 minutes.

2. Add garlic, red chili and spices and sauté until fragrant, about 1 to 2 minutes.

3. Add sweet potatoes and stock. Bring to a boil, and boil for about 5 minutes. Reduce to a simmer and allow to cook until potatoes are fork tender, about 10 to 15 minutes.

4. Add remaining ingredients. Using a hand immersion blender, blend until completely smooth.

5. To serve, ladle 2 cups (500 mL) of soup into each soup bowl. Top with sesame brittle and a drizzle of pesto (if using).

Sriracha Sesame Brittle

6 SERVINGS	24 SERVINGS	INGREDIENTS
1 Tbsp (15 mL)	¼ cup (60 mL)	coconut oil
½ cup (125 mL)	2 cups (500 mL)	sesame seeds
2 Tbsp (30 mL)	½ cup (125 mL)	maple syrup
2 Tbsp (30 mL)	½ cup (125 mL)	sriracha or other favourite hot sauce

1. Preheat oven to 300F (150C) and line a baking sheet with parchment paper.

2. Heat coconut oil in a small pot over medium heat. Once coconut oil has completely melted, add sesame seeds. Stir and allow sesame seeds to become fragrant, about 3 minutes.

3. Turn off heat and use a spatula to fold in maple syrup and hot sauce. Pour onto the parchment-lined baking sheet, ensuring that the brittle is about ¼ inch (0.6 cm) thick. For 24 servings use three parchment-lined baking sheets.

4. Place in oven and bake for 24 minutes, or until hard (rotating trays halfway through). Once it cools, the brittle should break easily when bent.

Cilantro Pesto

6 SERVINGS	24 SERVINGS	INGREDIENTS
4 cups (1 L)	16 cups (4 L)	cilantro, tightly packed
¼ cup (60 mL)	1 cup (250 mL)	ground blanched almonds
¼ cup (60 mL)	1 cup (250 mL)	nutritional yeast
¼ cup (60 mL)	1 cup (250 mL)	extra-virgin olive oil
¼ cup (60 mL)	1 cup (250 mL)	water
1	4	lime, juiced
1 clove	4 cloves	garlic
¼ tsp (1 mL)	1 tsp (5 mL)	salt

1. In a food processor, combine all pesto ingredients. Process until smooth, about 4 minutes.

Waldorf Salad with Pomegranate and Pistachio

This salad is beautiful and can easily be prepared ahead of time to lighten your lunch or dinner load. Just leave the dressing on the side and dress five minutes before serving. Using pre-cut slaw mixes would save even more time. This take on a classic Waldorf salad is fresh, crunchy, sweet and sour, and has a moreish quality—although it's also healthy as heck.

Per 4 cups/301 g serving: 240 calories; 8 g total fat; 37 g total carbs; 8 g fibre; 26 g sugar; 5 g protein; 300 mg sodium.

6 SERVINGS	24 SERVINGS	INGREDIENTS
¾ head (about 10 cups/2.5 L)	1 large head (about 40 cups/10 L)	purple or green cabbage (or a combination of both colours), thinly sliced
2	8	Granny Smith apples, diced
2 cups (500 mL)	4 cups (1 L)	pomegranate seeds (about 1 pomegranate)
¼ cup (60 mL)	1 cup (250 mL)	chopped pistachios
⅓ cup (80 mL)	1⅓ cups (350 mL)	chopped walnuts
¾ bunch	3 bunches	mint, cut in chiffonade
½ bunch	2 bunches	parsley, chopped
3 Tbsp (45 mL)	¾ cup (180 mL)	Dijon mustard
3 Tbsp (45 mL)	¾ cup (180 mL)	maple syrup
1 Tbsp (15 mL)	¼ cup (60 mL)	fresh lemon zest
¼ cup (60 mL)	1 cup (250 mL)	fresh lemon juice
¼ tsp (1 mL)	1 tsp (5 mL)	salt

1. In a large salad bowl, combine cabbage, apple, pomegranate seeds, pistachios, walnuts, mint and parsley.

2. In a small bowl, whisk together the remaining ingredients.

3. When ready to serve, add dressing to salad bowl and toss.

Pot Pies Three Ways

PREPARATION TIME 25 minutes

COOKING TIME 25 to 30 minutes

Pot pies are the ultimate comfort food, and aside from filling you with hearty warmth they can also be good for you! These healthful pot pie recipes are a modern twist on the traditional freezer-friendly pot pies the local church ladies prepared for a community of eaters in my youth. They include all kinds of health-promoting foods, such as whole grains, legumes, orange and green vegetables, allium vegetables and herbs and spices.

6 SERVINGS	24 SERVINGS	INGREDIENTS
Crust		
4 cups (1 L)	16 cups (4 L)	spelt flour
1 tsp (5 mL)	4 tsp (20 mL)	baking powder
1 tsp (5 mL)	4 tsp (20 mL)	onion powder
½ tsp (2.5 mL)	2 tsp (10 mL)	salt
1 cup (250 mL)	4 cups (1 L)	coconut oil
1⅓ cups (350 mL)	5⅓ cups (1.35 L)	water
1 Tbsp (15 mL)	⅓ cup (80 mL)	apple cider vinegar

1. Preheat oven to 375F (190C) and grease individual 5-inch pie plates.

2. In a large bowl, combine flour, baking powder, onion powder and salt.

3. Cut in coconut oil until fully incorporated. (Clumps of coconut oil will form when you are kneading the dough. This is normal and will result in a flaky crust.)

4. Make a well in the centre of the mixture and add the water and apple cider vinegar. Thoroughly combine.

5. Knead into dough. To adjust consistency, add additional flour if needed. Cover with a damp cloth, set aside and allow to rest for 15 minutes.

6. Prepare your choice of filling (see recipes on pages 50–52).

7. Divide the dough mixture into 6 balls (or 24 balls if making 24 servings). On a well-floured surface, take two-thirds of each ball and roll out to ¼-inch (0.6 cm) thickness. Place into the 5-inch pie plates.

8. Fill each pie to the top with 1 cup (250 mL) pot pie filling.

9. Roll out the remaining third of each ball into a circle and place on top of each pot pie. Pinch to secure the pastry's edges, and press down edges with a fork. Then use a knife to make 3 slits in the top to release steam. Brush tops with soy milk. Repeat with the remaining dough and pot pie filling. Once completed, place on a baking sheet and cook in the oven for 25 to 30 minutes until the crust is golden brown.

TIP

For large 9-inch pies: Split dough into 3 balls (or 12 if making 24 servings). Roll out two-thirds of a ball. Place in a 9-inch pie plate. Roll out the remaining third of that ball. Set aside for top crust. Repeat with the remaining balls. Add 2 cups (500 mL) of filling to each pie shell and place top crust on each pot pie. Pinch to secure the pastry's edges, and press down edges with a fork. Then use a knife to make 3 slits in the top to release steam. Brush tops with soy milk and bake in the oven for 45 to 50 minutes.

Continued...

Cream of Chickpea

Per 1 pie (424 g):
790 calories; 45 g total fat; 75 g total carbs; 16 g fibre; 5 g sugar; 21 g protein; 490 mg sodium.

6 SERVINGS	24 SERVINGS	INGREDIENTS
1¾ cups (430 mL)	5 cups (1.25 L)	unsweetened soy milk (6 servings: reserve 2 Tbsp/30 mL for brushing the top crusts) and (24 servings: reserve ½ cup/125 mL for brushing the top crusts)
1 cup (250 mL)	4 cups (1 L)	silken or soft tofu
3 Tbsp (45 mL) (about 1 lemon)	¾ cup (180 mL) (about 4 lemons)	fresh lemon juice
3 Tbsp (45 mL)	¾ cup (180 mL)	nutritional yeast
4½ tsp (20 mL)	5 Tbsp (75 mL)	grapeseed oil
1	4	onion, diced
2	8	carrots, diced
1 stalk	4 stalks	celery, diced
¼ head	1 head	garlic, minced
2 tsp (10 mL)	3 Tbsp (45 mL)	dried thyme
1 tsp (5 mL)	4 tsp (20 mL)	ground cumin
½ tsp (2.5 mL)	2 tsp (10 mL)	ground turmeric
1½ cups (375 mL)	6 cups (1.5 L)	sliced white button mushrooms
1 (540 mL) can	3 (796 mL) cans	chickpeas, drained, rinsed and mashed
1 small head	4 small heads	broccoli, cut into small florets, stems diced
¼ bunch	1 bunch	parsley, chopped
¾ tsp (4 mL)	3 tsp (15 mL)	salt
½ tsp (2.5 mL)	2 tsp (10 mL)	black pepper

1. In a blender, working in batches, if necessary, combine soy milk, tofu, lemon juice and nutritional yeast. Blend until smooth and set aside.

2. Heat oil in a large stockpot over medium heat. Add onions and sauté for 4 minutes (10 minutes for 24 servings), or until translucent.

3. Add carrots, celery, garlic, thyme, cumin and turmeric and cook until fragrant, about 2 to 3 minutes (7 minutes for 24 servings).

4. Add mushrooms and sauté until just softened, about 4 minutes (8 minutes for 24 servings).

5. Add the tofu sauce and chickpeas. Bring to a boil then reduce heat and simmer until sauce has thickened, about 10 minutes (15 minutes for 24 servings).

6. Add broccoli and cook for another 5 minutes.

7. Stir in parsley, salt and pepper and remove from heat.

Lentil, Spinach and Onion

Per 1 pie (450 g):
790 calories; 41 g total fat;
87 g total carbs; 16 g fibre;
4 g sugar; 17 g protein;
500 mg sodium.

6 SERVINGS	24 SERVINGS	INGREDIENTS
1 Tbsp (15 mL)	¼ cup (60 mL)	grapeseed oil
1½	6	large onions, diced
4 cloves	16 cloves	garlic, pureed
2	8	large russet potatoes, diced
3 cups (750 mL)	12 cups (3 L)	vegetable stock
1 Tbsp (15 mL)	¼ cup (60 mL)	tapioca starch
2 cups (500 mL)	8 cups (2 L)	cooked brown lentils
4½ tsp (22.5 mL)	6 Tbsp (90 mL)	tamari
5 cups (1.25 L)	20 cups (5 L)	spinach
1 Tbsp (15 mL)	¼ cup (60 mL)	finely chopped fresh thyme
½ tsp (2.5 mL)	2 tsp (10 mL)	sea salt
¼ tsp (1 mL)	1 tsp (5 mL)	black pepper

TIP

For a variation on this recipe,
try diced celeriac or turnip in
lieu of potatoes.

1. Heat oil in a medium stockpot over medium-high heat. Add onions and garlic. Sauté until fragrant, about 3 minutes (10 minutes for 24 servings).

2. Stir in potatoes and 2 cups (500 mL) of stock (or 8 cups/2 L for 24 servings). Cover with lid and bring to a boil. Once boiling, reduce heat and simmer for 15 minutes or until potatoes are tender.

3. Meanwhile whisk together tapioca starch and remaining vegetable stock in a large bowl to form a slurry.

4. Stir in slurry, lentils and tamari and bring back up to a simmer. Allow tapioca starch to thicken and reduce liquid, about 10 to 12 minutes.

5. Stir in spinach, thyme, salt and pepper and remove from heat.

Miso, Mushroom and Edamame

PREPARATION TIME 15 to 20 minutes
COOKING TIME 55 minutes

Per 1 pie (417 g):
780 calories; 42 g total
fat; 81 g total carbs;
13 g fibre; 5 g sugar;
16 g protein; 510 mg
sodium.

6 SERVINGS	24 SERVINGS	INGREDIENTS
1 Tbsp (15 mL)	¼ cup (60 mL)	grapeseed oil
1	4	onion, thinly sliced
5 cups (1.25 L)	3 lbs (1.4 kg)	sliced mixed mushrooms, such as cremini, shiitake and oyster
4 cloves	16 cloves	garlic, pureed
2	8	large russet potatoes, diced
2 cups (500 mL)	12 cups (3 L)	low-sodium vegetable stock
3 Tbsp (45 mL)	¾ cup (180 mL)	red miso paste
¼ cup (60 mL)	1 cup (250 mL)	water
2 Tbsp (30 mL)	¼ cup (60 mL)	tapioca starch
1½ cups (375 mL)	6 cups (1.5 L)	shelled edamame, fresh or frozen
2 Tbsp (30 mL)	½ cup (125 mL)	rice vinegar
½ tsp (2.5 mL)	2 tsp (10 mL)	sea salt
¼ tsp (1 mL)	1 tsp (5 mL)	black pepper
2	8	green onions, thinly sliced

1. Heat oil in a medium stockpot over medium-high heat. Add onions and mushrooms and sauté until onions are translucent and mushrooms are browned, about 8 minutes (12 minutes for 24 servings).

2. Add garlic and sauté until fragrant, about 1 minute (3 minutes for 24 servings).

3. Stir in potatoes and vegetable stock. Cover with lid and bring to a simmer. Reduce heat and simmer for 15 minutes (25 minutes for 24 servings), or until potatoes are tender.

4. Meanwhile, whisk together miso paste, water and tapioca starch in a small bowl to form a slurry and set aside.

5. When potatoes are tender, stir in miso slurry, edamame, rice vinegar, salt and pepper. Bring back to a simmer and cook until edamame are cooked through, about 2 minutes (5 minutes for 24 servings). Remove from heat and garnish with green onions.

Brussels Sprouts with Roasted Apples and Shiitake Bacon

PREPARATION TIME 10 minutes for 6 servings and 20 minutes for 24 servings
COOKING TIME 50 minutes

The combination of sweet, savoury and salty in this protein- and fibre-rich side dish is a good excuse to make a large batch for your next sit-down meal. Cruciferous vegetables such as Brussels sprouts are filled with antibacterial and anti-inflammatory properties and provide health benefits related to cancer prevention and management.

Per 1 cup/615 g serving: 380 calories; 13 g total fat; 62 g total carbs; 18 g fibre; 31 g sugar; 14 g protein; 500 mg sodium.

6 SERVINGS	24 SERVINGS	INGREDIENTS
3 lbs (1.4 kg)	12 lbs (5.4 kg)	Brussels sprouts, ends removed and halved or quartered depending on size
4	16	large gala apples, cut in large dice (similar in size to the cut sprouts)
¼ cup (60 mL)	1 cup (250 mL)	grapeseed oil
½ tsp (2.5 mL)	2 tsp (10 mL)	dried thyme
½ tsp (2.5 mL)	2 tsp (10 mL)	dried rosemary
½ tsp (2.5 mL)	2 tsp (10 mL)	sea salt
3 lbs (1.4 kg)	12 lbs (5.4 kg)	shiitake mushrooms, stems removed, thinly sliced
1 Tbsp (15 mL)	¼ cup (60 mL)	smoked paprika
3 Tbsp (45 mL)	¾ cup (180 mL)	maple syrup
4½ tsp (22.5 mL)	6 Tbsp (90 mL)	tamari
Garnish		
3 Tbsp (45 mL)	¾ cup (180 mL)	blanched ground almonds
¼ tsp (1 mL)	1 tsp (5 mL)	sea salt

1. Preheat oven to 400F (205C). Line baking sheet(s) with parchment paper.

2. In a large bowl, combine Brussels sprouts and apples, along with half of the oil and the thyme, rosemary and salt. Toss together until sprouts and apples are evenly coated.

3. Distribute onto the prepared pan(s) and cover with foil. Ensure that they are not overcrowded. Bake for 15 minutes. Remove foil and continue to bake uncovered for another 35 minutes or until the Brussels sprouts are golden brown and crispy.

4. Meanwhile, place a large sauté pan over medium-high heat. Once heated, add mushrooms and remaining oil. You will need to sauté in batches if preparing 24 servings, which prevents overcrowding and steaming in the pan, ensuring crispier mushrooms. (When doing so, divide the paprika, maple syrup and tamari up as well to make sure each mushroom gets coated with flavour.) Sauté until crispy and golden brown, about 8 to 10 minutes. Stir in paprika, maple syrup and tamari and sauté for another 2 minutes. Remove from heat and set aside.

5. In a small bowl, combine ground almonds and salt.

6. Remove Brussels sprouts from oven and transfer to serving plates. Top with shiitake bacon and sprinkle with the ground almond mixture.

Butterscotch Squash Coffee Cake

Yes, squash in cake, we have gone there! This decadent and kid-friendly cake could be your show-stopping moment at the next holiday meal. There are many reasons to hop on the orange vegetable cake bandwagon, including the high fibre and antioxidant content, but ultimately this cake is just plain delicious. Share it far and wide! Note: If buttercup squash is out of season and difficult to source, feel free to replace it with butternut squash, at a 1:1 ratio. Other varieties such as kabocha will make the cake too dry. And don't forget to reserve some puree for the glaze.

Per 1 slice/98 g serving:
310 calories; 20 g total fat;
31 g total carbs; 4 g fibre;
13 g sugar; 3 g protein;
320 mg sodium.

12 SERVINGS	24 SERVINGS	INGREDIENTS
Dry Ingredients		
2 cups (500 mL)	4 cups (1 L)	whole grain spelt flour
3 Tbsp (45 mL)	6 Tbsp (90 mL)	ground flaxseed
2 tsp (10 mL)	4 tsp (20 mL)	ground cinnamon
2 tsp (10 mL)	1 Tbsp (15 mL)	baking powder
1 tsp (5 mL)	2 tsp (10 mL)	baking soda
¼ tsp (1 mL)	½ tsp (2.5 mL)	ground nutmeg
¼ tsp (1 mL)	½ tsp (2.5 mL)	salt
¼ cup (60 mL)	½ cup (125 mL)	pecans, chopped
Wet Ingredients		
1¼ cups (300 mL)	2½ cups (625 mL)	buttercup squash puree
½ cup (125 mL)	1 cup (250 mL)	grapeseed oil
½ cup (125 mL)	1 cup (250 mL)	maple syrup
⅓ cup (80 mL)	⅔ cup (160 mL)	water
1 Tbsp (15 mL)	2 Tbsp (30 mL)	apple cider vinegar
1 Tbsp (15 mL)	2 Tbsp (30 mL)	freshly grated ginger
1 tsp (5 mL)	2 tsp (10 mL)	vanilla extract
Butterscotch Glaze		
¼ cup (60 mL)	½ cup (125 mL)	coconut oil
½ cup (125 mL)	1 cup (250 mL)	coconut milk
¼ cup (60 mL)	½ cup (125 mL)	maple syrup
1 Tbsp (15 mL)	2 Tbsp (30 mL)	buttercup squash puree
1 tsp (5 mL)	2 tsp (10 mL)	vanilla extract
Garnish		
3 Tbsp (45 mL)	⅓ cup (80 mL)	toasted pecans, chopped

Continued . . .

1. Preheat oven to 350F (180C) and grease one 9-inch bundt cake pan or two 9-inch bundt cake pans if making 24 servings. (If bundt cake pans are not available use one 9-inch cake pan for 12 servings or two 9-inch cake pans for 24 servings. Line the bottoms of the cake pans with parchment paper and reduce baking time to 30 minutes.)

2. In a large mixing bowl, combine dry ingredients and mix thoroughly. Make sure the pecans are nicely coated to prevent them from falling into the bottom of the pan.

3. In a small mixing bowl, combine wet ingredients and whisk thoroughly.

4. Add the wet ingredients to the dry and mix until combined. Do not overmix.

5. Evenly distribute batter into greased bundt cake pan(s). Bake for 45 to 50 minutes or until a toothpick inserted into the centre(s) comes out clean. Remove from oven and allow to cool completely in pan(s) on a cooling rack. (It is important that the cakes cool completely before removing them from their pans, or else they may fall apart.)

6. Meanwhile, make the butterscotch glaze. Heat a medium saucepan over medium heat, then add the coconut oil.

7. Once melted, whisk in the remaining glaze ingredients, then reduce heat and allow to simmer for 3 to 5 minutes. Occasionally whisk the glaze to ensure it is not sticking to the pan's sides or bottom. Set aside and allow to cool, about 10 minutes.

8. Once the cake(s) and sauce have completely cooled, carefully flip the cake pan(s) over onto cake plate(s). Drizzle with the butterscotch glaze and sprinkle with toasted pecans. Slice and serve!

Cinnamon Bun Cookies

PREPARATION TIME 20 minutes
COOKING TIME 12 minutes

Why choose between cinnamon buns and cookies when you can have it all! These freezable circles of pure joy not only provide you with a good source of fibre per cookie, but also your daily dose of sweetness. This recipe is a family and supper club favourite.

Per 1 cookie/43 g serving: 210 calories; 15 g total fat; 17 g total carbs; 2 g fibre; 6 g sugar; 3 g protein; 45 mg sodium.

24 SERVINGS — INGREDIENTS

1 cup (250 mL)	coconut oil
½ cup (125 mL)	maple syrup
1 tsp (5 mL)	vanilla extract
2½ cups (625 mL)	spelt flour
2 Tbsp (30 mL)	ground flaxseed
½ tsp (2.5 mL)	salt

Cinnamon Filling

3 Tbsp (45 mL)	coconut oil
2 Tbsp (30 mL)	spelt flour
1 Tbsp (15 mL)	cinnamon
2 tsp (10 mL)	maple syrup
1 tsp (5 mL)	vanilla extract

Cashew Cream Icing

1 cup (250 mL)	cashews
¼ cup (60 mL)	water
3 Tbsp (45 mL)	maple syrup
2 Tbsp (30 mL)	coconut oil
1 tsp (5 mL)	vanilla extract

1. Preheat oven to 375F (190C) and line two baking sheets with parchment paper.

2. In a medium bowl, use a hand mixer to combine coconut oil, maple syrup and vanilla. Mix until fully combined, about 2 minutes.

3. In a large bowl, whisk together flour, flaxseed and salt. Using the hand mixer, slowly mix the wet ingredients into the dry.

4. Transfer the dough onto a flat, dry and floured surface. Using a rolling pin, roll out the dough to a 12 × 12-inch (30 × 30-cm) square.

5. In a small bowl, whisk together the cinnamon filling ingredients. Using an offset spatula, evenly spread the filling onto the dough, covering the entire surface all the way to the edges. Roll the dough into a tight log, wrap in parchment paper and place in the freezer for 20 minutes, until the dough is firm and sliceable.

6. Once the dough is firm, slice the log evenly into 24 cookies and place on the prepared baking sheets.

7. Bake for 12 minutes or until cookies are golden brown. Remove from oven and allow to cool on a cooling rack.

8. Meanwhile, combine all icing ingredients in a food processor. Process until smooth and then drizzle over the cookies. (If you plan to package these cookies, allow the icing to set before doing so. Or you can package the cookies and icing separately and ice the cookies before serving.)

The Ultimate Chocolate Protein Powder

Short on time during the holiday season? This luxurious, make-ahead recipe for protein-rich chocolate heaven in a glass is a great way to healthfully fuel your tank during a busy time of year. It makes a great grab-and-go breakfast or snack. The protein powder provides 11 g of protein per serving, and when unsweetened soy milk is added the total is 18 g per serving. The powder also happens to be dead easy to make, as well as being high in phytonutrients: polyphenols, omega-3 fatty acids and vitamins C and E.

Per ⅓ cup/71 g serving:
340 calories; 21 g total fat;
28 g total carbs; 19 g fibre;
2 g sugar; 16 g protein;
120 mg sodium.

6 SERVINGS	24 SERVINGS	INGREDIENTS
1 cup (250 mL)	4 cups (1 L)	chia seeds
⅔ cup (160 mL)	2½ cups (625 mL)	cacao powder or cocoa powder
⅔ cup (160 mL)	2⅔ cups (660 mL)	hemp seeds
¼ cup (60 mL)	1 cup (250 mL)	maca powder
¼ tsp (1 mL)	1½ tsp (7.5 mL)	stevia (optional)

For making a smoothie (1 serving)
1 cup frozen berries of choice
1 cup of milk alternative of choice

1. In a spice grinder or high-powered flour grinder, combine all the protein powder ingredients and grind until they form a smooth flour. (If you do not have a spice grinder or flour grinder, mix all the dry ingredients together and just add to smoothies before blending or use as a topper for your morning cereal or breakfast bowl.)

2. When making a smoothie, add ¼ cup (60 mL) of protein powder to berries and milk alternative in a blender. Blend until smooth, and enjoy.

3. To store powder, keep in a resealable bag or jar in the freezer.

TIP

If you plan to leave the stevia out of the powder, you can replace it by adding 1 tsp (5 mL) honey or maple syrup to your smoothie before blending. Or adjust the sweetness to your liking!

Grandma's butter tarts, Dad's chowder, Mom's mac and cheese, canned peaches and strawberry jam, the church ladies' pot pies, Chappie's deep dish pizza—my comfort food list could go on for a while. These are the types of foods we turn to when we need a feeling of security, of being looked after, and a reminder of unconditional love. The following recipes, many of which can be made ahead for a friend or loved one, can serve as a warm hug for someone who is having a hard day. When you're in need of a comforting meal, turn to these warming soups, hearty mains and simple desserts for an easy-to-prepare taste of home.

**SAMPLE MENU FOR A
COMFORTING GET-TOGETHER**

SOUP
*Okra and Oyster Mushroom Gumbo
with Red and White Beans*

SALAD
Fresh Vegan Caesar Salad

MAIN
Mac and Cheese with Coconut Bacon

DESSERT
*Maple Caramel Sauce with Granny
Smith Apples and Toasted Walnuts*

Comforting
Classics

Okra and Oyster Mushroom Gumbo with Red and White Beans

PREPARATION TIME 20 minutes
COOKING TIME 40 minutes for 6 servings
and 60 minutes for 24 servings

Filled with all the things that warm you from head to toe—including health-promoting chilies, beans, greens and colourful veggies—this gumbo invites you to grab crusty whole grain bread, your coziest sweater and your favourite people on a chilly night and dig in.

Per 1⅔ cups/400 mL serving: 310 calories; 4 g total fat; 60 g total carbs; 13 g fibre; 12 g sugar; 12 g protein; 490 mg sodium.

6 SERVINGS	24 SERVINGS	INGREDIENTS
1 Tbsp (15 mL)	¼ cup (60 mL)	olive oil
1½ cups (375 mL)	5 cups (1.25 L)	diced yellow onions
1 cup (250 mL)	4 cups (1 L)	diced carrots
⅔ cup (160 mL)	2⅔ cups (660 mL)	diced celery
¼ cup (60 mL)	¾ cup (180 mL)	diced shallots
2 cups (500 mL)	8 cups (2 L)	sliced king oyster mushrooms, cut crosswise
2 cups (500 mL)	8 cups (2 L)	chopped okra, fresh or frozen, in ¼-inch (0.6 cm) pieces
1 cup (250 mL)	3 cups (750 mL)	diced green peppers
½ head	2 heads	garlic, minced
1	4	large red chili, minced
1 Tbsp (15 mL)	¼ cup (60 mL)	dried thyme
2 tsp (10 mL)	2 Tbsp (30 mL)	ground cumin
2	6	bay leaves
½ cup (125 mL)	2 cups (500 mL)	uncooked long-grain brown rice
2½ cups (625 mL)	8 cups (2 L)	diced white potatoes
2½ cups (625 mL)	10 cups (2.5 L)	canned diced tomatoes, no added salt
2 cups (500 mL)	4 cups (1 L)	crushed tomatoes
3 cups (750 mL)	8 cups (2 L)	low-sodium vegetable stock
1 cup (250 mL)	4 cups (1 L)	cooked white kidney beans, drained and rinsed
1 cup (250 mL)	4 cups (1 L)	cooked red kidney beans, drained and rinsed
4 sprigs	14 sprigs	parsley, chopped
1 Tbsp (15 mL)	¼ cup (60 mL)	dulse flakes (optional)
1 tsp (5 mL)	4 tsp (20 mL)	salt
¼ tsp (1 mL)	2 tsp (10 mL)	ground black pepper
¼ tsp (1 mL)	2 tsp (10 mL)	cayenne (optional)
2	8	green onions, thinly sliced

1. Heat a large stockpot over medium-high heat, then add oil. Once heated, add onions, carrots, celery and shallots. Sauté for 5 to 7 minutes, until fragrant.

2. Add oyster mushrooms and sauté for 7 minutes (12 minutes for 24 servings), or until slightly brown.

3. Add okra, green peppers, garlic, chilies, thyme, cumin and bay leaves. Sauté until fragrant, about 4 minutes (10 minutes for 24 servings).

4. Stir in rice and sauté for 2 to 3 minutes. Stir in potatoes, tomatoes and stock.

5. Bring to a boil, then reduce to a simmer. Cover and cook until potatoes are fork tender and rice is al dente, about 20 to 25 minutes. Stir occasionally to avoid rice sticking to the bottom.

6. Add beans, parsley, dulse flakes (if using), salt and pepper, and cayenne (if using). Heat through, about 3 minutes.

7. Remove bay leaves, top with green onions and serve with multigrain bread.

Bean and Squash Soup with Kamut Dumplings

PREPARATION TIME 45 minutes for 6 servings and 60 minutes for 24 servings
COOKING TIME 30 minutes for 6 servings and 45 minutes for 24 servings

This dish is a beautiful bean- and whole-grain-filled take on a classic, creamy Rastafarian family recipe. It is everything you will want after a long, lonely day and is best enjoyed in big fancy bowls with your favourite people.

Per 1⅓ cup/325 mL serving: 300 calories; 10 g total fat; 46 g total carbs; 10 g fibre; 5 g sugar; 11 g protein; 470 mg sodium.

6 SERVINGS	24 SERVINGS	INGREDIENTS
Kamut Dumplings		
1½ cups (375 mL)	6 cups (1.5 L)	kamut flour
¼ tsp (1 mL)	1 tsp (5 mL)	salt
¾ cup (180 mL)	3 cups (750 mL)	coconut milk
Soup		
1 Tbsp (15 mL)	¼ cup (60 mL)	grapeseed oil
¾ cup (180 mL) (about 1 onion)	3½ cups (875 mL) (about 4 onions)	finely chopped onions
6 cloves	2 large heads	garlic, minced
2¼ cups (560 mL)	9 cups (2.2 L)	seeded and diced tomatoes
1 tsp (5 mL)	4 tsp (20 mL)	salt
1 Tbsp (15 mL)	¼ cup (60 mL)	finely chopped fresh thyme
1 bunch	4 bunches	green onions, finely chopped
2 cups (500 mL)	8 cups (2 L)	cooked red kidney beans, drained and rinsed
½ (400 mL) can	2 (400 mL) cans	coconut milk (stir first to mix water and cream)
1½ cups (375 mL)	6 cups (1.5 L)	vegetable stock
1 cup (250 mL)	4 cups (1 mL)	peeled and diced butternut squash
¼ tsp (1 mL)	1 tsp (5 mL)	ground allspice
2 cups (500 mL)	8 cups (2 L)	baby spinach, chopped

TIP

Adjust the consistency of the dumplings during kneading by adding extra flour if the dough is too sticky, or water if it is too dry.

1. In a large bowl, combine kamut flour and salt. Make a well in the centre.

2. Add coconut milk and knead for 15 minutes, until dough is firm. Divide dough into 8 pieces and roll into tube shapes. Set aside.

3. Heat a large stockpot over medium-high heat, then add oil. Once heated, add onions and cook until soft, about 3 minutes (or 9 minutes for 24 servings).

4. Add garlic, tomatoes, salt and thyme and cook until fragrant, about 2 minutes (or 7 minutes for 24 servings).

5. Stir in green onions, beans, coconut milk and stock. Bring to a boil, then lower heat and simmer for 5 minutes (or 12 minutes for 24 servings).

6. Add squash and allspice and continue to cook on low heat for 15 minutes. Add dumplings and continue to cook for 5 more minutes (10 to 15 minutes for 24 servings), until squash is softened and dumplings are cooked through.

7. Remove from heat and stir in spinach. Serve with crusty whole grain bread for dipping.

Fresh Vegan Caesar Salad

Plant-based Caesar salad is a must-have comfort food staple in your recipe repertoire. Throughout my life Caesar salads have always been a go-to when feeding large crowds, from farm family gatherings to meals for soup kitchens, out-of-the cold-programs to Gilda's Club dinners. And this version is miles ahead in terms of its nutritional profile and comes equipped with the creaminess and rich flavour we all love.

Per 2½ cup/165 g serving: 150 calories; 8 g total fat; 16 g total carbs; 5 g fibre; 2 g sugar; 5 g protein; 330 mg sodium.

6 SERVINGS	24 SERVINGS	INGREDIENTS
Dressing		
¼ tsp (1 mL)	1 tsp (5 mL)	lemon zest
¼ cup (60 mL)	1 cup (250 mL)	fresh lemon juice
2 Tbsp (30 mL)	½ cup (125 mL)	organic unsweetened soy milk
4½ tsp (22.5 mL)	6 Tbsp (90 mL)	nutritional yeast
2 Tbsp (30 mL)	¼ cup (60 mL)	extra-virgin olive oil
5 tsp (25 mL)	7 Tbsp (105 mL)	ground flaxseed
1 tsp (5 mL)	4 tsp (20 mL)	Dijon mustard
¼ tsp (1 mL)	1 tsp (5 mL)	pureed garlic
¼ tsp (1 mL)	1 tsp (5 mL)	dulse flakes (optional)
¼ tsp (1 mL)	1 tsp (5 mL)	sea salt
Cashew Parmesan (optional)		
2½ Tbsp (37 mL)	¾ cup (180 mL)	raw cashews
2 Tbsp (30 mL)	½ cup (125 mL)	nutritional yeast
½ tsp (2.5 mL)	2 tsp (10 mL)	fresh lemon juice
¼ tsp (1 mL)	½ tsp (2.5 mL)	salt
Salad		
¼ cup (60 mL)	1 cup (250 mL)	thinly sliced sun-dried tomatoes
3 Tbsp (45 mL)	¾ cup (180 mL)	capers
2 cups (500 mL)	8 cups (2 L)	whole grain croutons
15 cups (3.75 L)	60 cups (15 L)	hearty salad greens, such as kale, Swiss chard or romaine lettuce, loosely packed

1. In a Mason jar, combine all dressing ingredients and shake vigorously until thoroughly combined. Set aside.

2. For cashew parmesan, if using: In a food processor, combine cashews, nutritional yeast, lemon juice and salt. Process until smooth. Set aside.

3. In a large salad bowl, combine leafy greens with sundried tomatoes, capers, croutons and parmesan, if using. When ready to serve, drizzle with dressing and toss until salad is coated.

Traditional Greek Salad with Tofu Feta

PREPARATION TIME: 25 to 30 minutes

Greek salads always remind me of time well spent with family and using up all the goodies in Grandma's garden. This one's got cucumbers, red onions, olives and crunchy, fresh bell peppers, topped with salty, melt-in-your-mouth tofu feta. A modern, protein-rich version of an old classic, it is a great way to start off a cozy dinner with those plant-based-eating skeptics. And to make it a meal, top this delicious salad with falafel.

Per 2 cups/259 g serving: 170 calories; 12 g total fat; 11 g total carbs; 3 g fibre; 5 g sugar; 7 g protein; 400 mg sodium.

6 SERVINGS	24 SERVINGS	INGREDIENTS
Dressing		
1 (350 g) package	4 (350 g) packages	extra-firm tofu, drained, half crumbled and half cut into ¼-inch cubes
2 Tbsp (30 mL)	¾ cup (180 mL)	fresh lemon juice
2 cloves	8 cloves	garlic, pureed
¼ cup (60 mL)	1 cup (250 mL)	red wine vinegar
¼ cup (60 mL)	1 cup (250 mL)	oregano, chopped
2 Tbsp (30 mL)	½ cup (125 mL)	olive oil
½ tsp (2.5 mL)	2 tsp (10 mL)	black pepper (optional)
½ tsp (2.5 mL)	2 tsp (5 mL)	sea salt
Salad		
5	20	small Roma tomatoes, cut into sixths
1	4	green pepper, thinly sliced
1	4	medium English cucumber, halved lengthwise and sliced
1	4	red pepper, thinly sliced
½	2	small red onion, thinly sliced
½ cup (125 mL)	2 cups (500 mL)	pitted kalamata olives, quartered

1. In a small bowl, combine all dressing ingredients. Add all the tofu and mix to coat evenly. Allow to marinate for 20 minutes.

2. In a large salad bowl, combine all salad ingredients. When ready to serve, add the marinated tofu and dressing to the salad and toss. Serve with toasted whole wheat or multigrain pita.

Eggplant Moussaka

PREPARATION TIME 20 minutes
COOKING TIME 1 hour

This make-ahead Greek classic can be dressed up or down and has been served for a wide variety of occasions, from casual potlucks to my wedding. Aside from being a meaty meatless alternative, lentils are high in protein, fibre, folate and iron and deserve to be the star of your next meal.

Per 1 slice/207 g serving: 170 calories; 7 g total fat; 19 g total carbs; 5 g fibre; 5 g sugar; 9 g protein; 420 mg sodium.

6 SERVINGS	24 SERVINGS	INGREDIENTS
½ eggplant (about 250 g)	2 eggplants (about 1 kg)	sliced into ¼-inch-thick (0.6-cm-thick) disks
¾ tsp (4 mL)	1 Tbsp (15 mL)	sea salt, divided
1½ tsp (7.5 mL)	2 Tbsp (30 mL)	extra-virgin olive oil, divided
1 (400 mL) can	2 (798 mL) cans	diced tomatoes, juice drained and reserved
½ cup (125 mL)	1¾ cups (430 mL)	dry brown lentils
½	2	onion, diced
1 Tbsp (15 mL)	¼ cup (60 mL)	dried oregano
¼ tsp (1 mL)	1 tsp (5 mL)	black pepper
175 g	2 (350 g) packages	firm tofu, crumbled
⅓ cup (80 mL)	1½ cups (375 mL)	unsalted blanched almonds or cashews, soaked in hot water for 1 hour, water discarded
½ cup (125 mL)	2 cups (500 mL)	water
3–4 cloves	1 head	garlic, peeled
2½ Tbsp (37 mL)	⅔ cup (160 mL)	fresh lemon juice
1 sprig	4 sprigs	parsley, finely chopped

1. Preheat oven to 375F (190C) and line baking sheet(s) with parchment paper.

2. Lay eggplant slices flat on a clean counter. Sprinkle with ¼ tsp (1 mL) salt for 6 servings or 1 tsp (5 mL) salt for 24 servings. Allow to sit for 5 minutes then pat dry with a towel. Arrange eggplant in a single layer on prepared baking sheet(s) and brush tops with ½ tsp (2.5 mL) oil for 6 servings or 2 tsp (10 mL) oil for 24 servings. Place in oven for 10 minutes or until slightly brown. Flip and bake for another 10 minutes. Remove from oven and set aside.

3. Using the reserved tomato juice, cook lentils according to package directions, using additional water if needed. The lentils should cook to about 1¼ cups (310 mL) for 6 servings and 5 cups (1.25 L) for 24 servings.

4. Heat a large sauté pan over medium heat, then add remaining oil. Once heated, add onions and sauté until translucent, about 3 to 5 minutes.

5. Add cooked lentils and oregano. Sauté until fragrant, about 3 minutes.

6. Add tomatoes to the lentil mixture. Sauté until liquid has evaporated, about 5 to 7 minutes. Season with pepper and ¼ tsp (1 mL) salt for 6 servings or 1 tsp (5 mL) salt for 24 servings. Set aside.

7. Meanwhile, combine tofu, soaked nuts, water, garlic, lemon juice and remaining salt in a food processor. Blend until completely smooth.

8. To assemble: In one to four 9 × 13-inch baking dishes, evenly distribute and spread the lentil mixture. Layer the eggplant onto it and then top with the almond mixture. Cover with foil and bake for 15 minutes. Remove foil and bake for another 30 to 35 minutes, or until the topping starts to turn golden. Garnish with fresh parsley.

Mac and Cheese with Coconut Bacon

PREPARATION TIME 1 hour for 6 servings
and 1½ hours for 24 servings
COOKING TIME 1 hour

Every great home cook, student, caretaker, grandparent and boyfriend needs a go-to, leaves-you-dreaming-about-it, plant-based mac and cheese recipe in their repertoire. This is mine. Aside from being unforgettable, this dish is packed with loads of whole grains, orange veggies and mountains of garlic. To up your culinary nutrition game, the sweet, smoky and salty coconut bacon can also be used on sandwiches or sprinkled on salads and pastas. Note: If the large coconut flakes are difficult to locate, blanched sliced almonds can be substituted.

Per 1 slice/387 g serving with coconut bacon: 780 calories; 42 g total fat; 89 g total carbs; 15 g fibre; 13 g sugar; 24 g protein; 470 mg sodium.

6 SERVINGS	24 SERVINGS	INGREDIENTS
Mac and Cheese		
1 (about 340 g)	4 (about 1.35 kg)	small butternut squash, peeled, halved and seeded
1 head	4 heads	garlic, top removed
500 g	2 kg	whole grain elbow macaroni, gluten free if desired
4 tsp (20 mL)	5 Tbsp (75 mL)	extra-virgin olive oil
5 cups (1.25 L)	20 cups (5 L)	stemmed and sliced shiitake mushrooms
2 cups (500 mL)	5 (400 mL) cans	coconut milk
2 cups (500 mL)	8 cups (2 L)	low-sodium vegetable stock
1 cup (250 mL)	4 cups (1 L)	cashews, soaked for 30 minutes, water discarded
2 tsp (10 mL)	3 Tbsp (45 mL)	lemon zest
3 Tbsp (45 mL)	¾ cup (180 mL)	fresh lemon juice
¼ cup (60 mL)	1 cup (250 mL)	almond meal or ground blanched almonds
½ cup (125 mL)	2 cups (500 mL)	nutritional yeast
2 tsp (10 mL)	8 tsp (40 mL)	Dijon mustard
1 tsp (5 mL)	4 tsp (20 mL)	sea salt
½ tsp (2.5 mL)	2 tsp (10 mL)	black pepper
Garnish		
⅛ bunch	½ bunch	parsley, roughly chopped
—	—	Coconut Bacon (see recipe on following page)

1. Preheat oven to 400F (205C) and line a baking sheet (or two if needed) with parchment paper.

2. Place butternut squash and head(s) of garlic on prepared baking sheet(s). Bake in the oven for 45 minutes or until tender.

3. Meanwhile, cook pasta according to package directions. Drain and thoroughly rinse with cold water. Evenly distribute among one to four 9 × 13-inch baking dishes.

4. Heat a sauté pan over medium heat, then add oil. Once heated, add mushrooms and sauté until fragrant, about 5 minutes (10 minutes for 24 servings). Remove from heat and set aside.

5. When the squash and garlic are ready, remove from the oven and allow to cool slightly. Reduce oven to 350F (180C).

6. Once the squash and garlic are cooled, carefully remove the skins from the garlic and add squash and garlic to a blender with remaining mac and cheese ingredients. Process until completely smooth. (For 24 servings the sauce will need to blended in batches.)

7. Pour all of the sauce over the pasta and combine until all noodles are completely coated with sauce. Top with mushrooms and bake in the oven for 30 minutes. It may look like there is excess sauce, but the pasta will absorb it during baking—make sure to use it all!

8. Remove from the oven. Sprinkle with parsley and coconut bacon and serve.

Coconut Bacon

6 SERVINGS	24 SERVINGS	INGREDIENTS
1 cup (250 mL)	4 cups (1 L)	large unsweetened, sulphite-free coconut flakes
1 tsp (5 mL)	4 tsp (20 mL)	smoked paprika
1 Tbsp (15 mL)	¼ cup (60 mL)	maple syrup
2 tsp (10 mL)	8 tsp (40 mL)	low-sodium tamari
½ tsp (2.5 mL)	2 tsp (10 mL)	grapeseed oil

1. Preheat oven to 325F (160C) and line a baking sheet (or two) with parchment paper.

2. In a medium bowl, combine all ingredients and gently toss. Ensure that the coconut flakes are completely coated and the paprika is mixed in.

3. Evenly spread the coconut on prepared baking sheet(s) in a single layer. Place in the oven and bake for 10 to 12 minutes (up to 18 minutes for 24 servings), stirring after 6 minutes, taking care not to burn the flakes. Check every 2 to 3 minutes for the last half of the baking time. When the flakes are crispy, remove from oven and allow to cool. Once cooled, use immediately or store in a glass jar for up to 3 weeks.

Mushroom and Lentil Shepherd's Pie

PREPARATION TIME 20 minutes for 6 servings and 30 minutes for 24 servings
COOKING TIME 50 minutes

The epitome of comfort eats, this shepherd's pie is made up of pillowy mounds of garlicky mashed potatoes atop veg, sautéed mush-rooms, whole grains and stick-to-your-ribs lentils, all bathed in a velvety, herbed tamari gravy. Be certain to invite over those friends and family members who claim to have an endless appetite.

Per 1 piece/407 g serving: 350 calories; 11 g total fat; 51 g total carbs; 8 g fibre; 8 g sugar; 11 g protein; 530 mg sodium.

6 SERVINGS	24 SERVINGS	INGREDIENTS
Bottom		
5 tsp (25 mL)	¼ cup + 3 Tbsp (105 mL)	olive oil, divided
2 cups (500 mL)	8 cups (2 L)	diced onions
2 tsp (10 mL)	3 Tbsp (45 mL)	pureed garlic
1¾ cups (430 mL)	7 cups (1.75 L)	diced carrots
1½ stalks	6 stalks	celery, diced
1½ tsp (7.5 mL)	2 Tbsp (30 mL)	tomato paste
1 Tbsp (15 mL)	¼ cup (60 mL)	dried basil
1½ tsp (7.5 mL)	2 Tbsp (30 mL)	ground coriander
1 tsp (5 mL)	4 tsp (20 mL)	paprika
1 tsp (5 mL)	4 tsp (20 mL)	dried rosemary
1 tsp (5 mL)	4 tsp (20 mL)	dried thyme
½ tsp (2.5 mL)	2 tsp (10 mL)	ground cumin
1 cup (250 mL)	4 cups (1 L)	cooked brown lentils
½ cup (125 mL)	2 cups (500 mL)	cooked quinoa
1 tsp (5 mL)	4 tsp (20 mL)	sea salt
¼ tsp (1 mL)	1 tsp (5 mL)	black pepper
2¼ cups (560 mL)	9 cups (2.25 L)	halved cremini mushrooms
¾ cup (180 mL)	3 cups (750 mL)	green peas, fresh or frozen
Topping		
4 (about 1 kg)	16 (about 4 kg)	white potatoes
¾ cup (180 mL)	3 cups (750 mL)	unsweetened soy milk
5 cloves	1 head	roasted garlic, peeled
½ tsp (2.5 mL)	2 tsp (10 mL)	extra-virgin olive oil
⅛ tsp (0.6 mL)	½ tsp (2.5 mL)	salt
⅛ tsp (0.6 mL)	½ tsp (2.5 mL)	black pepper
Garnish		
⅛ bunch	½ bunch	parsley, chopped
Gravy		
2 Tbsp (30 mL)	½ cup (125 mL)	extra-virgin olive oil
½ cup (125 mL)	2 cups (500 mL)	finely chopped cremini mushrooms
8 tsp (40 mL)	⅔ cup (160 mL)	flour (such as brown rice, whole wheat or spelt)
1½ tsp (7.5 mL)	2 Tbsp (30 mL)	dried herbs (such as basil, thyme and/or rosemary)
1 cup (250 mL)	4 cups (1 L)	water
1½ tsp (7.5 mL)	2 Tbsp (30 mL)	tamari
1 clove	4 cloves	garlic, pureed
⅛ tsp (0.6 mL)	½ tsp (2.5 mL)	salt
¼ tsp (1 mL)	1 tsp (5 mL)	black pepper

Continued...

If freezing, freeze after assembly (do not bake). Lay parchment paper on the top and cover tightly with plastic wrap. To prepare, remove from freezer, allow to thaw in the fridge overnight and bake, covered, for 50 minutes.

1. Preheat oven to 400F (205C) and grease one 8 × 8-inch baking pan if making 6 servings or two 9 × 13-inch baking pans if making 24 servings.

2. Heat a third of the oil in a large sauté pan over medium heat. Add the onions and sauté until translucent, about 3 to 5 minutes.

3. Add garlic and sauté until fragrant, about 1 to 2 minutes.

4. Add carrots and celery. Sauté until vegetables are tender, about 10 to 12 minutes.

5. Add tomato paste, basil, coriander, paprika, rosemary, thyme and cumin and cook until fragrant, about 3 to 4 minutes.

6. Remove from heat and pour into a large bowl. Add the lentils, quinoa, salt and pepper and thoroughly combine. Divide mixture into prepared baking dish(es) and evenly pat down to form the bottom layer of the shepherd's pie(s). Set aside.

7. Using the same sauté pan, heat the remaining oil over medium heat. Add the mushrooms and sauté until golden brown, about 3 to 4 minutes. Remove from heat and evenly distribute over the bottom layer(s), followed by the peas.

8. For the topping, quarter the potatoes and boil or steam until fork tender. Allow to cool slightly.

9. Combine potatoes, milk, garlic, oil, salt and pepper in a large bowl. Using a masher, mash until relatively smooth. Using a rubber spatula, evenly spread the potato mixture over the pea and mushroom layer. Bake in the oven, uncovered, for 40 minutes, until the edges are golden and crispy. Remove from oven and sprinkle with fresh parsley.

10. In the meantime, make the gravy. Heat a saucepan over medium heat, then add oil. Once heated, add mushrooms and sauté until slightly brown, about 4 minutes.

11. Stir in flour and herbs. Sauté for 5 minutes, until fragrant. Switch to a whisk, and slowly whisk in the water, making sure there are no flour clumps. Continue whisking, allowing gravy to gently simmer and thicken, for about 3 to 4 minutes.

12. Whisk in the tamari, garlic, salt and pepper and simmer until gravy reaches desired consistency. Whisk in more water, 1 Tbsp (15 mL) at a time, if needed. Remove from heat and serve 2 Tbsp (30 mL) with each serving of shepherd's pie.

Maple Caramel Sauce with Granny Smith Apples and Toasted Walnuts

PREPARATION TIME 10 minutes

COOKING TIME 5 to 7 minutes

Sticky sweetness at its best! This maple caramel sauce, otherwise known as ooey-gooey drippy heaven on earth, is perfectly paired with flavonoid-rich, sweet and sour Granny Smith apples and topped off with walnuts laden with vitamin E and omega-3s.

Per 8 pieces/118 g serving: 220 calories; 13 g total fat; 24 g total carbs; 4 g fibre; 17 g sugar; 3 g protein; 3 mg sodium.

6 SERVINGS	24 SERVINGS	INGREDIENTS
¼ cup (60 mL)	1 cup (250 mL)	maple syrup
½ tsp (2.5 mL)	2 tsp (10 mL)	vanilla extract
1 Tbsp (15 mL)	¼ cup (60 mL)	arrowroot powder
3	12	Granny Smith apples, cored and each cut into 16 slices

Garnish		
1 cup (250 mL)	4 cups (1 L)	toasted walnuts, chopped

1. In a small saucepan over medium heat, whisk together maple syrup, vanilla and arrowroot powder. Whisk continuously until the sauce has thickened, about 5 to 7 minutes.

2. Transfer sauce to a heatproof bowl. Chill in the freezer for 15 minutes, stirring once after 5 minutes.

3. To serve, use a dessert spoon to drizzle caramel sauce over the apples and sprinkle with walnuts.

Spiced Banana Cakes
with Orange Frosting

PREPARATION TIME 15 minutes

COOKING TIME 25 to 30 minutes

This is not your typical banana cake recipe. It is full of functional, health-promoting foods like fibre and antioxidant-rich whole grains, nuts, flaxseed and spices. Aside from their great taste and nutrient-dense ingredients, these cakes are the perfect food for curling up with hot ginger tea. They are also kid-approved, freezer-friendly and easy to digest.

Per 1 piece/91 g serving: 200 calories; 5 g total fat; 34 g total carbs; 5 g fibre; 15 g sugar; 4 g protein; 125 mg sodium.

8 SERVINGS	24 SERVINGS	INGREDIENTS
Dry Ingredients		
1 cup (250 mL)	3 cups (750 mL)	spelt flour
1 Tbsp (15 mL)	⅓ cup (80 mL)	almond flour
2 Tbsp (30 mL)	6 Tbsp (90 mL)	chopped unsweetened dark chocolate
1 Tbsp (15 mL)	⅓ cup (80 mL)	ground flaxseed
2 tsp (10 mL)	2 Tbsp (30 mL)	baking powder
2 tsp (10 mL)	6 tsp (90 mL)	ground cinnamon
1 tsp (5 mL)	1 Tbsp (15 mL)	ground nutmeg
½ tsp (2.5 mL)	2 tsp (10 mL)	baking soda
⅛ tsp (0.6 mL)	½ tsp (2.5 mL)	salt
Wet Ingredients		
2	6	ripe bananas
¼ cup (60 mL)	¾ cup (180 mL)	maple syrup
½ cup (125 mL)	1½ cups (375 mL)	unsweetened soy milk
2 tsp (10 mL)	2 Tbsp (30 mL)	apple cider vinegar
2 tsp (10 mL)	2 Tbsp (30 mL)	vanilla extract
Icing		
2 tsp (10 mL)	2 Tbsp (30 mL)	orange zest
⅓ cup (80 mL)	1 cup (250 mL)	fresh orange juice
(about ½ orange)	(about 2 oranges)	
¼ cup (60 mL)	¾ cup (180 mL)	whole pitted dates
¼ cup (60 mL)	¾ cup (180 mL)	unsalted dry-roasted cashews
Garnish		
2 Tbsp (30 mL)	6 Tbsp (90 mL)	shaved or melted dark chocolate

1. Preheat oven to 350F (180C). Grease muffin pans with coconut oil and set aside.

2. In a large bowl, whisk together the dry ingredients. Set aside.

3. In a separate bowl, use a fork to thoroughly mash bananas until smooth. Add the remaining wet ingredients and whisk until smooth.

4. Add the wet ingredients to the dry ingredients and mix until combined.

5. Distribute a heaping ⅓ cup (80 mL) of batter into each muffin cup.

6. Place into the oven and bake for 25 minutes or until an inserted toothpick comes out clean. Remove from oven and allow cakes to cool on a cooling rack.

7. Meanwhile, in a food processor, combine all icing ingredients and process until smooth, about 2 minutes. For best results, refrigerate icing for 30 minutes to harden slightly before application.

8. Once cooled, ice the cakes and sprinkle with shaved (or drizzle with melted) chocolate.

Spelt and Coconut Waffles with Raspberries and Coconut Mousse

PREPARATION TIME 20 minutes
COOKING TIME 10 minutes for 6 servings
and 20 minutes for 24 servings

Now you can have your greens and eat waffles too! Blending leafy greens into smoothies, muffins, cakes and even waffles is an innovative way to squeeze in those extra nutrients and phytonutrients! This recipe is particularly kid-friendly, and always a popular choice for easy Sunday brunches.

Per 1 waffle/177 g serving: 400 calories; 18 g total fat; 55 g total carbs; 7 g fibre; 30 g sugar; 7 g protein; 230 mg sodium.

6 SERVINGS	24 SERVINGS	INGREDIENTS
Coconut Mousse		
⅔ cup (160 mL)	2⅔ cups (660 mL)	coconut fat from chilled coconut milk
1 Tbsp (15 mL)	¼ cup (60 mL)	maple syrup
2¼ tsp (11 mL)	3 Tbsp	cocoa powder (optional)
½ tsp (2.5 mL)	2 tsp (10 mL)	vanilla extract
Dry Ingredients		
1½ cups (375 mL)	6 cups (1.5 L)	spelt flour
4 tsp (20 mL)	⅓ cup (80 mL)	baking powder
¼ tsp (1 mL)	1 tsp (5 mL)	sea salt
½ tsp (2.5 mL)	2 tsp (10 mL)	ground cinnamon
4 tsp (20 mL)	⅓ cup (80 mL)	ground flaxseed
Wet Ingredients		
3	12	Medjool dates, pitted, chopped and soaked in hot water for 10 minutes
1 cup (250 mL)	4 cups (1 L)	unsweetened soy milk
⅔ cup (160 mL)	2⅔ cups (660 mL)	coconut milk
2¼ tsp (11 mL)	3 Tbsp (45 mL)	vanilla extract
3 Tbsp (45 mL)	¾ cup (180 mL)	grapeseed oil
½ cup (125 mL)	2 cups (500 mL)	drained steamed spinach, packed
Garnish		
¾ cup (180 mL)	3 cups (750 mL)	fresh raspberries
3 Tbsp (45 mL)	¾ cup (180 mL)	toasted pumpkin seeds
1½ tsp (7.5 mL)	2 Tbsp (30 mL)	cocoa powder (optional)

TIP

To reduce fat, substitute any nut or soy milk for the coconut milk in the waffles.

1. To prepare the mousse, whisk together coconut fat, maple syrup, cocoa powder (if using) and vanilla extract in a small bowl.

2. Cover the bowl with plastic wrap and place in the refrigerator to chill.

3. Turn on the waffle iron to preheat.

4. In a large bowl, whisk together all dry ingredients.

5. Drain the soaked dates and place in a blender. Add the remaining wet ingredients and blend until smooth.

6. Pour the wet ingredients into the dry and whisk until there is no visible flour remaining.

7. Grease preheated waffle maker using ½ tsp (7.5 mL) grapeseed oil per 2 waffles.

8. Scoop ½ cup (125 mL) batter onto each waffle mould on the waffle maker. Close lid and cook until lightly brown. Repeat with remaining batter.

9. When ready to serve, top each waffle with 2 tablespoons (30 mL) coconut mousse and garnish with raspberries, pumpkin seeds and a dust of cocoa powder (if using).

Turmeric Ginger Latte

PREPARATION TIME 5 minutes

COOKING TIME 10 minutes

This warming and beautiful beverage is liquid anti-inflammatory gold. It is loaded with turmeric, combined with buttery coconut oil, spicy ginger, vitamin-E-rich almond milk and a touch of sweet, floral cardamom. It is luxury and comfort in a mug. Cheers!

Per 1 cup/250 mL serving: 70 calories; 4.5 g total fat; 6 g total carbs; 1 g fibre; 3 g sugar; 1 g protein; 190 mg sodium.

6 SERVINGS	24 SERVINGS	INGREDIENTS
1½ tsp (7.5 mL)	2 Tbsp (30 mL)	coconut oil
1 Tbsp (15 mL)	¼ cup (60 mL)	ground turmeric
1½ tsp 7.5 mL)	2 Tbsp (30 mL)	ground ginger or grated fresh ginger
¼ tsp (1 mL)	1½ tsp (7.5 mL)	ground cardamom
¼ tsp (1 mL)	1½ tsp (7.5 mL)	black pepper
6 cups (1.5 L)	24 cups (6 L)	unsweetened almond milk
4 tsp (20 mL)	6 Tbsp (90 mL)	maple syrup

1. Heat a saucepan over medium heat, then add coconut oil.

2. Once oil has melted, whisk in turmeric, ginger, cardamom and pepper. Toast until fragrant, about 1 minute.

3. Whisk in almond milk. Bring to a simmer and continue to simmer until flavours meld.

4. Sweeten with maple syrup and enjoy!

A sunny stroll, picnics in the park, endless dips in the pool, lake or ocean, and all the fresh local produce you can carry home from the farmers' market! Summer can be a busy social time or simply a time to relax and take things a little slower. Whatever way you do the season, remember to replenish your electrolytes, move your body in the summer sun and get your fill of in-season goods packed with vitamins and phytochemicals. This section offers light and refreshing summery fare, made for barbecuing, dining al fresco, packing up for a stroll through the woods or just cooling off and enjoying the best the season has to offer.

**SAMPLE MENU FOR
A PERFECT SUMMERY PICNIC**

SOUP
Cucumber and Lime Gazpacho

SALAD
Watermelon, Mint, Feta and Arugula Salad

MAIN
*Curried Chickpea Salad Sandwiches
with Turmeric Garlic Parsnip Fries*

DESSERT
Raspberry Key Lime Pie

Picnic Basket and Barbecue Favourites

Cucumber and Lime Gazpacho

Nothing beats a refreshing gazpacho on a sweltering hot summer day! Pour it in a Mason jar and throw it into a cooler for an instant meal on the beach, at the next family picnic or when travelling. It's my favourite way to take advantage of fresh, local produce.

Per 1½ cups/375 mL serving: 120 calories; 5 g total fat; 18 g total carbs; 6 g fibre; 6 g sugar; 4 g protein; 340 mg sodium.

6 SERVINGS	24 SERVINGS	INGREDIENTS
1	4	avocado, cut in small dice
1	5	large English cucumber, cut in small dice
1	5	green pepper, seeded and cut in small dice
1	5	red pepper, seeded and cut in small dice
1	5	green chili pepper, seeded and minced
1 bunch	5 bunches	green onions, minced
½ bunch	5 bunches	basil, stems removed, cut in chiffonade
½ head	2 heads	garlic, pureed
4 tsp (20 mL)	⅓ cup (80 mL)	lime zest
⅓ cup (80 mL) (about 2 limes)	1¾ cups (430 mL) (about 10 limes)	fresh lime juice
2½ cups (625 mL)	10 cups (2.5 L)	low-sodium vegetable stock
1¼ cups (310 mL)	5 cups (1.25 L)	tomato juice
¾ cup (180 mL)	2 (398 mL) cans	canned artichoke hearts, drained and rinsed, cut in small dice
½ cup (125 mL)	2 cups (500 mL)	white wine vinegar
½ tsp (2.5 mL)	2 tsp (10 mL)	sea salt
Garnish		
¼ bunch	1 bunch	basil, cut in chiffonade

1. Combine all ingredients in a large stockpot. Taste and adjust seasoning if necessary.

2. Chill in refrigerator for 1 to 2 hours before serving. Garnish with basil.

Crisp Watercress Salad with Tempeh and Mango

PREPARATION TIME 25 minutes

COOKING TIME 20 minutes

This is the epic salad you need to make for those who shy away from leafy green consumption. It is not only striking in appearance and flavour, but it is one of the most nutrient- and anti-inflammatory- packed recipes in this book. Moreover, it is rich in omega-3 fatty acids, flavonoids, polyphenols and isoflavones, and high in potassium, calcium, iron and vitamins A, C and E. It also contains a whopping 30 g of protein per serving. It is the perfect fuel to share with your workout pal after your outdoor summer sessions!

Per 3½ cups/354 g serving: 680 calories; 53 g total fat; 31 g total carbs; 4 g fibre; 8 g sugar; 30 g protein; 460 mg sodium.

6 SERVINGS	24 SERVINGS	INGREDIENTS
Salad		
½ cup (125 mL)	2 cups (500 mL)	coconut oil, melted and divided
750 g	3 kg	tempeh, cut into ¼-inch (0.6 cm) cubes
1½ tsp (7.5 mL)	2 Tbsp (30 mL)	ground turmeric
¼ tsp (1 mL)	1 tsp (5 mL)	black pepper
1 tsp (5 mL)	4 tsp (20 mL)	sea salt, divided
½ cup (125 mL)	2 cups (500 mL)	oat flour (or grind whole rolled oats)
¼ cup (60 mL)	1 cup (250 mL)	ground flaxseed
1½ tsp (7.5 mL)	2 Tbsp (30 mL)	ground coriander
¾ tsp (4 mL)	1 Tbsp (15 mL)	ground ginger
8 cups (2 L)	32 cups (8 L)	watercress, packed, cut into bite-sized pieces and kept cold
1	4	red pepper, thinly sliced
2 cups (500 mL)	8 cups (2 L)	thinly sliced red cabbage
1 cup (250 mL)	4 cups (1 L)	mango pieces, fresh or frozen, cut into ¼-inch (0.6 cm) cubes
½ bunch	2 bunches	cilantro, stems removed and leaves separated
Vinaigrette		
½ cup (125 mL)	2 cups (500 mL)	grapeseed oil
½ cup (125 mL)	2 cups (500 mL)	apple cider vinegar
1 Tbsp (15 mL)	¼ cup (60 mL)	maple syrup
¼ tsp (1 mL)	1 tsp (5 mL)	salt
½ tsp (2.5 mL)	2 tsp (10 mL)	grated ginger

1. In a medium bowl, toss together half of the coconut oil with the tempeh, turmeric, black pepper and a quarter of the salt.

2. In another bowl, combine oat flour (or ground oats), ground flaxseed, coriander, ginger and another quarter of the salt. Roll the marinated tempeh into the breading until completely coated. (For best results, divide both the breading and the tempeh into two portions and do in two batches.)

3. Heat a large sauté pan over medium heat, then add remaining coconut oil. Once heated, add tempeh and lightly fry until golden and crispy, about 2 minutes per side, working in batches if needed. Transfer hot tempeh to a large mixing bowl and toss with the remaining salt.

4. Combine remaining salad ingredients in a large bowl.

5. In a small bowl, whisk together vinaigrette ingredients.

6. Add dressing to salad, toss and then top with tempeh.

Watermelon, Mint, Feta and Arugula Salad

This is summer in a bowl: fresh, crisp, sweet, refreshing and colourful. The sweet, juicy watermelon cut with salty tofu feta and topped off with peppery arugula will have you sharing this nutrient-dense recipe far and wide.

Per 2 cups/231 g serving: 250 calories; 19 g total fat; 7 g total carbs; 2 g fibre; 8 g sugar; 9 g protein; 350 mg sodium.

6 SERVINGS	24 SERVINGS	INGREDIENTS
Salad		
1 small	1 large	watermelon, rind and seeds removed, cut into ½-inch (1.25 cm) cubes
½ bunch	2 bunches	mint, cut in chiffonade
6 cups (1.5 L)	24 cups (6 L)	arugula
Dressing		
1 (350 g) package	4 (350 g) packages	extra-firm tofu, drained and crumbled
1 Tbsp (15 mL)	¼ cup (60 mL)	lemon zest
¼ cup (60 mL) (about 1 lemon)	¾ cup (180 mL) (about 4 lemons)	fresh lemon juice
¾ cup (180 mL)	3 cups (750 mL)	thinly sliced red onions
2 cloves	8 cloves	garlic, pureed
¼ cup (60 mL)	1 cup (250 mL)	red wine vinegar
¼ cup (60 mL)	1 cup (250 mL)	chopped fresh basil
3 Tbsp (45 mL)	½ cup (125 mL)	olive oil
½ tsp (2.5 mL)	2 tsp (10 mL)	black pepper (optional)
1 tsp (5 mL)	4 tsp (20 mL)	salt
Garnish		
¾ cup (180 mL)	3 cups (750 mL)	toasted walnuts, chopped

1. In a large bowl, combine all salad ingredients and set aside.

2. In a medium bowl, combine all dressing ingredients. Let stand for 20 minutes so tofu can marinate and flavours can meld.

3. When ready to serve, add dressing to salad and toss. Garnish with walnuts.

Curried Chickpea Salad Sandwiches with Turmeric Garlic Parsnip Fries

PREPARATION TIME 15 minutes
COOKING TIME 40 minutes

This satisfyingly creamy sandwich, with homemade mayo and an assortment of crunchy and sweet vegetables, proves beyond doubt that a plant-based diet can be equal parts indulgent and health promoting.

Per 1 sandwich/347 g serving with fries:
510 calories; 17 g total fat; 67 g total carbs; 15 g fibre; 4 g sugar; 19 g protein; 490 mg sodium.

6 SERVINGS	24 SERVINGS	INGREDIENTS
1 head	4 heads	garlic
2 Tbsp (30 mL)	½ cup (125 mL)	grapeseed oil, divided
1½ cups (375 mL)	6 cups (1.5 L)	diced sweet potatoes, cut into ½-inch (1.25 cm) cubes
1 Tbsp (15 mL)	¼ cup (60 mL)	curry powder
1½ tsp (7.5 mL)	2 Tbsp (30 mL)	ground coriander
1½ tsp (7.5 mL)	2 Tbsp (30 mL)	ground cumin
1½ tsp (7.5 mL)	2 Tbsp (30 mL)	paprika
1½ tsp (7.5 mL)	2 Tbsp (30 mL)	ground turmeric
3 cups (750 mL)	12 cups (3 L)	unsalted canned chickpeas, drained and rinsed
¼ cup (60 mL)	1 cup (250 mL)	tahini
1½ Tbsp (22 mL)	6 Tbsp (90 mL)	nutritional yeast
1½ tsp (7.5 mL)	2 Tbsp (30 mL)	lemon zest
2 Tbsp (30 mL)	½ cup (125 mL)	fresh lemon juice
1 stalk	4 stalks	celery, diced
¾ cup (180 mL)	3 cups (750 mL)	thinly sliced green onions
⅛ bunch	½ bunch	parsley, finely chopped
½ cup (125 mL)	1 cup (250 mL)	vegan mayo
1 tsp (5 mL)	4 tsp (20 mL)	sea salt
¼ tsp (1 mL)	1 tsp (5 mL)	black pepper
12 slices	48 slices	multigrain bread
½ head	2 heads	Boston lettuce, leaves separated
1	4	beefsteak tomato, thinly sliced

1. Preheat oven to 375F (190C). Line a baking sheet with parchment paper.

2. Cut off the top(s) of the head(s) of garlic. Lightly drizzle with a quarter of the grapeseed oil. Place on the prepared baking sheet. Set aside.

3. Toss sweet potatoes with curry, coriander, cumin, paprika, turmeric and remaining oil. If room permits, spread evenly on same baking sheet with garlic. (If making 24 servings, use an additional lined baking sheet.) Roast for 40 minutes, or until sweet potatoes are fork tender and garlic is golden and soft. Allow to cool before removing garlic skins.

4. In a food processor, combine roasted garlic, chickpeas, tahini, nutritional yeast and lemon zest and juice. Pulse 5 to 8 times (or 15 to 18 times if making 24 servings) until ingredients are incorporated and chickpeas are slightly broken down, but still chunky.

5. In a large bowl, mix together sweet potatoes, chickpeas, celery, green onions, parsley and mayo. Add salt and pepper. Cover and refrigerate for 20 minutes, or overnight.

6. Divide among half the bread slices, topping with Boston lettuce, tomatoes and the rest of the bread.

Turmeric Garlic Parsnip Fries

PREPARATION TIME 10 minutes
COOKING TIME 30 minutes

6 SERVINGS	24 SERVINGS	INGREDIENTS
16	48	small parsnips (about 1 kg), cut into ¼-inch (0.6 cm) french fries
¼ cup (60 mL)	¾ cup (180 mL)	grapeseed oil
2 tsp (10 mL)	2 Tbsp (30 mL)	garlic powder
2 tsp (10 mL)	2 Tbsp (30 mL)	ground turmeric
2 Tbsp (30 mL)	6 Tbsp (90 mL)	dried thyme or dried oregano
½ tsp (2.5 mL)	2 tsp (10 mL)	salt
¼ tsp (1 mL)	1 tsp (5 mL)	black pepper

1. Preheat oven to 400F (205C). Line two baking sheets with parchment paper.

2. In a large bowl, combine parsnips with oil and toss until evenly coated. Add garlic powder, turmeric and thyme (or oregano) and toss.

3. Transfer parsnips to prepared baking sheets and spread evenly. Bake for 15 minutes.

4. Carefully flip parsnip fries and return to oven to bake for another 15 minutes, until golden brown.

5. Working quickly, transfer baked parsnip fries to a large bowl and toss with salt and pepper. Serve immediately with the sandwiches.

Red Bean and Fennel Sausages with Sweet Onion Mustard and Cultured Veg

PREPARATION TIME 10 to 15 minutes

COOKING TIME 30 minutes to 1 hour

Cue up the BBQ! Even when eating for optimal health, barbecues are still a viable option. Of course, healthiness has every-thing to do with what you select to put on yours. This recipe is a first-rate, plant-based option for all of your summer gath-erings, and the sausages can be made ahead and frozen—perfect for last-minute BBQ invites. Serve them up on home-baked buns with the tangy sweet onion mustard and probiotic-rich cultured veg as described below, or slice them to add to your favourite pasta dish or pizza. Note that the cultured vegetables and the mustard are best prepared a few days in advance.

Per 1 sausage/234 g serving with bun, mustard and cultured veg: 460 calo-ries; 15 g total fat; 48 g total carbs; 11 g fibre; 5 g sugar; 32 g protein; 420 mg sodium.

6 SERVINGS	24 SERVINGS	INGREDIENTS
1 cup (250 mL)	2 (540 mL) cans	canned red kidney beans, drained and rinsed
1 cup (250 mL)	4 cups (1 L)	water
1 cup (250 mL)	4 cups (1 L)	vital wheat gluten flour
¼ cup (60 mL)	1 cup (250 mL)	nutritional yeast
1½ tsp (7.5 mL)	2 Tbsp (30 mL)	toasted fennel seeds
1 tsp (5 mL)	4 tsp (20 mL)	black pepper
1 tsp (5 mL)	4 tsp (20 mL)	onion powder
½ tsp (2.5 mL)	2 tsp (10 mL)	sea salt
¼ tsp (1 mL)	1 tsp (5 mL)	ground thyme
½ head	2 heads	garlic, minced
1 Tbsp (15 mL)	¼ cup (60 mL)	extra-virgin olive oil
1 Tbsp (15 mL)	¼ cup (60 mL)	tamari
6	24	Sesame Spelt Buns (see recipe on page 105)
6 Tbsp (90 mL)	1½ cups (375 mL)	Sweet Onion Mustard (see recipe on page 104)
1 cup (250 mL)	4 cups (1 L)	Cultured Vegetables (see recipe on page 104)

1. Preheat oven to 400F (205C).

2. In a food processor, combine beans and water and process until completely smooth, working in batches if needed. Transfer to a large bowl.

3. In a large bowl, mix together dry sausage ingredients.

4. In a small bowl, whisk together the garlic, oil and tamari. Stir into the bean puree. Add wet ingredients to dry ingredients and mix well to fully incorporate.

5. Using a ⅓ cup (80 mL) measure, scoop out a ball of the sausage mixture onto a small sheet of aluminum foil and form into a 5-inch (12.5 cm) log. Tightly wrap and then twist ends to create a sausage. Repeat with remaining mixture.

6. Line the wrapped sausages in a single layer on baking sheets. Bake sausages until the outsides of the sausages are browned and feel firm to the touch, about 30 minutes for 6 servings and 1 hour for 24 servings. Remove from oven and set aside to cool slightly.

7. Carefully remove the foil packaging from the sausages and serve on buns with mustard and cultured veg. To freeze sausages, allow to cool completely then remove from foil, transfer to resealable bags and freeze for up to 6 months.

Sweet Onion Mustard

PREPARATION TIME 15 minutes

24 SERVINGS	INGREDIENTS
⅔ cup (160 mL)	white wine vinegar
3 Tbsp (45 mL)	maple syrup
5 Tbsp (75 mL)	brown mustard seeds
½ cup (125 mL)	minced sweet onion
¼ tsp (1 mL)	sea salt

1. In a small bowl, combine all ingredients and allow to soak for 30 minutes at room temperature.

2. Transfer to blender and blend on high until mustard becomes smooth and creamy, about 5 minutes.

3. Store remaining mustard in an airtight container and keep refrigerated for up to 2 weeks.

Cultured Vegetables

PREPARATION TIME 15 minutes

24 SERVINGS	INGREDIENTS
2 cups (500 mL)	grated carrots, lightly packed
1 cup (250 mL)	grated beets, packed
½ cup (125 mL)	thinly sliced cabbage, packed (reserve 2 large leaves)
1 cup (250 mL)	water
4 cloves	garlic
¼ tsp (1 mL)	sea salt
¼ bunch	dill, chopped

TIP

The cultured veg also tastes great in salads and on sandwiches and wraps.

1. In a large bowl, combine carrots, beets and cabbage. Remove 1 cup (250 mL) of vegetables and add them to a blender with the water, garlic and salt.

2. Blend until vegetables become a smooth juice. Toss vegetables and chopped dill with blended juice until coated.

3. Tightly pack mixture into a 16-ounce Mason jar, leaving about 1½ inches (3.75 cm) at the top of the jar. Top with reserved cabbage leaves and tightly close lid.

4. Allow the mixture to sit for 3 to 4 days in a 68F (20C) room away from sunlight.

5. When ready, open the jar over a sink. Refrigerate and use within 3 weeks.

Sesame Spelt Buns

PREPARATION TIME 10 minutes
COOKING TIME 25 minutes

6 SERVINGS	24 SERVINGS	INGREDIENTS
2 cups (500 mL)	8 cups (2 L)	spelt flour
1 cup (250 mL)	4 cups (1 L)	almond flour (or use spelt flour)
2 Tbsp (10 mL)	½ cup (125 mL)	ground flaxseed
1½ tsp (7.5 mL)	2 Tbsp (30 mL)	baking powder
¼ tsp (1 mL)	2 tsp (10 mL)	sea salt
2 tsp (10 mL)	8 tsp (40 mL)	maple syrup
⅔ cup (160 mL)	2⅔ cups (660 mL)	water
Topping		
1½ tsp (7.5 mL)	2 Tbsp (30 mL)	white and black sesame seeds

1. Preheat oven to 375F (190C). Line baking sheet(s) with parchment paper.

2. In a large bowl, combine spelt flour, almond flour, flaxseed, baking powder and salt.

3. In a medium bowl, mix together maple syrup and water.

4. Add the wet ingredients to the dry ingredients and mix well by hand for 2 to 3 minutes until a sticky-firm dough is formed. Allow dough to rest for 25 minutes, covered, at room temperature.

5. Using a ⅓ cup (80 mL) measure, scoop balls of dough onto a cutting board and shape into rolls. Arrange them on prepared baking sheet(s), and slightly flatten. Lightly press sesame seeds onto the tops so that they stick.

6. Bake for 25 minutes or until a toothpick comes out clean.

7. Transfer buns onto a cooling rack. Allow to completely cool before slicing lengthwise.

Zucchini Noodles with Sunflower Basil Pesto

PREPARATION TIME 5 minutes
COOKING TIME 40 minutes (optional)

Sweet and tangy roasted cherry tomatoes and bold basil pesto tossed with ribbons of fresh zucchini and topped with hemp parmesan—this dish is a thing of summer beauty. It's guaranteed to be popular with guests of all ages and is high in fibre, iron, vitamin E and phyto-nutrients like polyphenols, carotenoids and flavo-noids. Make a large batch of the pesto and freeze it to prolong the summer sunshine into the fall and winter months.

Per 2½ cups/310 g serving: 200 calories; 12 g total fat; 14 g total carbs; 4 g fibre; 7 g sugar; 8 g protein; 200 mg sodium.

6 SERVINGS	24 SERVINGS	INGREDIENTS
2 cups (500 mL)	8 cups (2 L)	cherry tomatoes, halved
4 tsp (20 mL)	⅓ cup (80 mL)	extra-virgin olive oil, divided
3 cups (750 mL)	12 cups (3 L)	fresh basil
½ cup (125 mL)	2 cups (500 mL)	sunflower seeds
3 Tbsp (45 mL)	¾ cup (180 mL)	fresh lemon juice
¾ head	3 heads	garlic, chopped
8	32	small zucchini, spiralized or cut into long, thin strips using a vegetable peeler

Vegan Parmesan

6 SERVINGS	24 SERVINGS	INGREDIENTS
6 Tbsp (90 mL)	1½ cups (375 mL)	hemp seeds
3 Tbsp (45 mL)	¾ cup (180 mL)	nutritional yeast
¾ tsp (4 mL)	1 Tbsp (15 mL)	sea salt

1. Preheat oven to 350F (180C). Line a baking sheet (or two) with parchment paper.

2. Place tomatoes in a large bowl. Drizzle with half of the oil. Evenly spread tomatoes on prepared baking sheet(s). Bake 35 to 40 minutes until tender and slightly brown. Remove from oven, set aside and allow to cool. (Alternatively, the tomatoes could be left raw in the dish.)

3. Meanwhile, in a small bowl, thoroughly combine vegan parmesan ingredients. Measure out ¼ cup (60 mL) for the pesto (or 1 cup/250 mL for 24 servings) and set aside the remainder for garnish.

4. In a food processor, combine basil, vegan parmesan, sunflower seeds, lemon juice and garlic. Begin to process while slowly drizzling in the remainder of the oil. Process until smooth, about 3 to 4 minutes.

5. In a large bowl, toss zucchini noodles with pesto. Transfer to a serving bowl, top with roasted tomatoes and sprinkle with remaining vegan parmesan.

Raspberry Key Lime Pie

This sweet and sour masterpiece will be a summer staple in your recipe repertoire moving forward. In addition to its visual appeal and unique flavour profile, this pie can be made in advance, is kid friendly, and is high in fibre, protein, potassium and vitamins C and E, as well as healthy fats.

Per 1 slice/207 g serving: 440 calories; 26 g total fat; 53 g total carbs; 14 g fibre; 35 g sugar; 8 g protein; 10 mg sodium.

6 SERVINGS	24 SERVINGS	INGREDIENTS
Shell		
15	60	Medjool dates, pitted
½ cup (125 mL)	2 cups (500 mL)	whole almonds
½ cup (125 mL)	2 cups (500 mL)	whole walnuts
6 Tbsp (90 mL)	1½ cups (375 mL)	ground flaxseed
2 Tbsp (30 mL)	½ cup (125 mL)	hemp seeds
Filling		
1½ cups (375 mL)	6 cups (1.5 L)	raspberries
2	8	avocados, pitted and skin removed
3 Tbsp (45 mL)	¾ cup (180 mL)	maple syrup
2 tsp (10 mL)	3 Tbsp (45 mL)	lime zest
½ cup (125 mL)	1½ cups (375 mL)	fresh lime juice
(about 4 limes)	(about 12 limes)	
Garnish		
½ cup (125 mL)	2 cups (500 mL)	raspberries
1 Tbsp	¼ cup (60 mL)	toasted coconut flakes (optional)

1. Line the bottom of a 9-inch pie plate with parchment paper (or line four 9-inch pie plates if making 24 servings). Set aside.

2. In a food processor, combine dates, almonds, walnuts, ground flaxseed and hemp seeds and process until crumbly. (You will need to work in batches when making 24 servings.)

3. Press the mixture into prepared plate(s), making sure to press evenly up the walls and along the base(s). Set aside.

4. Add raspberries to a saucepan over medium heat and cook for 7 to 10 minutes, or until mashed raspberries have a jam-like consistency.

5. Transfer the raspberry filling to the prepared crust(s) and spread evenly.

Allow this layer to cool in the fridge for 15 to 20 minutes.

6. Meanwhile, in a blender, combine avocados, maple syrup and lime juice and zest. Blend until smooth and fluffy, about 5 minutes, taking breaks to avoid the blender overheating. (Work in batches if making 24 servings.)

7. Pour the avocado filling onto the raspberry layer and gently spread to the edges. Garnish with raspberries and coconut flakes (if using). Gently lay parchment paper on top, then cover with aluminum foil and place into the freezer to chill until set, about 3 hours.

8. Remove from the freezer and allow to thaw slightly before cutting.

Almond Apricot
Blueberry Smoothie

Sipping on ice-cold beverages while soaking up a scorcher of a day (in the shade of a leafy tree or big umbrella, of course) is the quintessential image of summer. For a picture-perfect, health-promoting scenario, this apricot blueberry smoothie, rich in fibre, polyphenols, omega-3 fatty acids and vitamins A, C and E, is best served with fresh, light and nutritious eats. And enjoyed with a new friend—or three! If apricots aren't in season, you can use half the number of fresh peaches instead.

Per 1 cup/250 mL serving:
150 calories; 8 g total fat;
15 g total carbs; 4 g fibre;
9 g sugar; 4 g protein;
90 mg sodium.

6 SERVINGS	24 SERVINGS	INGREDIENTS
4	16	fresh apricots, pitted
2 cups (500 mL)	8 cups (2 L)	frozen blueberries
1	4	medium ripe banana
3 cups (750 mL)	12 cups (3 L)	unsweetened almond or soy milk
2 Tbsp (30 mL)	½ cup (125 mL)	almond butter (or other nut butter)
1 tsp (5 mL)	8 tsp (40 mL)	vanilla extract
¼ cup (60 mL)	1 cup (250 mL)	hemp seeds

1. Place all ingredients in a blender and blend until smooth, about 5 minutes. (Work in batches if needed.) Serve in tall glasses.

Lemon, Mint and Ginger Slush

Slushies are refreshing reminders of playful childhood summers. This ginger-laced version of the perpetual favourite is very easy to drink and contains abundant electrolytes, phytonutrients and antioxidants. For a fun twist, try adding other fibre-rich fruit like blackberries, strawberries or raspberries.

Per 1½ cups/375 mL serving: 110 calories; 0.2 g total fat; 29 g total carbs; 1 g fibre; 23 g sugar; 0.5 g protein; 20 mg sodium.

6 SERVINGS	24 SERVINGS	INGREDIENTS
⅔ cup (160 mL)	2⅔ cups (660 mL)	maple syrup
3 cups (750 mL)	12 cups (3 L)	water
1½ cups (375 mL) (about 8 lemons)	6 cups (1.5 L) (about 32 lemons)	fresh lemon juice
5 cups (1.25 L)	20 cups (5 L)	ice
1½ cups (375 mL)	6 cups (1.5 L)	mint leaves
1 Tbsp (15 mL)	¼ cup (60 mL)	freshly grated ginger

1. Combine all ingredients in a blender and blend until all the ice has been crushed, about 4 minutes. (For 24 servings you will need to blend in batches.)

Wintertime on our family farm meant ice skating on homemade rinks, serious downhill sledding, constructing snow fortresses and endless snow shovelling. Clearly all of these outdoor activities needed to be fuelled by satisfying, stick-to-your-ribs fare: think soups, stews, roasted veg, homemade bread and soul-warming baked goods. And when the outside fun had been exhausted, it was all about getting dry and cozy by the fireplace with a steaming hot beverage. Escape from the elements with favourites of the season, from creamy soups to a twist on sweet potato pie, and enjoy a few lighter takes on cold-weather fare, including hearty and satisfying winter salads.

SAMPLE MENU FOR
A WARMING WINTER MEAL

SOUP
Creamy Cauliflower and Potato Soup

SALAD
Winter Coleslaw with Orange Vinaigrette

MAIN
Falafel Sliders with Kale Tabbouleh,
Spicy Tahini Sauce and Papaya Chutney

DESSERT
Strawberry and Hazelnut Streusel Cake
with a Maple Vanilla Glaze

Warming Meals for Cold Days

Creamy Cauliflower and Potato Soup

PREPARATION TIME 30 minutes
COOKING TIME 30 minutes

Don't be deceived by the recipe title: this is a unique, health-enhanced take on the classic winter soup. As it contains healthy servings of both leafy greens and orange vegetables it is rich in B vitamins and phytonutrients, specifically flavonoids and carotenoids. Make it on Sunday for the week ahead and be certain to share it with your lunch-less co-worker.

Per 1⅔ cups/400 mL serving: 280 calories; 14 g total fat; 31 g total carbs; 9 g fibre; 6 g sugar; 12 g protein; 520 mg sodium.

6 SERVINGS	24 SERVINGS	INGREDIENTS
1 tsp (5 mL)	4 tsp (20 mL)	grapeseed oil
1 cup (250 mL)	4 cups (1 L)	diced onions
4 tsp (20 mL)	⅓ cup (80 mL)	minced garlic
2 cups (500 mL)	8 cups (2 L) (about 4 medium)	diced sweet potatoes
1½ cups (375 mL)	6 cups (1.5 L) (about 4 medium)	diced white potatoes
4 cups (1 L)	16 cups (4 L)	low-sodium vegetable stock
1 Tbsp (15 mL)	¼ cup (60 mL)	dried thyme
¾ tsp (4 mL)	1 Tbsp (15 mL)	ground rosemary
1 cup (250 mL)	4 cups (1 L)	nutritional yeast
1 head	4 heads	cauliflower (about 700 g), chopped into small florets
1½ cups (375 mL)	6 cups (1.5 L)	coconut milk
1¼ tsp (6 mL)	5 tsp (25 mL)	salt
¼ tsp (1 mL)	1 tsp (5 mL)	white pepper
3½ cups (875 mL)	14 cups (3.5 L)	baby spinach, tightly packed
2 Tbsp (30 mL)	½ cup (125 mL)	apple cider vinegar
Garnish		
3 sprigs	12 sprigs	thyme, stems removed
1	3	green onion, thinly sliced (optional)

1. Heat oil in a large stockpot over medium-high heat. Add onions and sauté until translucent, about 5 minutes.

2. Stir in garlic and potatoes and sauté until garlic is fragrant, about 3 minutes.

3. Add vegetable stock, thyme and rosemary and bring to a simmer. Reduce heat and allow to simmer for 10 minutes.

4. Stir in nutritional yeast and cauliflower and simmer for another 8 to 10 minutes, or until cauliflower is fork tender.

5. Remove half of the soup and puree until smooth with a hand immersion blender. (If using a regular blender to puree the soup, make sure to take breaks and release steam from the top.) The 24-serving recipe will need to be blended in batches. Pour soup back into the pot and stir in coconut milk, salt and pepper.

6. Stir in spinach and allow to wilt, about 4 minutes. Remove soup from heat and stir in apple cider vinegar. Top with fresh thyme and green onions (if using) when ready to serve.

Winter Vegetable Borscht

PREPARATION TIME 20 to 25 minutes

COOKING TIME 45 minutes for 6 servings
and 55 minutes for 24 servings

Loaded with winter vegetables and beans, this robust borscht is equal parts hearty and flavourful. With a perfect pop of citrus and dill, this is a quintessential warm and cozy meal.

Per 1⅓ cups/325 mL serving: 180 calories; 6 g total fat; 28 g total carbs; 7 g fibre; 8 g sugar; 5 g protein; 350 mg sodium.

6 SERVINGS	24 SERVINGS	INGREDIENTS
1½ tsp (7.5 mL)	2 Tbsp (30 mL)	grapeseed oil
½	2	onion, cut into small dice
2 Tbsp (30 mL)	1 head	finely minced garlic
1 stalk	4 stalks	celery, cut into small dice
1	4	leek, white part only, sliced
¼ head	1 head	red cabbage, thinly shredded
2	8	red beets, cut into medium dice
1 small	2 large	carrot, cut into medium dice
1 small	2 large	parsnip, cut into medium dice
1½ cups (375 mL)	6 cups (1.5 L)	chopped sweet potatoes, cut into medium dice
2 tsp (10 mL)	2 Tbsp (30 mL)	tomato paste
4 cups (1 L)	16 cups (4 L)	low-sodium vegetable stock
1	1	spice bag: 1 bay leaf, 2 sprigs thyme, 3 peppercorns and 2 stems parsley tied together in a cheesecloth
½ cup (125 mL)	2 cups (500 mL)	cooked red kidney beans
½ cup (125 mL)	2 cups (500 mL)	cooked white kidney beans
¾ tsp (4 mL)	1 Tbsp (15 mL)	salt
½ tsp (2.5 mL)	2 tsp (10 mL)	black pepper (optional)
¼ bunch	1 bunch	parsley leaves, finely chopped, divided
¼ bunch	1 bunch	dill, finely chopped, divided
1½ tsp (7.5 mL)	2 Tbsp (30 mL)	lemon zest
2 tsp (10 mL)	3 Tbsp (45 mL)	fresh lemon juice
¾ cup (180 mL)	3 cups (750 mL)	unsweetened non-dairy yogurt (optional)

1. Heat oil in a large stockpot over medium heat. Add onions and garlic. Sauté until translucent, about 3 to 4 minutes.

2. Add celery, leeks and cabbage. Sauté until fragrant, about 5 to 7 minutes.

3. Add beets, carrots, parsnips and sweet potatoes. Sauté until slightly softened, about 8 minutes (or 15 minutes for 24 servings).

4. Stir in tomato paste and cook for 2 minutes.

5. Add vegetable stock and spice bag. Bring to a boil then turn down heat and simmer until root vegetables are fork tender, about 20 minutes.

6. Add beans, salt and pepper. Simmer until beans are heated through, about 5 minutes.

7. Turn off heat. Remove half of the soup and puree until smooth with a hand immersion blender. (If using a regular blender to puree the soup, take breaks and release steam from the top.) The 24-serving recipe will need to be blended in batches.

8. Stir in half of the parsley, half of the dill and all of the lemon zest.

9. Garnish each serving with a dollop of non-dairy yogurt and a sprinkling of parsley and dill.

Winter Coleslaw with Orange Vinaigrette

Salads are not just for summer, and this winter-ized coleslaw proves just that. This will be your new favourite go-to salad: mounds of cruci-ferous cabbage, beets and honey-sweet pears tossed in orange vinaigrette, all topped off with decadent hazelnuts, fresh parsley and sour cranberries. To save time or add even more flavours, pre-cut slaw mix can be used instead of the cabbage—just follow the volume measurements.

Per 1¾ cups/242 g serving:
200 calories; 8 g total fat;
30 g total carbs; 6 g fibre;
20 g sugar; 3 g protein;
135 mg sodium.

6 SERVINGS	24 SERVINGS	INGREDIENTS
Salad		
2 large	8 large	Bartlett pears, cored and julienned
1 medium	4 medium	golden (or red) beet, peeled and julienned
1 small (about 5 cups/1.25 L)	4 small (about 18 cups/4.5 L)	green cabbage, thinly sliced
2 cups (500 mL)	8 cups (2 L)	thinly sliced red onions
Dressing		
1 Tbsp (15 mL)	¼ cup (60 mL)	orange zest
½ cup (125 mL) (about 1 orange)	2 cups (500 mL) (about 4 oranges)	fresh orange juice
3 Tbsp (45 mL)	¾ cup (180 mL)	apple cider vinegar
2 Tbsp (30 mL)	½ cup (125 mL)	extra-virgin olive oil
1 tsp (5 mL)	4 tsp (20 mL)	Dijon mustard
1 tsp (5 mL)	4 tsp (20 mL)	maple syrup
¼ tsp (1 mL)	1 tsp (5 mL)	salt
Garnish		
¼ cup (60 mL)	1 cup (250 mL)	toasted hazelnuts, chopped
⅓ cup (80 mL)	1⅓ cups (350 mL)	unsweetened dried cranberries
3 Tbsp (45 mL)	¾ cup (180 mL)	stemmed and chopped parsley

1. In a large salad bowl, combine all of the salad ingredients.

2. In a small bowl, whisk together all dressing ingredients. Pour over salad and toss.

3. Top with hazelnuts, cranberries and parsley.

Tahini Dill Dressing

This creamy and dreamy dressing is a fun and flavourful way to reinvent those winter root vegetables, whether they are roasted, spiralized or just straight up raw! Or serve it over spring greens, cucumber slices and spiralized carrots topped with microgreens and roasted sunflower seeds—this dressing is super-adaptable. And making your own dressing from scratch is an easy way to minimize the consumption of unwanted sugar and salt and unhealthy fat. This is high in the antioxidant vitamin C, and is a source of fibre, protein and healthy fats.

Per ⅓ cup/80 mL serving: 280 calories; 21 g total fat; 20 g total carbs; 2 g fibre; 8 g sugar; 7 g protein; 60 mg sodium.

8 SERVINGS	24 SERVINGS	INGREDIENTS
¼ tsp (1 mL)	¾ tsp (4 mL)	lemon zest
½ cup (125 mL) (about 2 large lemons)	1½ cups (375 mL) (about 6 large lemons)	fresh lemon juice
⅓ cup (80 mL)	1 cup (250 mL)	tahini paste
3 Tbsp (45 mL)	½ bunch (about ½ cup/125 mL)	chopped fresh dill
1 Tbsp (15 mL)	3 Tbsp (45 mL)	maple syrup
¼ tsp (1 mL)	¾ tsp (4 mL)	pureed garlic
Pinch	¼ tsp (1 mL)	sea salt

1. In a large bowl, combine all the ingredients. Whisk until thoroughly blended and serve with your choice of raw or cooked vegetables. Store in refrigerator for 2 to 3 days.

Falafel Sliders with Kale Tabbouleh, Spicy Tahini Sauce and Papaya Chutney

PREPARATION TIME 30 minutes
COOKING TIME 40 minutes

Inspiringly beautiful, this fresh and colourful take on a Middle Eastern staple is designed to kick any winter blues that come your way. Aside from their wow factor, these sliders are a very high source of fibre and protein and manageable for little hands, and the falafels freeze like a dream. You can also use the falafels on their own as a salad topper, for instance with our Traditional Greek Salad (page 72).

Per 1 slider/135 g serving:
260 calories; 10 g total fat;
36 g total carbs; 7 g fibre;
6 g sugar; 11 g protein;
490 mg sodium.

6 SERVINGS	24 SERVINGS	INGREDIENTS
Falafel Sliders		
1 Tbsp (15 mL)	¼ cup (60 mL)	ground flaxseed
4½ tsp (22 mL)	6 Tbsp (90 mL)	water
1½ tsp (7.5 mL)	2 Tbsp (30 mL)	olive oil
¼ cup (60 mL)	1 cup (250 mL)	finely chopped onions
2 cloves	6 cloves	garlic, minced
2 cups (500 mL)	8 cups (2 L)	cooked chickpeas
2 Tbsp (30 mL)	½ cup (125 mL)	low-sodium vegetable stock
2 Tbsp (30 mL)	½ cup (125 mL)	chopped curly parsley leaves
½ cup (125 mL)	2 cups (500 mL)	chickpea flour
½ tsp (2.5 mL)	2 tsp (10 mL)	baking powder
1 tsp (5 mL)	4 tsp (20 mL)	ground cumin
¼ tsp (1 mL)	1 tsp (5 mL)	chili powder (optional)
¼ tsp (1 mL)	1½ tsp (7.5 mL)	sea salt
⅛ tsp (0.6 mL)	½ tsp (2.5 mL)	black pepper
—	—	Papaya Chutney (see recipe on page 127)
6	24	mini pitas
Kale Tabbouleh		
½ cup (125 mL)	2 cups (500 mL)	roughly chopped curly parsley
½ cup (125 mL)	2 cups (500 mL)	roughly chopped kale
2 Tbsp (30 mL)	½ cup (125 mL)	finely chopped red onions
2 Tbsp (30 mL)	½ cup (125 mL)	finely diced red pepper
2 tsp (10 mL)	3 Tbsp (45 mL)	olive oil
1 tsp (5 mL) (about ⅛ lemon)	1½ Tbsp (22 mL) (about ¾ lemon)	fresh lemon juice
¼ tsp (1 mL)	1 tsp (5 mL)	sea salt
⅛ tsp (0.6 mL)	½ tsp (2.5 mL)	black pepper
Spicy Tahini Sauce		
3 Tbsp (45 mL)	¾ cup (180 mL)	tahini
2 Tbsp (30 mL)	½ cup (125 mL)	water
1 Tbsp (15 mL) (about ½ lemon)	¼ cup (60 mL) (about 2 lemons)	fresh lemon juice
2 tsp (10 mL)	3 Tbsp (40 mL)	maple syrup
1 clove	4 cloves	garlic, pureed
⅛ tsp (0.6 mL)	½ tsp (2.5 mL)	sea salt
⅛ tsp (0.6 mL)	½ tsp (2.5 mL)	cayenne

Continued...

1. Preheat oven to 375F (190C). Line baking sheet(s) with parchment paper and set aside.

2. In a small bowl, mix ground flaxseed with water. Set aside to allow to thicken.

3. Heat a medium sauté pan over medium heat, then add oil. Once heated, add onions and sauté until soft, about 3 to 5 minutes. Add garlic and chickpeas and sauté until garlic is fragrant, about 1 to 2 minutes.

4. In a food processor, combine the onion and chickpea mixture, the flaxseed mixture and the vegetable stock, parsley, chickpea flour, baking powder, cumin, chili powder (if using), salt and pepper. Process until the ingredients are thoroughly combined. (For 24 servings you will need to process in batches.)

5. Take a heaping ¼ cup (60 mL) of the mixture and form into a ball. Place on a prepared baking sheet. Repeat with remaining mixture, spacing the balls an inch apart.

6. Transfer to the oven and bake for 40 minutes, flipping the falafels after 20 minutes. Remove from oven. If freezing, allow falafels to cool and then place into a resealable container or bag. Store in the freezer for up to 3 months.

7. Meanwhile, in a medium bowl, thoroughly combine all kale tabbouleh ingredients. Set aside.

8. For the spicy tahini sauce, whisk together all ingredients in a small bowl until smooth. Set aside. Then prepare the papaya chutney (see recipe).

9. To assemble the falafel sliders, open the mini pitas and spread spicy tahini on the bottom. Layer with kale tabbouleh, a falafel and some more spicy tahini, then top with papaya chutney. (You can also serve the sliders with your favourite hot sauce and non-dairy yogurt.)

Papaya Chutney

Per ⅓ cup/80 mL serving: 60 calories; 1 g total fat; 14 g total carbs; 2 g fibre; 9 g sugar; 1 g protein; 50 mg sodium.

6 SERVINGS	24 SERVINGS	INGREDIENTS
1 tsp (5 mL)	4 tsp (20 mL)	grapeseed oil
3 cloves	12 cloves	garlic, pureed
1	4	jalapeno, seeded and minced
1 tsp (5 mL)	4 tsp (20 mL)	coriander seeds, crushed
½ tsp (2.5 mL)	2 tsp (10 mL)	yellow mustard seeds, cracked
1 small (about 3 cups/750 mL)	4 small (about 12 cups/3 L)	ripe papaya, cut into ¼-inch (0.6 cm) dice
1 Tbsp (15 mL)	¼ cup (60 mL)	lime zest
4 tsp (20 mL) (about 1 lime)	⅓ cup (80 mL) (about 3 limes)	fresh lime juice
1 Tbsp (15 mL)	¼ cup (60 mL)	apple cider vinegar
1 Tbsp (15 mL)	¼ cup (60 mL)	pureed ginger
1 Tbsp (15 mL)	¼ cup (60 mL)	maple syrup
½ cup (125 mL)	2 cups (500 mL)	water
⅛ tsp (0.6 mL)	¾ tsp (4 mL)	salt

1. Heat a saucepan over medium heat, then add oil. Once heated, add garlic, jalapenos, coriander and mustard seeds and sauté until fragrant, about 1 minute (3 minutes for 24 servings).

2. Add the remaining ingredients, except salt, and stir. Bring to a boil, reduce heat and allow to simmer for 20 minutes, stirring occasionally.

3. When the chutney has reduced by a third and is thick and viscous, remove from heat and stir in salt.

Warm Farro Salad with Spicy Citrus Dressing

PREPARATION TIME 15 to 20 minutes

COOKING TIME 40 to 45 minutes

I bestow upon you a fun and fancy way to eat your broccoli and whole grains in one vibrant and nutritionally sound dish! This salad is complete with nutty farro, beautifully bitter broccoli, crunchy seeds and tart and chewy cranberries, all tossed in a punchy citrus dressing and topped with fresh, fragrant cilantro.

Per 1 cup/237 g serving: 320 calories; 12 g total fat; 45 g total carbs; 7 g fibre; 10 g sugar; 11 g protein; 290 mg sodium.

6 SERVINGS	24 SERVINGS	INGREDIENTS
½ cup (125 mL)	2 cups (500 mL)	pumpkin seeds
1½ cups (375 mL)	6 cups (1.5 L)	farro
3 cups (750 mL)	12 cups (3 L)	water
½ cup (125 mL)	2 cups (500 mL)	diced shallots
2	8	bay leaves
2½ cups (625 mL)	10 cups (2.5 L)	small broccoli florets
4½ tsp (22 mL)	6 Tbsp (90 mL)	ground cumin
4½ tsp (22 mL)	6 Tbsp (90 mL)	ground coriander
3 Tbsp (45 mL)	¾ cup (180 mL)	extra-virgin olive oil
2 tsp (10 mL) (about ½ lime)	⅓ cup (80 mL) (about 2 limes)	fresh lime juice
1½ tsp (7.5 mL)	2 Tbsp (30 mL)	lime zest
2 Tbsp (30 mL) (about ½ orange)	½ cup (125 mL) (about 2 oranges)	fresh orange juice
1½ tsp (7.5 mL)	2 Tbsp (30 mL)	orange zest
1½ tsp (7.5 mL)	2 Tbsp (30 mL)	black pepper (optional)
½ tsp (2.5 mL)	2 tsp (10 mL)	chili flakes (optional)
½ cup (125 mL)	2 cups (500 mL)	unsweetened dried cranberries
¾ tsp (4 mL)	3 tsp (15 mL)	sea salt
Garnish		
¼ bunch	1 bunch	cilantro, stemmed

1. Preheat oven to 350F (180C). Line a baking sheet with parchment paper. Evenly spread pumpkin seeds on it and toast for about 10 minutes, or until slightly brown, tossing halfway. Remove from oven and set aside to cool.

2. Meanwhile, in a pot, combine farro, water, shallots and bay leaves. Bring to a boil over medium heat.

3. Once boiling, cover the pot and turn the heat to low. Simmer for 25 minutes, or until the farro is tender.

4. Place the broccoli florets in the pot on top of the farro and steam for 6 minutes. Once the broccoli is tender, remove bay leaves, drain excess liquid (if necessary) and transfer the farro and broccoli mixture to a large bowl to cool slightly.

5. Meanwhile, in a small sauté pan over low heat, toast cumin and coriander, stirring occasionally, until fragrant, about 5 minutes.

6. In a medium bowl, whisk together olive oil, lime juice and zest, orange juice and zest, toasted spices and pepper and chili flakes (if using).

7. Toss the farro mixture with the pumpkin seeds, cranberries, dressing and salt. Garnish with cilantro leaves and serve.

Caramelized Onion, Pear and Arugula Focaccia

PREPARATION TIME 1 hour 40 minutes
COOKING TIME 45 minutes

Every carbohydrate or bread lover's dream has come true in this celebration of all things caramelized and whole grain. It is an impeccable combination of sweet, sour, savoury, salty and peppery!

Per 1 slice/267 g serving: 380 calories; 19 g total fat; 47 g total carbs; 11 g fibre; 10 g sugar; 10 g protein; 190 mg sodium.

6 SERVINGS	24 SERVINGS	INGREDIENTS
Focaccia		
2¼ tsp (11 mL)	2 Tbsp + ¾ tsp (34 mL)	active dry yeast
¾ cup + 2 Tbsp (210 mL)	3⅓ cups (830 mL)	lukewarm water, 105–115F (49–55C)
¼ tsp (1 mL)	1½ tsp (7.5 mL)	honey
1 cup (250 mL)	4 cups (1 L)	whole grain flour
1 cup + 1 Tbsp (265 mL)	4¼ cups (1.05 L)	spelt flour
3 Tbsp (45 mL)	¾ cup (180 mL)	extra-virgin olive oil
½ tsp (2.5 mL)	2¼ tsp (11 mL)	kosher salt
Toppings		
3 Tbsp (45 mL)	¾ cup (180 mL)	extra-virgin olive oil, divided
2 cups (500 mL) (about 1 large onion)	7½ cups (1.9 L) (about 4 large onions)	thinly sliced onions
1¼ cups (310 mL) (about 1 pear)	5 cups (1.25 L) (about 4 pears)	thinly sliced Bosc pear
3 cups (750 mL)	9 cups (2.25 L)	arugula
Balsamic Reduction		
½ cup (125 mL)	2 cups (500 mL)	balsamic vinegar
2 tsp (10 mL)	2 Tbsp + 2 tsp (40 mL)	honey

Continued...

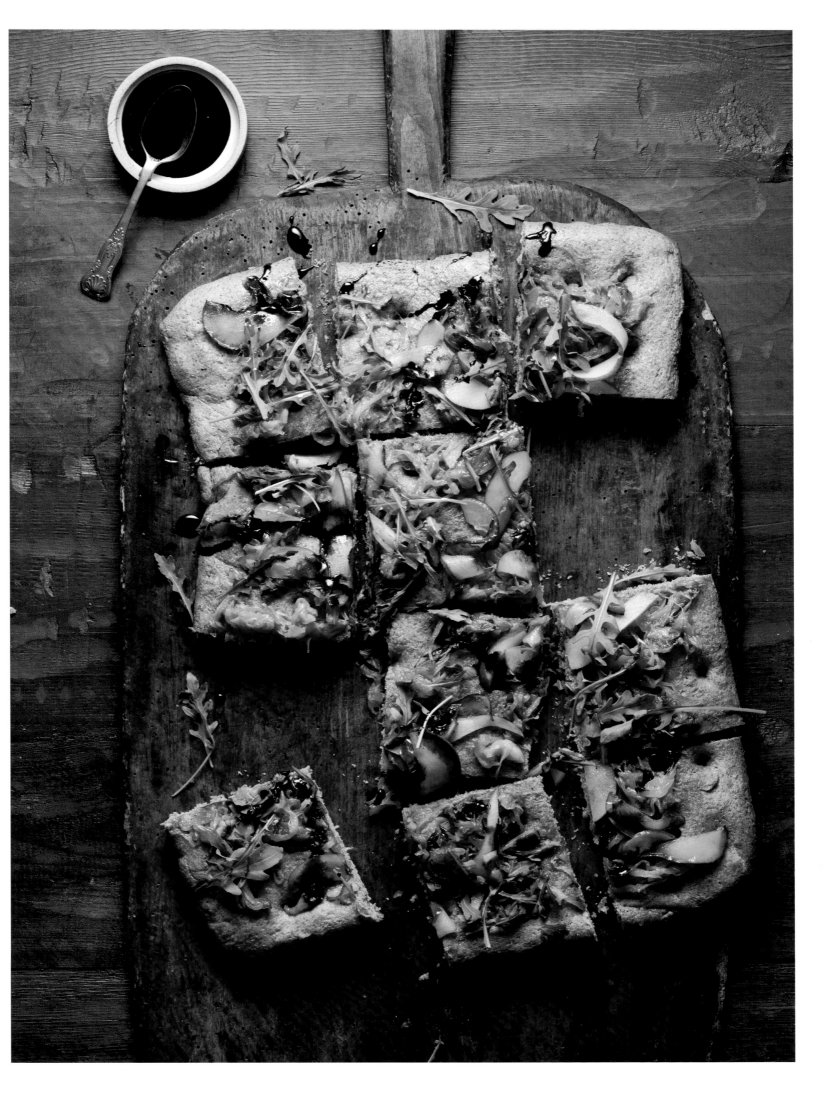

1. Preheat oven to 425F (220C). Grease pan(s), line with parchment paper and then grease parchment paper. (For 6 servings, use one 8 × 8-inch (20 × 20 cm) baking pan and for 24 servings use two 9 × 13-inch (22.5 × 32.5 cm) baking pans.)

2. In a small bowl, combine yeast, water and honey and stir to dissolve the honey. Set aside for 5 minutes in a draft-free place.

3. Sift the two flours together in a medium bowl. Set aside.

4. In the bowl of a stand mixer, combine the yeast mixture, the oil and half of the flour. Using a dough hook attachment, knead the dough for 5 minutes on medium speed. (Depending upon the size of your mixer, the dough may need to be prepared in batches for 24 servings.)

5. Add the remaining flour and salt and knead for another 5 minutes, until the dough has released from the side of the bowl and a ball forms. If the dough is too dry, add 1 tsp (5 mL) water at a time. If it is too wet, add 1 tsp (5 mL) flour until dough ball forms.

6. Transfer the dough to a lightly oiled bowl. (You may need more than one bowl if making 24 servings.) Cover with plastic wrap and let rest 1 hour in a warm, draft-free place.

7. Meanwhile, prepare the toppings. In a sauté pan over medium-low heat, heat 1 Tbsp (15 mL) oil for 6 servings and ¼ cup (60 mL) oil for 24 servings. Add sliced onions. Stir occasionally until onions are caramelized, about 30 minutes (1 hour for 24 servings). Remove from heat and set aside to cool.

8. In a large bowl, gently toss sliced pears with 1 Tbsp (15 mL) oil for 6 servings or ¼ cup (60 mL) for 24 servings.

9. To make the reduction, combine vinegar and honey in a small saucepan over medium-high heat and bring to a boil. Lower heat and simmer until the mixture has reduced by half or is thick enough to coat the back of a spoon, about 7 to 10 minutes. Set aside to cool and thicken further.

10. Transfer dough to prepared baking pan(s) and spread to the edges. Cover with plastic wrap and allow to rest for 20 minutes or until dough almost fully bounces back when gently pressed.

11. Poke holes in the top of the dough using your fingers. Brush the remaining oil over the dough. Evenly scatter caramelized onions on top, followed by the pears. Bake until edges are golden, about 30 minutes for 6 servings and 45 minutes for 24 servings.

12. Remove from oven and allow to cool on a rack. When ready to serve, scatter arugula on top and drizzle with balsamic reduction. Cut into slices and serve immediately.

Strawberry and Hazelnut Streusel Cake with a Maple Vanilla Glaze

Serve this dessert when you would like to impress your loved ones or guests. In my house it's known as the all-purpose cake because it's been used for almost every occasion, from holiday dinners to birthdays to baby showers to celebratory brunches. Don't be fooled by the decadent use of hazelnuts, maple syrup and straw-berries, as it is packed with whole grains, flaxseed, healthy fats and heaps of phytochemicals.

Per 1 piece/68 g serving: 150 calories; 7 g total fat; 21 g total carbs; 3 g fibre; 11 g sugar; 2 g protein; 100 mg sodium.

12 SERVINGS	24 SERVINGS	INGREDIENTS
Dry Ingredients		
1 cup (250 mL)	2 cups (500 mL)	whole wheat or spelt flour
4½ tsp (22 mL)	3 Tbsp (45 mL)	ground flaxseed
1 tsp (5 mL)	2 tsp (10 mL)	ground cinnamon
1 tsp (5 mL)	2 tsp (10 mL)	baking powder
½ tsp (2.5 mL)	1 tsp (5 mL)	baking soda
⅛ tsp (0.6 mL)	¼ tsp (1 mL)	sea salt
Wet Ingredients		
¼ cup (60 mL)	½ cup (125 mL)	grapeseed oil
3 Tbsp (45 mL)	⅓ cup (80 mL)	maple syrup
¼ cup (60 mL)	½ cup (125 mL)	water
½ cup (125 mL) (about 1 small banana)	1 cup (250 mL) (about 2 small bananas)	mashed banana
1½ tsp (7.5 mL)	1 Tbsp (15 mL)	apple cider vinegar
1 tsp (5 mL)	2 tsp (10 mL)	vanilla extract
Garnish		
1½ cups (375 mL)	3 cups (750 mL)	sliced strawberries, divided
⅓ cup (80 mL)	⅔ cup (160 mL)	chopped dates
¼ cup (60 mL)	½ cup (125 mL)	toasted hazelnuts, chopped, divided
Streusel Glaze		
¼ cup (60 mL)	½ cup (125 mL)	chopped dates
¼ cup (60 mL)	½ cup (125 mL)	water
1½ tsp (7.5 mL)	1 Tbsp (15 mL)	maple syrup
¼ tsp (1 mL)	½ tsp (2.5 mL)	vanilla extract

Continued...

1. Preheat oven to 350F (180C). Lightly grease one 8 × 8-inch (20 × 20 cm) cake pan if making 12 servings or two 8 × 8-inch cake pans if making 24 servings. Bundt pan(s) would work well here too. You would put the garnish in the bottom of the the pan instead of on the top of the cake. Set pan(s) aside.

2. In a large mixing bowl, combine all dry ingredients.

3. In a small mixing bowl, combine all wet ingredients.

4. Add the wet ingredients to the dry and thoroughly mix.

5. Carefully fold in half of the strawberries, all the dates and half of the hazelnuts until fully incorporated.

6. Evenly distribute mix into prepared pan(s). Place in the oven for 30 to 35 minutes, or until an inserted toothpick comes out clean. Remove from oven and set aside to cool.

7. Meanwhile, in a blender, puree all glaze ingredients until smooth. Set aside at room temperature.

8. When ready to serve, drizzle cake with streusel glaze and sprinkle with remaining hazelnuts. Slice and serve with remaining strawberries.

Sweet Potato Pie Parfaits

PREPARATION TIME 15 to 20 minutes
COOKING TIME 18 to 20 minutes + 1 hour
for baking sweet potatoes

Here, we vamp up the often underappreciated parfait by marrying it with classic sweet potato pie ingredients, then top it all off with creamy coconut yogurt and crunchy pumpkin seed granola. Not only is this an easy make-ahead breakfast or dessert that everyone will request again and again, but it is also very high in fibre, iron and vitamin A, and a good source of potassium, calcium and healthy fats. Any leftover granola topping can be stored in a resealable bag and enjoyed as a snack or atop your morning breakfast.

Per 1½ cups/325 g serving: 540 calories; 23 g total fat; 75 g total carbs; 12 g fibre; 24 g sugar; 12 g protein; 135 mg sodium.

6 SERVINGS	24 SERVINGS	INGREDIENTS
Parfait		
4 small or 2 large	16 small or 8 large	sweet potatoes
2 Tbsp (30 mL)	½ cup (125 mL)	maple syrup
1 tsp (5 mL)	4 tsp (20 mL)	vanilla extract
1 tsp (5 mL)	4 tsp (20 mL)	ground cinnamon
¼ tsp (1 mL)	1 tsp (5 mL)	ground allspice
¼ tsp (1 mL	1 tsp (5 mL)	ground nutmeg
⅛ tsp (0.6 mL)	½ tsp (2.5 mL)	ground cardamom
1 (400 mL) can	4 (400 mL) cans	light coconut milk
1½ cups (375 mL)	6 cups (1.5 L)	coconut yogurt or yogurt of your choice
Topping		
2 cups (500 mL)	8 cups (2 L)	whole rolled oats
¾ cup (180 mL)	3 cups (750 mL)	pecans
¼ cup (60 mL)	1 cup (250 mL)	raw pumpkin seeds
¼ cup (60 mL)	1 cup (250 mL)	hemp seeds
2 Tbsp (30 mL)	½ cup (125 mL)	maple syrup
1 tsp (5 mL)	4 tsp (20 mL)	ground cinnamon
½ cup (125 mL)	2 cups (500 mL)	chopped dates

1. Preheat oven to 375F (190C) and line baking sheets with parchment paper.

2. Cut sweet potatoes in half lengthwise. Arrange face down on prepared baking sheets and bake 1 hour, or until fork tender. Set aside to cool slightly.

3. Meanwhile, in a large bowl, combine all topping ingredients and mix until oats, nuts and seeds are completely coated in syrup. Evenly distribute on another lined baking sheet and bake in the oven for 18 to 20 minutes, or until mixture is toasted and slightly brown. Remove from oven and allow to cool.

4. In a food processor, combine sweet potatoes, maple syrup, vanilla and spices. (Work in batches if needed for 24 servings.) Puree until completely smooth, about 4 to 5 minutes.

5. Remove half of the puree and set aside. Add coconut milk to the puree in the food processor and process until coconut milk is completely mixed in, about 3 minutes. Remove from processor and set aside.

6. In 12-ounce Mason jars, layer ingredients in the following order and amounts: ¼ cup (60 mL) sweet potato puree, ½ cup (125 mL) coconut milk and sweet potato puree, and ¼ cup (60 mL) yogurt. Seal with lids or plastic wrap and refrigerate until ready to eat.

7. When ready to serve, top each parfait with ½ cup (125 mL) topping and enjoy.

Matcha Mint Chocolate Chip Shakes

PREPARATION TIME 10 to 15 minutes

The ways to use polyphenol-rich green tea and cacao are endless, and this shake is an example of chocolatey ingenuity. Frozen bananas make a beautifully sweet and creamy base, and with the addition of mint leaves this shake is best described as a sip of fresh winter air.

Per 1 cup/250 mL serving: 190 calories; 6 g total fat; 28 g total carbs; 6 g fibre; 14 g sugar; 6 g protein; 45 mg sodium.

6 SERVINGS	24 SERVINGS	INGREDIENTS
4 large	16 large	frozen bananas
3 cups (750 mL)	12 cups (3 L)	unsweetened soy milk
½ cup (125 mL)	2 cups (500 mL)	mint leaves, packed
⅓ cup (80 mL)	1⅓ cups (350 mL)	cacao nibs
1 Tbsp (15 mL)	¼ cup (60 mL)	maple syrup
1 Tbsp (15 mL)	¼ cup (60 mL)	matcha powder
1 tsp (5 mL)	4 tsp (20 mL)	vanilla extract
Garnish		
½ bunch	2 bunches	mint leaves
2 Tbsp (30 mL)	½ cup (125 mL)	cacao nibs

1. Combine all ingredients in a blender. Blend until mint leaves are fully incorporated and texture is relatively smooth, but still leaving some cacao nibs for a bit of texture and crunch. Alternatively, you can add the cacao nibs after blending for a chunkier and greener shake. (For 24 servings, blending will have to be done in batches. Follow the 6-serving quantities and repeat 4 times.)

2. Garnish each shake with mint leaves and 1 tsp (5 mL) cacao nibs.

Myth: rich and indulgent food has to be unhealthy. This could not be further from the truth, particularly when you focus on whole, plant-based foods. And with the use of high-fibre, flavourful fruits and vegetables, nut and seed butters, plant-based milks, spices from around the world, and hearty legumes, grains and mushrooms, you can make any dish healthful and still have it be an indulgent treat. This section offers fresh and delicious twists on take-out favourites, including Kung Pao Chickpeas, Raw Pad Thai Salad and pho transformed into a wrap.

SAMPLE MENU FOR
AN INDULGENT CURRY DINNER

BEVERAGE
Mango Turmeric Lassi

SOUP
Yam and Coconut Curry Soup

MAIN
Mango Almond Curry

DESSERT
Spicy Chocolate-Dipped Oranges

Healthy Take-Out Twists

Yam and Coconut Curry Soup

This soup satisfies all forms of cravings, from the velvety coconut base to its mildly sweet yam flavour, from the satisfying heartiness of the lentils to the slightly salty roasted chickpeas that give this dish a nice crunchy finish. If you would like a thicker, "creamier" soup, only add a quarter of the vegetable stock.

Per 1¼ cups/415 g serving: 420 calories; 14 g total fat; 62 g total carbs; 17 g fibre; 11 g sugar; 15 g protein; 600 mg sodium.

6 SERVINGS	24 SERVINGS	INGREDIENTS
1 (400 mL) can	4 (400 mL) cans	chickpeas, drained and rinsed
2 Tbsp (30 mL)	½ cup (125 mL)	extra-virgin olive oil, divided
1½ tsp (7.5 mL)	2 Tbsp (30 mL)	sea salt, divided
½ tsp (2.5 mL)	2 tsp (10 mL)	black pepper (optional), divided
⅔ cup (160 mL)	2⅔ cups (660 mL)	diced onions
½ head	2 heads	garlic, minced
2 Tbsp (30 mL)	½ cup (125 mL)	minced ginger
1 Tbsp (15 mL)	¼ cup (60 mL)	curry powder
¾ tsp (4 mL)	1 Tbsp (15 mL)	cayenne
4 cups (1 L) (about 2 to 3 yams)	16 cups (4 L) (about 8 to 12 yams)	chopped yams, cut into small dice
2 cups (500 mL)	8 cups (2 L)	low-sodium vegetable stock
2 (400 mL) cans	8 (400 mL) cans	light coconut milk
1 cup (250 mL)	4 cups (1 L)	dry red lentils

1. Preheat oven to 400F (205C). Line a baking sheet (or two if making 24 servings) with parchment paper.

2. Using a clean kitchen towel, pat chickpeas dry. In a large bowl, toss chickpeas with half each of the oil, salt and pepper.

3. Spread chickpeas evenly onto the prepared baking sheet(s). Bake for 40 minutes (55 to 60 minutes for 24 servings), stirring halfway through the baking time. Bake until chickpeas are crispy on the outside and slightly soft on the inside. Remove and set aside to cool slightly.

4. Heat a large pot over medium heat then add remaining oil. Once heated, add onions and cook until translucent, about 2 to 3 minutes. Add garlic, ginger, curry powder and cayenne and sauté until fragrant.

5. Add the yams and vegetable stock, and bring to a simmer. Allow to cook until yams are tender, about 10 to 12 minutes. Stir occasionally.

6. Add coconut milk and lentils. Stir once and allow to simmer for 25 minutes, covered.

7. Once the lentils are soft, remove the soup from heat and carefully use a hand immersion blender to puree until completely smooth. (If using a regular blender, work in batches as needed and make sure to take breaks to release the heat from the blender.)

8. Stir in remaining salt and pepper.

9. Top with roasted chickpeas and serve!

Raw Pad Thai Salad

Red bell peppers, yellow and green zucchini, green broccoli, orange (or yellow or purple!) carrots—eating the rainbow is quite easy when you have a recipe that focuses on raw vegetables! When the picking is ripe and you want to highlight the bounty of the harvest, this is the dish. It is not only vibrant in colour, but in flavour. And the tangy dressing and sweet and sour tofu make it taste like you are indulging in something saved only for special occasions.

Per 1¼ cups/271 g serving: 190 calories; 9 g total fat; 19 g total carbs; 5 g fibre; 11 g sugar; 9 g protein; 260 mg sodium.

6 SERVINGS	24 SERVINGS	INGREDIENTS
Tofu		
2 Tbsp (30 mL)	½ cup (125 mL)	tamari
1 Tbsp (15 mL)	¼ cup (60 mL)	tamarind paste
1½ tsp (7.5 mL)	2 Tbsp (30 mL)	maple syrup
1 clove	4 cloves	garlic, minced
175 g	2 (350 g) packages	extra-firm organic tofu, cut into ½-inch (1.25 cm)cubes
Salad		
2 small	8	green zucchini, spiralized or peeled into long strips
2 medium	6 large	carrots, spiralized or peeled into long strips
1	4	yellow zucchini, spiralized or peeled into long strips
1	4	red pepper, julienned
½ head	2 heads	broccoli, cut into small florets and stems peeled and diced
½ bunch	2 bunches	basil, cut in chiffonade
½ bunch	2 bunches	green onions, thinly sliced
Dressing		
¼ cup (60 mL)	1 cup (250 mL)	raw, natural almond butter
1 Tbsp (15 mL)	¼ cup (60 mL)	tamarind paste
¼ cup (60 mL)	1 cup (250 mL)	water
1 tsp (5 mL)	1 Tbsp (15 mL)	lime zest
1 Tbsp (15 mL) (about 1 lime)	¼ cup (60 mL) (about 2 limes)	fresh lime juice
2 Tbsp (30 mL)	½ cup (125 mL)	maple syrup
Garnish		
2 Tbsp (30 mL)	½ cup (125 mL)	crushed almonds
—	—	Cilantro leaves (optional)

TIP

For an extra boost of flavour, add 1 julienned green mango to 6 servings and 4 julienned green mangoes to 24 servings.

1. Preheat oven to 375F (190C). Line two (or more) baking sheets with parchment paper and set aside.

2. In a large bowl whisk together tamari, tamarind paste, maple syrup and garlic.

3. Add tofu and coat with marinade. Set aside for 15 minutes.

4. Evenly distribute tofu on the baking sheets. Bake for 20 to 25 minutes until most of the liquid has been absorbed. Remove from oven and set aside to cool.

5. Meanwhile, toss the salad ingredients together in a large salad bowl and set aside.

6. In a small mixing bowl, whisk together the dressing ingredients until smooth.

7. When ready to serve, combine the dressing and salad and toss until everything is completely coated. Top with tofu, crushed almonds and cilantro leaves (if using).

Thai Noodle Salad with Spicy Roasted Almonds

PREPARATION TIME 15 minutes
COOKING TIME 10 minutes

Nothing feels more satisfying than slurping up a giant bowl of noodles. Serve this warm or cold depending upon the weather, or your mood.

Per 1½ cups/123 g serving: 260 calories; 12 g total fat; 32 g total carbs; 4 g fibre; 5 g sugar; 7 g protein; 140 mg sodium.

6 SERVINGS	24 SERVINGS	INGREDIENTS
Spicy Almonds		
½ cup (125 mL)	2 cups (500 mL)	dry-roasted almonds
1½ tsp (7.5 mL)	2 Tbsp (30 mL)	maple syrup
1½ tsp (7.5 mL)	2 Tbsp (30 mL)	your favourite hot sauce (no sugar added)
Salad		
150 g	600 g	purple potato vermicelli (or rice vermicelli or glass noodles), uncooked
1 small	2 large	carrot, spiralized or peeled into ribbons
1 cup (250 mL)	4 cups (1 L)	thinly sliced red cabbage, tightly packed
½ cup (125 mL)	2 cups (500 mL)	sugar snap peas, julienned
½ cup (125 mL)	2 cups (500 mL)	frozen shelled edamame, thawed
1	6	green onion, thinly sliced
Dressing		
¼ tsp (1 mL)	1 tsp (5 mL)	lime zest
3 Tbsp (45 mL) (about 1 lime)	¾ cup (180 mL) (about 4 limes)	fresh lime juice
3 Tbsp (45 mL)	¾ cup (180 mL)	natural, unsalted almond butter
3 Tbsp (45 mL)	¾ cup (180 mL)	water
1 Tbsp (15 mL)	¼ cup (60 mL)	rice wine vinegar
2 tsp (10 mL)	2 Tbsp (30 mL)	maple syrup
½	2	red chili, seeded and minced
½ tsp (2.5 mL)	2 tsp (10 mL)	pureed ginger
¼ tsp (1 mL)	1 tsp (5 mL)	sea salt
Garnish		
⅛ bunch	½ bunch	cilantro, chopped
1½ tsp each	2 Tbsp each	black and white sesame seeds

TIP

You can swap out the almonds and almond butter for your favourite nuts and nut butter. Or if a nut allergy is present, use tahini in lieu of almond butter and top with the sesame brittle from the Sweet Potato and Tahini Soup recipe (page 43).

1. Preheat oven to 375F (190C) and line a baking sheet with parchment paper.

2. In a small bowl, toss together almonds, maple syrup and hot sauce. Evenly distribute on baking sheet and roast for 10 to 12 minutes, or until nuts are slightly toasted and fragrant. Remove from oven and set aside.

3. Meanwhile, boil water and cook noodles according to package directions. Once cooked, drain and rinse under cold water to stop the noodles from cooking. Ensure that excess water has been completely drained.

4. Transfer noodles to a large bowl, along with the carrots, cabbage, snap peas, edamame and green onions. Toss together and set aside.

5. Whisk together all dressing ingredients.

6. When ready to serve, toss salad and dressing together, and top with chopped cilantro and sesame seeds. Garnish with spicy roasted almonds.

Mango Almond Curry

I dream of thick-sauced, sweet and spicy, vegetable-heavy curries daily. With the addition of sweet mango to this fiery, savoury dish the depth of flavour and nutrition are taken to another level. This curry could (and should!) be a weekly staple in your make-ahead recipe repertoire. It is rich in phytonutrients like allicin, carotenoids, curcumin and isoflavones, and is high in protein, potassium, calcium and iron. It's also an excellent source of fibre and vitamins A, C and E. Serve over a whole grain like brown rice or quinoa or enjoy with soba or brown rice noodles, all great sources of fibre.

Per 1½ cups/375 mL serving: 440 calories; 27 g total fat; 40 g total carbs; 11 g fibre; 22 g sugar; 17 g protein; 510 mg sodium.

6 SERVINGS	24 SERVINGS	INGREDIENTS
1 Tbsp (15 mL)	¼ cup (60 mL)	coconut oil, divided
1 (350 g) package	4 (350 g) packages	organic tofu, cut into ½-inch (1.25 cm) cubes
2 tsp (10 mL)	8 tsp (40 mL)	tamari
2½ cups (625 mL)	10 cups (2.5 L)	cubed eggplant
1¼ cups (300 mL)	5 cups (1.25 L)	diced carrots
1½ cups (375 mL)	6 cups (1.5 L)	diced onions
4 cloves	15 cloves	garlic, minced
4 tsp (20 mL)	5 Tbsp (75 mL)	ground turmeric
1½ tsp (7.5 mL)	2 Tbsp (30 mL)	ground cumin
1½ tsp (7.5 mL)	2 Tbsp (30 mL)	ground ginger
¾ tsp (4 mL)	1 Tbsp (15 mL)	chili flakes
1½ tsp (7.5 mL)	2 Tbsp (30 mL)	ground coriander
¾ tsp (4 mL)	1 Tbsp (15 mL)	ground cinnamon
3 cups (750 mL)	12 cups (3 L) (about 1 cabbage)	diced green cabbage
1½ cups (375 mL)	6 cups (1.5 L)	diced red peppers
1¼ cups (200 g)	5 cups (1.25 L)	frozen or fresh diced mangoes, cut in ½-inch (1.25 cm) cubes

Sauce

6 SERVINGS	24 SERVINGS	INGREDIENTS
⅔ cup (160 mL)	2½ cups (625 mL)	almond butter
2 cups (500 mL)	8 cups (2 L)	water
¼ cup (60 mL)	1 cup (250 mL)	maple syrup
1 tsp (5 mL)	4 tsp (20 mL)	sea salt
4 tsp (20 mL)	5 Tbsp (75 mL)	lime zest
¼ cup (60 mL) (about 2 limes)	1 cup (250 mL) (about 8 limes)	fresh lime juice

Garnish

6 SERVINGS	24 SERVINGS	INGREDIENTS
¼ bunch	1 bunch	green onions, thinly sliced
¼ bunch	1 bunch	cilantro, stems removed
½ cup (125 mL)	2 cups (500 mL)	unsalted dry-roasted almonds, chopped

Continued...

For 24 servings, depending upon the size of your sauté pan, it may be best to reserve 1 Tbsp (15 mL) coconut oil and sauté the cabbage and red peppers separately, then add in with the mangoes and tofu.

1. Heat a large sauté pan over medium-high heat, then add half of the oil. Once heated, add tofu and panfry until tofu is crispy. Don't flip tofu until it is brown or it will crumble. (Work in batches, if needed, for 24 servings.)

2. Drizzle tamari over tofu and sauté for another minute, or until tamari has been absorbed. Remove from heat and set aside.

3. Heat a large stockpot over medium heat, then add remaining oil. Once heated, add eggplant, carrots, onions and garlic. Sauté for 5 to 10 minutes or until onions are translucent and garlic is fragrant.

4. Stir in spices and sauté until fragrant, about 2 minutes.

5. In a small bowl, whisk together all sauce ingredients until completely combined.

6. Add cabbage, peppers and sauce to the stockpot. Stir to coat all vegetables, and continue to cook for another 5 to 7 minutes.

7. Add mangoes and tofu and heat through, about 4 minutes.

8. Transfer the curry to a serving dish (or dishes) and garnish with green onions, cilantro and almonds.

Kung Pao Chickpeas over Sesame-Fried Millet

Throw out that take-out menu, pick up this recipe and have a friends, family or community cooking session! Aside from tasting like your go-to Chinese take-out, this recipe is high in fibre, iron and vitamins A, C and E, as well as health-promoting phytonutrients like beta-glucan, carotenoids and polyphenols. You will want to make the larger quantity to ensure that there are leftovers for the rest of the week!

Per 1½ cups/331 g serving with sesame-fried millet: 370 calories; 15 g total fat; 46 g total carbs; 8 g fibre; 8 g sugar; 13 g protein; 500 mg sodium.

6 SERVINGS	24 SERVINGS	INGREDIENTS
Chickpea Marinade		
1 (540 mL) can	6 (540 mL) cans	chickpeas, drained and rinsed
2 Tbsp (30 mL)	½ cup (125 mL)	low-sodium tamari
1 Tbsp (15 mL)	¼ cup (60 mL)	rice vinegar
1 Tbsp (15 mL)	¼ cup (60 mL)	maple syrup
Sauce		
¼ cup (60 mL)	1 cup (250 mL)	rice vinegar
¼ cup (60 mL)	1 cup (250 mL)	low-sodium vegetable stock
3	12	red Thai chilies, minced
2 Tbsp (30 mL)	½ cup (125 mL)	almond or peanut butter
2 Tbsp (30 mL)	½ cup (125 mL)	low-sodium tamari
2 Tbsp (30 mL)	½ cup (125 mL)	tapioca starch
1½ tsp (7.5 mL)	2 Tbsp (30 mL)	sesame oil
¾ tsp (4 mL)	1 Tbsp (15 mL)	molasses
Stir-Fry		
1 tsp (5 mL)	4 tsp (20 mL)	sesame oil
1 cup (250 mL)	3¾ cups (930 mL) (about 8 stalks)	diced celery
1 cup (250 mL)	3½ cups (875 mL) (about 4 large carrots)	diced carrot
3 cups (750 mL)	12 cups (3 L)	halved then sliced white or brown mushrooms
4 cloves	16 cloves	garlic, minced
¾ cup (180 mL) (about ½ pepper)	3 cups (750 mL) (about 2 peppers)	diced red peppers
½ cup (125 mL)	2 cups (500 mL)	sugar snap peas, strings removed and halved
½ cup (125 mL)	2 cups (500 mL)	sliced bamboo shoots
½ cup (125 mL)	2 cups (500 mL)	sliced water chestnuts
3 cups (750 mL)	12 cups (3 L)	Sesame-Fried Millet (see recipe on following page)
Garnish		
¼ cup (60 mL)	1 cup (250 mL)	toasted almonds, chopped

Continued . . .

1. Combine all chickpea marinade ingredients in a medium bowl. Mix well and set aside.

2. In a small bowl, whisk together sauce ingredients. Set aside.

3. Heat a large wok over high heat, then add sesame oil. Once heated, add celery and carrots and sauté for 3 minutes (7 minutes for 24 servings).

4. Add mushrooms and garlic and sauté for 2 more minutes (5 minutes for 24 servings).

5. Add red peppers, snap peas, bamboo shoots and water chestnuts and sauté for another 2 minutes (5 minutes for 24 servings).

6. Add chickpeas with marinade and heat through, about 3 minutes.

7. Pour in sauce and heat through, about 3 minutes.

8. Remove from heat and scoop 1 cup (250 mL) Kung Pao chickpeas over ½ cup (125 mL) sesame-fried millet for each serving. Top with 1 Tbsp (15 mL) toasted almonds and a sprinkling of sesame seeds.

Sesame-Fried Millet

PREPARATION TIME   35 minutes
COOKING TIME   25 minutes

6 SERVINGS	24 SERVINGS	INGREDIENTS
1½ tsp (7.5 mL)	2 Tbsp (30 mL)	sesame oil
3 cups (750 mL)	12 cups (3 L)	cooked millet
¼ cup (60 mL)	1 cup (250 mL)	sliced green onions
⅛ tsp (0.6 mL)	½ tsp (2.5 mL)	salt

TIP

1 cup (250 mL) of dried millet will yield 3 cups (750 mL) cooked and 4 cups (1 L) will yield 12 cups (3 L).

1. Heat a large wok over high heat, then add oil. Once heated, add millet and sauté for 3 to 5 minutes.

2. Add green onions and sauté for 2 to 3 minutes.

3. Remove from heat and stir in salt.

Pho Noodle Wrap

Now you can easily experience your favourite Vietnamese noodle soup's sweet, spicy and complex flavours in a neat and tidy wrap. This make-ahead meal is ideal for sharing at your next office luncheon or as a fabulous, fuss-free option for that quick, on-the-go dinner. In addition to being convenient, it contains a plethora of functional foods, including cruciferous, orange and leafy green vegetables.

Per 1 wrap/233 g serving: 300 calories; 9 g total fat; 47 g total carbs; 5 g fibre; 9 g sugar; 13 g protein; 450 mg sodium.

6 SERVINGS	24 SERVINGS	INGREDIENTS
150 g (about 400 g cooked)	600 g (about 1.6 kg cooked)	dry brown rice noodles, cooked
3 Tbsp (45 mL)	¾ cup (180 mL)	tamari, divided
2 Tbsp (30 mL)	½ cup (125 mL)	sesame oil, divided
¾ tsp (4 mL)	1 Tbsp (15 mL)	ground cinnamon
¾ tsp (4 mL)	1 Tbsp (15 mL)	ground ginger
¾ tsp (4 mL)	1 Tbsp (15 mL)	garlic powder
3 Tbsp (45 mL)	¾ cup (180 mL)	maple syrup
3 Tbsp (45 mL)	¾ cup (180 mL)	rice wine vinegar
2 tsp (10 mL)	2½ Tbsp (37 mL)	lime zest
4 tsp (20 mL) (about 1 lime)	⅓ cup (80 mL) (about 4 limes)	fresh lime juice
1 (350 g) package	3 lbs (1.4 kg)	firm tofu, cut into long, ½-inch-thick (0.6 cm) strips
3 cups (750 mL)	12 cups (3 L)	stemmed and thinly sliced mushrooms
½ tsp (2.5 mL)	1½ tsp (7.5 mL)	black pepper
6 (10-inch)	24 (10-inch)	whole wheat wraps
Garnish		
1½ cups (375 mL)	6 cups (1.5 L)	thinly sliced red cabbage
1½ cups (375 mL)	6 cups (1.5 L)	grated carrots
¾ cup (180 mL)	3 cups (750 mL)	thinly sliced savoy cabbage
3 sprigs	12 sprigs	cilantro, stemmed
2 sprigs	8 sprigs	basil, stemmed
2	8	green onions, thinly sliced
—	—	Hot sauce of your choice (optional)

Continued . . .

1. In a medium bowl, toss noodles with a third each of the tamari and sesame oil. Set aside until ready to use.

2. In a small bowl, combine the cinnamon, ginger and garlic powder.

3. In a medium bowl, combine maple syrup, rice wine vinegar, the remaining tamari and lime zest and juice. Set aside until ready to use.

4. Heat a large sauté pan over medium heat, then add the remaining sesame oil. Once heated, add tofu and brown one side, about 4 minutes. Flip and brown other side, about 4 minutes. (If making 24 servings, work in batches, if needed.)

5. Sprinkle the spice mixture over the tofu and sauté until fragrant, about 1 minute.

6. Stir in mushrooms and sauté with tofu until brown, about 3 minutes (7 minutes for 24 servings).

7. Add the prepared sauce, making sure to coat the tofu and mushrooms. Season with pepper and remove from heat.

8. Store tofu and mushroom mixture separately from the toppings until ready to serve.

TO ASSEMBLE

Take 1 whole wheat wrap, warm it slightly in a dry pan (to make folding easier) and assemble wrap according to the following quantities:
- ¾ cup (180 mL) noodles
- ⅔ cup (160 mL) tofu-mushroom mixture
- ¼ cup (60 mL) red cabbage
- ¼ cup (60 mL) carrots
- 2 Tbsp (30 mL) savoy cabbage
- 5 leaves cilantro
- 4 leaves basil
- 1 Tbsp (15 mL) green onions
- Hot sauce (if using)

Repeat with the remaining wraps.

Raw Carrot Cake Pie with Whipped Cinnamon Orange Cream

Have your cake and eat some pie too! You really can have it all in one dessert—velvety, spiced carrot cake filling, chewy-sweet pecan crust and a vanilla-kissed coconut cream topping. There's (almost) no need to mention that each slice is a good source of fibre, protein, iron and vitamin A because you're going to want to eat it regardless.

Per 1 slice/156 g serving:
410 calories; 27 g total fat;
36 g total carbs;
5 g fibre; 25 g sugar;
8 g protein; 40 mg sodium.

6 SERVINGS	24 SERVINGS	INGREDIENTS
Crust		
⅔ cup (160 mL)	2⅔ cups (660 mL)	pitted dates
⅓ cup (80 mL)	1⅓ cups (350 mL)	chopped pecans
2 Tbsp (30 mL)	½ cup (125 mL)	pumpkin seeds
Filling		
2 cups (500 mL)	8 cups (2 L)	roughly chopped carrots
¼ cup (60 mL)	⅔ cup (160 mL)	fresh orange juice
(about 1 orange)	(about 2 large oranges)	
1 cup (250 mL)	4 cups (1 L)	cashews, soaked for 30 minutes
¼ cup (60 mL)	1 cup (250 mL)	maple syrup
2 Tbsp (30 mL)	½ cup (125 mL)	coconut oil
½ tsp (2.5 mL)	2 tsp (10 mL)	vanilla extract
¼ tsp (1 mL)	1 tsp (5 mL)	ground cinnamon
⅛ tsp (0.6 mL)	½ tsp (2.5 mL)	ground nutmeg
Topping		
1 (400 mL) can	3 (400 mL) cans	coconut milk, chilled overnight, cream separated and water removed
1½ tsp (7.5 mL)	1 tsp (5 mL)	maple syrup
¼ tsp (1 mL)	1 tsp (5 mL)	vanilla extract
¼ tsp (1 mL)	1 tsp (5 mL)	ground cinnamon
1½ tsp (7.5 mL)	2 Tbsp (30 mL)	orange zest
Garnish		
2 Tbsp (30 mL)	½ cup (125 mL)	finely chopped pumpkin seeds
2 Tbsp (30 mL)	½ cup (125 mL)	coarsely chopped pecans

Continued...

When making 4 pies, process the ingredients in batches so as not to exceed the capacities of the food processor and blender.

You can simplify serving by adding the whipped topping ahead of time. After the pie has been in the freezer for 1 hour to slightly firm up, gently smooth the topping over the carrot filling and top with garnish. Place pan(s) on a baking sheet, gently lay a parchment sheet on top and tightly wrap with plastic film. Return to freezer for 3 hours or until firm.

1. Grease a 9-inch (22.5 cm) cake pan (or four 9-inch pans if making 24 servings) with a little coconut oil and line bottom(s) with parchment paper.

2. In a food processor, combine all crust ingredients. Process into a crumbly, mealy dough, about 3 minutes. It should stick together when you press it between your fingers. (For 24 servings the crust ingredients will need to be processed in 4 batches.) Evenly press the crust into the bottoms and sides of the pan(s). (Using the bottom of a measuring cup helps.) The crust(s) should be tightly packed. Set aside.

3. Working in batches if needed, place carrots and orange juice in a blender and blend until smooth. Add the remaining filling ingredients and process until creamy and smooth, about 5 minutes. (If the blender starts to heat up, allow the machine to cool down before continuing.) Scrape down the sides of the blender with a spatula and process again if needed. Pour filling into the crust(s) and spread evenly. Place in freezer for 1 hour, to slightly firm up.

4. Meanwhile, combine topping ingredients in a mixing bowl. Using a hand mixer on medium speed, whip together until thick. Refrigerate topping until ready to serve.

5. Place pie pan(s) on a baking sheet. Gently lay a parchment sheet on top, and tightly wrap with plastic film. Chill in the freezer for 3 hours. The pie(s) will be firm to the touch when ready.

6. Once set, remove from freezer. Using a hot clean knife, slice each pie into 6 (or 24) pieces and serve each slice with a dollop of the topping and a sprinkle of pumpkin seeds and pecans.

Spicy Chocolate-Dipped Oranges

PREPARATION TIME 5 minutes

COOKING TIME 10 minutes

Making your own chocolate sauce and then dipping seasonal fruit in it is always very impressive when entertaining. This recipe is dead easy, has fancy garden party vibes, and is also good for you! The cocoa teamed up with the robust spices and buttery coconut oil make it that much more decadent, but they also double as functional foods providing health benefits. Use the sauce with oranges or other seasonal fruit, as a fondue, or freeze it in bar form for a rainy chocolate-less day.

Per 5 pieces/114 g serving: 300 calories; 25 g total fat; 22 g total carbs; 4 g fibre; 14 g sugar; 2 g protein; 4 mg sodium.

6 SERVINGS	24 SERVINGS	INGREDIENTS
⅔ cup (160 mL)	2½ cups (625 mL)	coconut oil
3 Tbsp (45 mL)	¾ cup (180 mL)	finely chopped fresh ginger
¾ tsp (4 mL)	1 Tbsp (15 mL)	ground cinnamon
Pinch of	½ tsp (2.5 mL)	cayenne
Pinch of	½ tsp (2.5 mL)	ground nutmeg
½ cup (125 mL)	2 cups (500 mL)	cocoa powder
¼ cup (60 mL)	1 cup (250 mL)	maple syrup
3 medium	12 medium	navel or blood oranges, peeled and separated into segments

1. Line baking sheet(s) with parchment paper and set aside.

2. Heat coconut oil in a small saucepan over medium-low heat. Whisk in ginger, cinnamon, cayenne and nutmeg. Once the spices are fragrant, about 2 minutes, slowly whisk in cocoa powder and cook for about 1 to 2 minutes, until fragrant.

3. Slowly whisk in maple syrup in a steady stream, until fully incorporated. Quickly remove from heat and set aside.

4. Carefully dip each orange segment into chocolate sauce and place on prepared baking sheet(s).

5. Allow to cool in the fridge for 20 minutes before serving.

TIP

Before the chocolate sets, you can sprinkle chocolate-covered oranges with coconut flakes or chopped nuts like walnuts or pistachios.

Vanilla Chai Chia Seed Pudding

PREPARATION TIME 5 minutes

Hop on the chia pudding bandwagon and reap the benefits of the seed's nutritional profile. Chia seeds are rich in fibre, omega-3 fatty acids, complete protein, calcium and vitamin E. They are also ideal for making a rich creamy pudding. This version takes traditional chai spices and perfectly pairs them with vanilla, a touch of maple syrup and tart, juicy raspberries.

Per 1 cup/235 g serving: 310 calories; 15 g total fat; 42 g total carbs; 19 g fibre; 19 g sugar; 9 g protein; 250 mg sodium.

6 SERVINGS	24 SERVINGS	INGREDIENTS
4 cups (1 L)	16 cups (4 L)	unsweetened almond milk
1 cup (250 mL)	4 cups (1 L)	chia seeds
8	24	dried, pitted dates
¼ cup (60 mL)	1 cup (250 mL)	maple syrup
¼ tsp (1 mL)	1½ tsp (7.5 mL)	ground cinnamon
¼ tsp (1 mL)	2 tsp (10 mL)	vanilla extract
¼ tsp (1 mL)	1 tsp	ground allspice
¼ tsp (1 mL)	1 tsp	ground cloves
⅛ tsp (0.6 mL)	½ tsp (2.5 mL)	black pepper
⅛ tsp (0.6 mL)	½ tsp (2.5 mL)	ground nutmeg
Garnish		
2 cups (500 mL)	8 cups (2 L)	fresh raspberries
2 Tbsp (30 mL)	½ cup (125 mL)	maple syrup

1. In a blender, combine all pudding ingredients and blend until completely smooth. (For 24 servings, follow the recipe for 6 servings and make 4 times.)

2. Pour into airtight container(s)—Mason jars work well—and chill for a minimum of 1 hour. (If you like, it can be stored overnight for a fast and easy breakfast treat!)

3. When ready to serve, pour into individual bowls and top each serving with ⅓ cup (80 mL) fresh berries and a drizzle (about 1 tsp/5 mL) of maple syrup.

Mango Turmeric Lassi

Up your lassi game by including one of the most anti-inflammatory foods known to human-kind: turmeric. This lassi, a whole food, contem-porary version of a tried-and-true classic, can be an indulgent jumpstart to the day or an ideal afternoon pick-me-up. You could also pair it with a spicy, vegetable-heavy curry atop whole grains to help calm and cool down your taste buds!

Per 1 cup/250 mL serving: 90 calories; 3 g total fat; 19 g total carbs; 5 g fibre; 13 g sugar; 1 g protein; 75 mg sodium.

6 SERVINGS	24 SERVINGS	INGREDIENTS
3 cups (750 mL)	12 cups (3 L)	frozen mango chunks
3 cups (750 mL)	12 cups (3 L)	water
2¼ cups (560 mL)	9 cups (2.25 L)	non-dairy yogurt
1½ tsp (7.5 mL)	2 Tbsp (30 mL)	ground turmeric
¼ tsp (1 mL)	¾ tsp (4 mL)	ground cardamom
Pinch of	1 tsp (5 mL)	black pepper
2 tsp (10 mL)	3 Tbsp (45 mL)	maple syrup or honey (optional)
Garnish		
Pinch of	½ tsp (2.5 mL)	ground cardamom

1. Combine all lassi ingredients in a blender and blend until smooth. (Work in batches to prepare 24 servings.)

2. Pour into glasses and garnish each with a pinch (about ⅛ tsp) of cardamom.

There are foods that you save for those extra-special occasions when your heart is full: weddings, anniversaries, birthdays, reunions, date nights. These dishes often include old family favourites or reflect traditions embraced by your family or community. The dishes in this section are wonderful for special occasions of all kinds, from large celebrations to more intimate dinner parties, and can be prepared in advance to let you enjoy time with your guests. The slightly sweet Roasted Tomato and Garlic Soup and fresh, crisp Apple, Fennel and Beet Salad are particular favourites of mine, as my partner and I served them on our wedding day. I hope they warm your heart like they do mine!

SAMPLE MENU FOR AN OCCASION TO REMEMBER

SOUP

Roasted Tomato and Garlic Soup

SALAD

*Apple, Fennel and Beet Salad with
Orange-Ginger Cider Vinaigrette*

MAIN

*Veggie Cannelloni with Cashew
Ricotta, Basil Pesto and Parmesan*

DESSERT

Black and Blue Cashew Cheesecake

Dinner Party Showstoppers

Roasted Tomato and Garlic Soup

PREPARATION TIME 15 minutes

COOKING TIME 1½ hours

Tomato soup is comfort food for the heart. It is a perfect raise-your-spirits-on-a-rainy-day dish. In addition to the phytonutrient-dense star of the show, tomatoes, this soup includes other health-promoting and soul-soothing ingredients, such as roasted carrots and garlic. The combination of these three antioxidant-rich powerhouses plus sweet onions and thyme, finished off with creamy coconut milk, feels like the power of 1,000 embraces. And in addition to soothing your soul, one bowl is a good source of potassium, calcium, fibre, iron and vitamins A, C and E.

Per 1½ cups/375 mL serving: 230 calories; 19 g total fat; 17 g total carbs; 4 g fibre; 7 g sugar; 4 g protein; 220 mg sodium.

6 SERVINGS	24 SERVINGS	INGREDIENTS
1 (796 mL) can	3 (796 mL) cans	whole tomatoes, drained and juices reserved
2 large	8 large	carrots, quartered
1 large head	4 large heads	garlic, top cut off
5 sprigs	20 sprigs	thyme
2 Tbsp (30 mL)	½ cup (125 mL)	extra-virgin olive oil, divided
1 large	4 large	sweet onion, diced
4 cups (1 L)	16 cups (4 L)	vegetable stock
1 (400 mL) can	4 (400 mL) cans	coconut milk
½ tsp (2.5 mL)	2 tsp (10 mL)	salt, divided
½ tsp (2.5 mL)	2 tsp (10 mL)	black pepper, divided
Garnish		
3 sprigs	12 sprigs	fresh thyme, leaves only
—	—	Crusty whole grain baguette slices (optional)
—	—	Homemade croutons or crostinis (optional)

1. Preheat oven to 400F (205C).

2. Add tomatoes, carrots, garlic head(s), thyme and half of the oil to a large roasting pan. Season with half of the salt and pepper and lightly toss.

3. Place roasting pan in the oven for 45 minutes, or until garlic is fully roasted.

4. Remove the garlic from the pan and allow to cool slightly. Remove the garlic skins and return to the pan.

5. Heat a large stockpot over medium-high heat, then add remaining oil. Once heated, add onions and sauté until soft, about 3 to 5 minutes.

6. Pour the roasted vegetables into the pot and stir to combine.

7. Add vegetable stock and reserved tomato juices. Reduce heat to medium and simmer for 25 to 30 minutes.

8. Add coconut milk and use a hand immersion blender to puree until smooth. (If using a regular blender, carefully work in batches as needed and take breaks to release heat and to avoid overheating the blender.)

9. Stir in remaining salt and pepper, garnish with fresh thyme and serve with crusty whole grain baguette slices or top with homemade croutons (if using).

Apple, Fennel and Beet Salad with Orange-Ginger Cider Vinaigrette

PREPARATION TIME 30 minutes

Fresh, crisp and slightly sweet, with a hint of tartness and licorice, this salad is a great way to begin a slow, sit-down meal with heartwarming company.

Per 3½ cups/241 g serving: 290 calories; 20 g total fat; 27 g total carbs; 7 g fibre; 16 g sugar; 6 g protein; 220 mg sodium.

6 SERVINGS	24 SERVINGS	INGREDIENTS
Dressing		
3 Tbsp (45 mL)	¾ cup (180 mL)	apple cider vinegar
1½ Tbsp (22 mL)	6 Tbsp (90 mL)	grapeseed oil
1 Tbsp (15 mL)	¼ cup (60 mL)	maple syrup
1½ tsp (7.5 mL)	2 Tbsp (30 mL)	pureed ginger
1 tsp (5 mL)	1 Tbsp (15 mL)	pureed garlic
1 Tbsp (15 mL)	¼ cup (60 mL)	orange zest
½ cup (125 mL) (about 1 orange)	2 cups (500 mL) (about 4–6 oranges)	fresh orange juice
½ tsp (2.5 mL)	1½ tsp (7.5 mL)	sea salt
Salad		
9 cups (2.2 L)	36 cups (9 L)	arugula
4 cups (1 L) (about 1 bulb fennel)	16 cups (4 L) (about 4 bulbs fennel)	julienned fennel, leaves reserved for garnish
1¼ cups (310 mL) (about 1 large beet)	5 cups (1.25 L) (about 4 large beets)	grated beets
3 cups (750 mL) (about 2 apples)	12 cups (3 L) (about 8 apples)	diced Granny Smith apples
Garnish		
1½ cups (375 mL)	6 cups (1.5 L)	toasted walnuts, chopped
1	4	orange, peeled and segmented
—	—	Fennel leaves

1. In a small bowl, whisk all dressing ingredients together until emulsified. Set aside.

2. Add all salad ingredients to a salad bowl and toss to combine.

3. When ready to serve, pour the dressing over the salad and toss. Garnish with walnuts, oranges and fennel leaves.

Creamy Dill and
Cannellini Bean Dip

Forget hummus—pass that creamy dill and cannellini bean dip, please! The cannellini bean, like the chickpea, is high in iron, fibre and protein, but cannellini beans tend to create a creamier consistency when pureed and are quite versatile as a result. Use them in soups, stews, salad dressings, pasta sauces, desserts and even smoothies for a comforting, velvety texture without all the cholesterol and unhealthy fats.

Per 3 Tbsp/50 g serving: 100 calories; 5 g total fat; 10 g total carbs; 2 g fibre; 0 g sugar; 4 g protein; 170 mg sodium.

6 SERVINGS	24 SERVINGS	INGREDIENTS
1¼ cups (310 mL)	5 cups (1.25 L)	canned cannellini or white kidney beans, drained and rinsed
3 Tbsp (15 mL)	¾ cup (180 mL)	chopped fresh dill
2 Tbsp (30 mL)	½ cup (125 mL)	extra-virgin olive oil
1 tsp (5 mL)	4 tsp (20 mL)	lemon zest
2 Tbsp (30 mL) (about ½ lemon)	½ cup (125 mL) (about 2 lemons)	fresh lemon juice
1 large clove	3–4 large cloves	garlic
½ tsp (2.5 mL)	2 tsp (10 mL)	salt
⅛ tsp (0.6 mL)	¼ tsp (1 mL)	black pepper

1. Place all dip ingredients in a food processor and blend until completely smooth, about 3 minutes. Serve with your favourite selection of fresh vegetables and crisp Kamut Crackers (see page 174).

TIP

To use as a dressing or a pasta sauce, add ½ cup (125 mL) water to the dip recipe to thin it out. If using as a pasta sauce, fill a large pot over low heat with warm noodles, add sauce and toss until completely coated and heated through.

Kamut Crackers

PREPARATION TIME 15 minutes

COOKING TIME 25 minutes

If you are not as familiar with whole grain kamut and its products, it's an ancient grain that is loaded with fibre, anti-oxidants, B vitamins and protein. It has a nice roasted nutty under-tone to it that rounds out breads, pastas and crackers beautifully. This recipe is the epitome of sharing food. Serve it before a meal with a variety of spreads and dips as you chit-chat or have it along with my cozy Roasted Tomato and Garlic Soup (page 168) and a deep, intimate conversation.

Per 4 crackers/89 g serving: 250 calories; 10 g total fat; 37 g total carbs; 5 g fibre; 2 g sugar; 5 g protein; 85 mg sodium.

6 SERVINGS	24 SERVINGS	INGREDIENTS
2½ cups (625 mL)	10 cups (2.5 L)	kamut flour
¼ tsp (1 mL)	1 tsp (5 mL)	sea salt
¼ cup (60 mL)	1 cup (250 mL)	coconut oil
¾ cup (180 mL)	2 cups (500 mL)	water
1 Tbsp (15 mL)	¼ cup (60 mL)	maple syrup

1. Preheat oven to 375F (190C) and line baking sheet(s) with parchment paper.

2. In a large bowl, combine flour and salt.

3. Using a pastry cutter or 2 forks, cut in coconut oil until incorporated. The mixture should be slightly crumbly, but still dry.

4. Make a well in the middle of the flour mixture and add the water and maple syrup. Fold in the flour, and knead until the liquid is completely incorporated and a dough has formed. If too dry, add 1 Tbsp (15 mL) cold water at a time. Divide dough into 2 balls (or 8 if making 24 servings), and cover with a lightly damp cloth. Allow to rest for 10 minutes.

5. Place a piece of parchment paper on your rolling surface. Sprinkle kamut flour on the surface and your rolling pin to prevent sticking. Roll out each dough ball to a ¼-inch (0.6 cm) thickness and use a knife to cut into 2 × 2-inch (5 × 5-cm) squares, about 24 pieces. Transfer parchment paper to a baking sheet. Slightly separate the pieces so that there is space between them. Repeat with remaining dough. Only bake 2 trays at a time and cover remaining dough until ready to bake to avoid drying out.

6. Bake for 20 to 25 minutes, flipping crackers halfway, until golden brown.

7. Allow the crackers to cool completely on a cooling rack. Store crackers in an airtight container until needed. Serve with Papaya Chutney (page 127) or Creamy Dill and Cannellini Bean Dip (page 172), or other spreads like pesto, hummus and tapenade.

TIP

To up the flavour profile, add a pinch of your favourite dried herbs and/or spices to the dry ingredients.

174   LONG TABLE

Caramelized Fennel, Sweet Potato and Pine Nut Cheese Pizza

PREPARATION TIME 1½ hours

COOKING TIME 1 hour

This recipe is not only best shared and eaten together, but best prepared together. It's a fun, tasty and healthy way to get your family or friends into the kitchen and involved in the dinner-making process. Children are likely to eat more vege-tables and try new things if they have had a hand in the meal's making. The pizza is great served as an appetizer or as the main event, but I highly recommend making more than you think you will need. Aside from its unique, moreish flavours, each slice contains high amounts of fibre, protein, potassium, iron and vita-mins A and C, in addition to being a source of calcium and vitamin E. Buon appetito!

Per 1 slice/267 g serving: 380 calories; 19 g total fat; 47 g total carbs; 11 g fibre; 10 g sugar; 10 g protein; 190 mg sodium.

6 SERVINGS	24 SERVINGS	INGREDIENTS
Crust		
⅔ cup (160 mL)	2⅔ cups (660 mL)	warm water
2 tsp (10 mL)	3 Tbsp (45 mL)	quick-rise instant yeast
2 cups (500 mL)	8 cups (2 L)	spelt flour
⅛ tsp (0.6 mL)	½ tsp (2.5 mL)	salt
Pizza Toppings		
1	4	sweet potato, thinly sliced
4 tsp (20 mL)	⅓ cup (80 mL)	grapeseed oil, divided
1 bulb	4 bulbs	fennel, thinly sliced
¼	1	red onion, thinly sliced
1 Tbsp (15 mL)	¼ cup (60 mL)	balsamic vinegar
2 tsp (10 mL)	8 tsp (40 mL)	maple syrup
½ cup (125 mL)	2 cups (500 mL)	fresh basil, cut in chiffonade
Pine Nut Cheese		
1 cup (250 mL)	4 cups (1 L)	pine nuts, soaked for 1 hour, water discarded
6 Tbsp (90 mL)	1 cup (250 mL)	water
1 Tbsp (15 mL)	¼ cup (60 mL)	minced red onion
2 tsp (10 mL)	3 Tbsp (45 mL)	apple cider vinegar
1 tsp (5 mL)	4 tsp (20 mL)	extra-virgin olive oil
1 clove	4 cloves	garlic, pureed
⅛ tsp (0.6 mL)	½ tsp (2.5 mL)	sea salt
1 Tbsp (15 mL)	¼ cup (60 mL)	finely chopped dill

Continued . . .

TIP

To save on cost, you can use blanched whole almonds instead of pine nuts in the cheese.

1. Preheat oven to 375F (190C) and line baking sheet(s) with parchment paper.

2. In a small bowl, mix together warm water and yeast. Set aside for 10 minutes.

3. In a medium bowl, mix together flour and salt.

4. Add water mixture to flour mixture. Knead until a smooth, elastic dough forms, about 3 minutes for 6 servings and 7 minutes for 24 servings. If the dough is too dry, add 1 Tbsp (15 mL) of water at a time until you reach desired texture. If making 24 servings, divide dough into 4 balls. Place in a bowl (or bowls) and cover with a damp cloth. Set aside in a warm place for 1½ hours to allow the dough to rise.

5. Meanwhile, add sweet potatoes and 1 tsp (5 mL) of oil (4 tsp/20 mL if making 24 servings) to a large bowl and toss until potatoes are coated. Lay flat and spread evenly on prepared baking sheet(s) and bake in the oven for 25 to 30 minutes, flipping halfway through, until fork tender. Remove from oven and set aside.

6. Increase the temperature of the oven to 500F (260C).

7. Heat a large sauté pan over medium-high heat, then add 2 tsp (10 mL) oil (or 8 tsp/40 mL for 24 servings). Once heated, add fennel and caramelize until golden brown, about 12 minutes (25 minutes for 24 servings). Reduce heat to low and allow to cook for an additional 12 minutes. When finished, remove from heat and stir in balsamic vinegar. Set aside.

8. Meanwhile, in a food processor, combine all cheese ingredients except for the dill. Process until completely smooth, about 5 minutes. Transfer to a small bowl. Stir in dill, cover and refrigerate until needed.

9. Roll out dough ball on a well-floured surface, forming crust for a 17-inch (42.5-cm) pizza. (Remember to flip the dough while rolling.) Fold over the edges of the crust and pinch into place. You will end up with a 15-inch (37.5-cm) pizza. Place on a baking sheet or pizza stone and brush the crust with 1 tsp (5 mL) oil. (If making 24 servings, repeat with rest of the dough.)

10. Now to top the pizza(s). Spread three-quarters of the pine nut cheese over the crust(s). Then evenly distribute the fennel, sweet potato and red onions. Add dollops of the remaining cheese all over the pizza(s), then drizzle with maple syrup and place in the oven. Bake for 10 minutes or until bottom of crust is slightly brown and crisp. Remove from oven and sprinkle with fresh basil. Cut each pizza into 12 slices.

Veggie Cannelloni with Cashew Ricotta, Basil Pesto and Parmesan

PREPARATION TIME 1½ hours

COOKING TIME 50 to 55 minutes

This is the dish that you will want to make if you are looking to impress someone, or propose to someone, or really for any of those epic, celebratory milestones in your life. Beautiful ribbons of zucchini stuffed with creamy cashew ricotta, hugged by tangy home-made tomato sauce and drizzled with a vibrant basil pesto—the layers of flavour built into this dish are noteworthy and perfect for sharing. Each serving is also nutrient dense, containing high levels of the antioxidants lycopene, allicin and vitamin C, as well as protein, fibre and iron.

Per 2 cannelloni/495 g serving: 630 calories; 42 g total fat; 43 g total carbs; 11 g fibre; 13 g sugar; 22 g protein; 450 mg sodium.

6 SERVINGS	24 SERVINGS	INGREDIENTS
Cashew Ricotta		
2½ cups (625 mL)	10 cups (2.5 L)	raw cashews, divided
1 tsp (5 mL)	4 tsp (20 mL)	extra-virgin olive oil
4 cups (1 L)	16 cups (4 L)	baby spinach
2 Tbsp (30 mL)	½ cup (125 mL)	fresh lemon juice
2 tsp (10 mL)	8 tsp (40 mL)	lemon zest
8 cloves	24 cloves	garlic
3 Tbsp (45 mL)	¾ cup (180 mL)	nutritional yeast
½ cup (125 mL)	2 cups (500 mL)	unsweetened milk alternative
¼ cup (60 mL)	1 cup (250 mL)	water
¼ tsp (1 mL)	1 tsp (5 mL)	salt
Tomato Sauce		
1 Tbsp (15 mL)	¼ cup (60 mL)	extra-virgin olive oil
1	4	onion, diced
4 cups (1 L)	16 cups (4 L)	canned crushed tomatoes
1 bunch	4 bunches	basil stems (leaves reserved for pesto), chopped
1	4	orange pepper, diced
¼ tsp (1 mL)	1 tsp (5 mL)	salt
½ tsp (2.5 mL)	2 tsp (10 mL)	black pepper
Veggie Noodles		
6 small	24 small	zucchini
Cashew Parmesan		
⅓ cup (80 mL)	1⅓ cups (350 mL)	raw cashews
¼ cup (60 mL)	1 cup (250 mL)	nutritional yeast
1 tsp (5 mL)	4 tsp (20 mL)	fresh lemon juice
¼ tsp (1 mL)	1 tsp (5 mL)	salt
Basil Pesto		
2 Tbsp (30 mL) (about ½ lemon)	½ cup (125 mL) (about 2 lemons)	fresh lemon juice
1 tsp (5 mL)	4 tsp (20 mL)	lemon zest
1 bunch	4 bunches	basil leaves
½ cup (125 mL)	2 cups (500 mL)	hemp hearts
3 cloves	12 cloves	garlic
¼ cup (60 mL)	1 cup (250 mL)	extra-virgin olive oil
¼ cup (60 mL)	1 cup (250 mL)	water
¼ tsp (1 mL)	1 tsp (5 mL)	salt

Continued . . .

1. For the cashew ricotta: Place the 2½ cups (625 mL) cashews (or 10 cups/2.5 L for 24 servings) in a stainless steel bowl and cover with boiling water. Allow to soak for 1 hour, or until softened. Drain and set aside.

2. For the tomato sauce: Heat a sauté pan over medium-high heat, then add oil. Once heated, add onions and sauté until soft and translucent, about 3 to 5 minutes.

3. Add canned tomatoes and basil stems and bring to a boil, then reduce heat and simmer for 10 minutes.

4. Add orange peppers and cook until soft, about 5 to 7 minutes. Finish with salt and pepper. Remove from heat and puree in a food processor until smooth, working in batches if needed.

5. Preheat oven to 400F (205C).

6. For noodles: Using a vegetable peeler, cut zucchini lengthwise into long wide ribbons. Set aside.

7. For the parmesan: In a food processor, combine cashews, nutritional yeast, lemon juice and salt. Process until smooth. Set aside.

8. For the basil pesto: Combine all ingredients in a high-speed blender and blend until smooth, about 4 minutes.

9. For ricotta mixture: Heat a sauté pan over medium heat, then add oil. Once heated, add spinach and sauté until wilted, about 3 to 4 minutes. Remove from heat and set aside.

10. Using a food processor, combine soaked cashews, lemon juice, lemon zest, garlic, nutritional yeast, milk alternative, water and salt. Process until smooth. Transfer from processor to a large bowl and fold in sautéed spinach. Set aside.

11. To assemble: Pour half of the tomato sauce into a 9 × 13-inch (22.5 × 32.5 cm) baking pan and set aside. (Or divide half of the total sauce among 4 pans if making 24 servings.)

12. On a clean surface, lay out 6 zucchini ribbons in a row overlapping vertically by ½ inch (1.25 cm). Top one end of the layered ribbons with a heaping ¼ cup (60 mL) of the cashew ricotta and roll to close. Place roll seam-side down in the prepared baking pan(s). Repeat with remaining zucchini ribbons and ricotta. (In total, the recipe for 6 servings makes 12 rolls and the one for 24 servings makes 48 rolls.)

13. Bake in oven for 30 to 35 minutes, or until sauce is bubbling. To serve, reheat the remaining tomato sauce and divide among individual plates. Place 2 zucchini rolls in sauce on each and top with pesto and parmesan.

Pasta with Mushroom Walnut Lentil Bites

PREPARATION TIME 20 minutes

COOKING TIME 35 minutes

This recipe always invokes the image of a romantic Italian eatery in my mind. Robust mushroom lentil bites atop a pile of tomatoey noodles topped with heaping mounds of almond parmesan and a side of (potentially seductive) company. This is an excellent "meaty" dish for the veg curious people in your life and a very freezer-friendly recipe.

Per 5 balls/192 g serving: 360 calories; 17 g total fat; 40 g total carbs; 11 g fibre; 3 g sugar; 14 g protein; 490 mg sodium.

6 SERVINGS	24 SERVINGS	INGREDIENTS
Lentil Bites		
1 cup (250 mL)	4 cups (1 L)	water
3 Tbsp (45 mL)	¾ cup (180 mL)	ground flaxseed
2 Tbsp (30 mL)	½ cup (125 mL)	grapeseed oil, divided
3 cups (750 mL)	12 cups (3 L)	stemmed and diced mixed mushrooms (portobello, shiitake, cremini)
1 cup (250 mL)	4 cups (1 L)	diced onions
4 cloves	16 cloves	garlic, pureed
1 Tbsp (15 mL)	¼ cup (60 mL)	dried basil
2 tsp (10 mL)	8 tsp (40 mL)	ground cumin
1 tsp (5 mL)	4 tsp (20 mL)	paprika
¼ tsp (1 mL)	1 tsp (5 mL)	cayenne (optional)
1 cup (250 mL)	4 cups (1 L)	walnuts, chopped
1 Tbsp (15 mL)	¼ cup (60 mL)	tamari
1½ cups (375 mL)	6 cups (1.5 L)	cooked brown lentils
1½ cups (375 mL)	6 cups (1.5 L)	whole grain spelt flour
1 Tbsp (15 mL) (about ½ lemon)	¼ cup (60 mL) (about 1 lemon)	fresh lemon juice
1 tsp (5 mL)	4 tsp (20 mL)	sea salt
¼ tsp (1 mL)	1 tsp (5 mL)	pepper
Tomato Sauce		
2¼ tsp (11 mL)	3 Tbsp (45 mL)	extra-virgin olive oil
1	3	onion, diced
3 cups (750 mL)	12 cups (3 L)	canned crushed tomatoes
1 bunch	3 bunches	basil stems, chopped
1	3	orange pepper, diced
¼ tsp (1 mL)	1 tsp (5 mL)	salt
½ tsp (2.5 mL)	2 tsp (10 mL)	black pepper
Almond Parmesan		
¼ cup (60 mL)	1 cup (250 mL)	raw cashews
¼ cup (60 mL)	1 cup (250 mL)	nutritional yeast
⅛ tsp (0.5 mL)	½ tsp (2.5 mL)	salt
1 lb	4 lbs	whole grain pasta of your choice, cooked

Continued...

These savoury lentil bites are also tasty served on whole grain sub sandwich buns with sautéed onions, bell peppers and marinara sauce.

To freeze, transfer cooled bites to a resealable bag or container and keep in the freezer for up to 6 months. When ready to use, remove from freezer and place on a parchment-lined baking sheet and bake in a 375F (190C) oven until heated through, about 20 minutes.

1. Preheat oven to 375F (190C). Line baking sheet(s) with parchment paper.

2. For the lentil bites: In a small bowl, mix together water and flaxseed. Set aside until gelatinous, about 10 minutes.

3. Meanwhile, heat a large sauté pan over medium-high heat, then add 1 Tbsp (15 mL) oil (¼ cup/60 mL for 24 servings). Once heated, add mushrooms and sauté until slightly brown, about 5 minutes (10 to 15 minutes for 24 servings).

4. Add onions, garlic, basil, cumin, paprika and cayenne (if using). Sauté until fragrant, about 3 minutes (6 minutes for 24 servings).

5. Add walnuts and sauté until slightly toasted, about 3 minutes (5 minutes for 24 servings).

6. Mix in tamari and remove from heat.

7. In a large mixing bowl, combine flaxseed mixture, mushroom mixture, cooked lentils, spelt flour, lemon juice, salt and pepper. Use your hands to knead the mixture and form a dough, ensuring that the flour and other ingredients are fully incorporated.

8. Roll dough into balls, using about 2 Tbsp (30 mL) of dough for each one. (In total, the recipe for 6 servings makes 30 balls and the one for 24 servings makes 120—5 bites per serving.) Arrange on prepared baking sheets and lightly brush with remaining oil.

9. Bake in the oven for 35 minutes, until tops are golden brown. (Or use oil to cook the bites in a large sauté pan over medium-high heat. Working in batches, cook each side for 3 to 4 minutes, covering the pan with a lid in between flipping.)

10. Meanwhile, for the tomato sauce: Heat a sauté pan over medium-high heat, then add oil. Once heated, add onions and sauté until soft and translucent, about 3 to 5 minutes.

11. Add canned tomatoes and basil stems and bring to a boil, then reduce heat and simmer for 10 minutes.

12. Add orange peppers and cook until soft, about 5 to 7 minutes. Finish with salt and pepper. Remove from heat and puree in a food processor until smooth, working in batches if needed.

13. For the parmesan: In a small bowl, whisk together parmesan ingredients. Set aside.

14. Serve lentil bites over whole grain pasta and tomato sauce and top with cashew parmesan.

Black and Blue Cashew Cheesecake

PREPARATION TIME 1 hour

COOKING TIME 5 minutes

This is a dessert you can share with the health food skeptics in your life. It is a soul-warming combination of creamy cashew filling and tart and tangy dark berry sauce piled onto a sweet and crumbly crust. It is also a great source of protein and is high in iron and heart-healthy fibre. The vitamin C present in this dessert also helps with the absorption of the non-heme iron present, making it more bioavailable to our bodies. This will become your go-to, make-ahead summer dessert as the children (or honourary children!) in your life will request it again and again.

Per 1 slice/176 g serving: 320 calories; 13 g total fat; 45 g total carbs; 7 g fibre; 22 g sugar; 9 g protein; 5 mg sodium.

TIP

If berries are in season, you can omit the maple syrup pureed with the berries and let them shine on their own!

6 SERVINGS	24 SERVINGS	INGREDIENTS
1 cup (250 mL)	4 cups (1 L)	rolled oats
3 Tbsp (15 mL)	¾ cup (180 mL)	ground flaxseed
¾ cup (180 mL)	3 cups (750 mL)	pitted dates
2 Tbsp (30 mL)	½ cup (125 mL)	water
1¼ cups (310 mL)	5 cups (1.25 L)	cashews, soaked overnight and drained
¾ cup (180 mL)	3 cups (750 mL)	silken or soft tofu
¼ cup (60 mL) (about 1 lemon)	1 cup (250 mL) (about 4 lemons)	fresh lemon juice
1 Tbsp (15 mL)	¼ cup (60 mL)	unsweetened soy milk
2 Tbsp (30 mL)	½ cup (125 mL)	maple syrup, divided
1 cup (250 mL)	4 cups (1 L)	blueberries, fresh or frozen, divided
1 cup (250 mL)	4 cups (1 L)	blackberries, fresh or frozen, divided
2 Tbsp (30 mL)	½ cup (125 mL)	lime zest
¼ cup (60 mL) (about 2 limes)	1 cup (250 mL) (about 8 limes)	fresh lime juice
Garnish		
1 Tbsp (15 mL)	¼ cup (60 mL)	chopped mint

1. Cut parchment paper to fit the bottom and sides of an 8-inch (20 cm) cake pan (or four 8-inch pans for 24 servings) and line the pan(s). Set aside.

2. In a food processor, combine the oats, ground flaxseed, dates and water and pulse until the mixture is crumbly and sticks together. (If making 24 servings you will need to process in two batches.)

3. Transfer to the prepared cake pan(s) and press the crust mixture evenly onto the bottom(s).

4. In a food processor, combine soaked cashews, tofu, lemon juice, soy milk and half the maple syrup and process until completely smooth. (If making 24 servings you will need to process in two batches.)

5. Pour the mixture into the cake pan(s) and spread evenly. Place in the freezer to set slightly.

6. Meanwhile, in a saucepan, combine half of the blueberries and half of the blackberries with lime juice, lime zest and remaining maple syrup and cook until soft, about 5 minutes for 6 servings and 10 minutes for 24 servings.

7. Transfer the cooked berries to a blender or food processor and blend until smooth. Allow the sauce to cool completely. (Alternatively, you can allow the cooked berries to cool completely and use them unpureed.)

8. Carefully remove the cheesecake(s) from the freezer. Gently spread the cooled berry sauce (or cooked berries) on the top. Place back into the freezer for 1½ to 2 hours, or until firm.

9. When ready to serve, allow to thaw slightly at room temperature for 15 minutes. Top with the remaining berries and garnish with chopped mint.

Cocoa Bean Pie with Raspberry Strawberry Coulis

PREPARATION TIME 15 minutes

COOKING TIME 35 minutes

Dark, rich cocoa and berries paired with robust black beans may seem sacrilegious, but trust me: this combination is nothing less than heavenly. The creaminess of the bean lends itself well to this dessert, making it seem like an indulgent treat rather than a healthy dish serving up high levels of iron, vitamin C, polyphenols, protein and fibre. The bright berry coulis is perfect for sharing during those treasured moments with loved ones.

Per 1 slice/252 g serving: 470 calories; 24 g total fat; 54 g total carbs; 11 g fibre; 28 g sugar; 11 g protein; 55 mg sodium.

TIPS

For ease of removal, use springform tart or cake pan(s), if available. Two-piece tart pans will make removing the pie(s) easier.

When making 24 servings, process ingredients in batches, so as not to exceed the capacity of the food processor.

6 SERVINGS	24 SERVINGS	INGREDIENTS
Crust		
⅔ cup (160 mL)	2⅔ cups (660 mL)	rolled oats
⅓ cup (80 mL)	1⅓ cups (350 mL)	pumpkin seeds
⅛ tsp (0.6 mL)	½ tsp (2.5 mL)	salt
½ cup (125 mL)	2 cups (500 mL)	pitted dates
2 Tbsp (30 mL)	½ cup (125 mL)	water
3 Tbsp (45 mL)	¾ cup (180 mL)	coconut oil
Filling		
½ cup (125 mL)	2 cups (500 mL)	chopped dark chocolate
3 Tbsp (45 mL)	¾ cup (180 mL)	coconut oil
1 (540 mL) can	3 (540 mL) cans	black beans, drained and rinsed
3 Tbsp (45 mL)	¾ cup (180 mL)	raw honey
½ cup (125 mL)	2 cups (500 mL)	warm water
Sauce		
1 cup (250 mL)	4 cups (1 L)	chopped strawberries, cut in small dice
2 cups (500 mL)	8 cups (2 L)	raspberries, divided
3 Tbsp (45 mL)	¾ cup (180 mL)	fresh lemon juice
1 tsp (5 mL)	4 tsp (20 mL)	honey

1. Line bottom(s) of one 9-inch (22.5 cm) tart pan for 6 servings (or four 9-inch tart pans for 24 servings) with parchment paper.

2. For crust: In a food processor, combine oats, pumpkin seeds and salt, and process until smooth.

3. Add dates and continue to process, then slowly add water and coconut oil. Process until fully incorporated. Press the crust mixture evenly along the bottom and sides of the pan(s). Set aside.

4. For filling: Using a double boiler, combine chocolate and coconut oil. Mix with a spatula until the ingredients have completely melted. Remove from heat.

5. Using a food processor, process black beans until smooth.

6. Add honey, warm water and the melted chocolate and oil mixture. Blend until completely smooth.

7. Pour the filling on top of the crust(s) and spread evenly. Transfer the tart(s) to the freezer and allow to chill until set, about 2 hours.

8. For the sauce: In a saucepan over medium heat, combine strawberries, half of the raspberries, lemon juice and honey and cook until soft, about 7 minutes for 6 servings and 12 minutes for 24 servings.

9. Transfer the berry mixture to a blender and blend on high until smooth. Strain the coulis through a fine-mesh sieve and allow to cool.

10. To serve, remove the tart(s) from the pan(s), garnish with remaining raspberries and serve with coulis.

Carrot and Ginger Orange Juice

PREPARATION TIME 10 minutes

If there ever was a beverage that encapsulated health and well-being this would be it. Each ingredient is packed with phytonutrients and anti-inflammatory properties aplenty! The recipe beautifully combines spicy ginger, slightly sweet carrots, sour oranges and bold and mildly bitter turmeric, and is finished off with the lingering sweetness of honey. If you prefer, omit the honey and pair this juice with a fibre- and protein-rich meal to avoid blood sugar spikes. Perfect served in midsummer over mountains of ice with soda water or straight up in the dead of winter to boost immunity and ward off pesky colds.

Per ½ cup/125 mL serving: 120 calories; 0.4 g total fat; 30 g total carbs; 4 g fibre; 21 g sugar; 2 g protein; 35 mg sodium

6 SERVINGS	24 SERVINGS	INGREDIENTS
5	15	carrots, peeled
8 large	24 large	oranges, peeled and cut into wedges
2-inch knob	6-inch knob	fresh ginger, peeled
1½ cups (375 mL)	4½ cups (1.125 L)	water, divided
3 Tbsp (45 mL)	½ cup + 1 Tbsp (140 mL)	honey
½ tsp (2.5 mL)	1½ tsp (7 mL)	ground turmeric
4 cups (1 L)	12 cups (3 L)	soda water (optional)

1. Using a juicer, juice carrots, orange and ginger. Stir in a third of the water and set aside. (If you do not have a juicer, blend the carrots and ginger very well with some water in a high-powered blender, in batches, then strain the mixture through a cheesecloth or sieve. Juice oranges separately with a squeezer or hand juicer.)

2. In a pot over gentle heat, combine the remaining water with the honey and turmeric, whisking until the honey has fully dissolved.

3. In a large bowl, whisk together juice(s) and the honey and turmeric mixture.

4. Pour over ice or chill in a jug in the refrigerator before serving. For a fun variation, add a ½ cup (125 mL) of soda water per serving!

TIP

Try adding spices like cinnamon or nutmeg, or increasing the amount of honey, for a different twist.

The explosive, happy energy that comes with celebratory moments is like no other. That feeling is what this section encapsulates in food form: bright, beautiful, bold in flavour. It's food worth sharing with teammates, coworkers, partners, friends and family in the spirit of pure merriment. These flexible and creative dishes turn every occasion into a celebration, and are perfect for a vibrant contribution to a community meal, an impromptu picnic, a pick-me-up for a friend, or just a moment of extra brightness during your day.

**SAMPLE MENU FOR
A CELEBRATION TO REMEMBER**

BEVERAGE
Lavender Lemonade

SOUP
*Creamy Corn Chowder with
Tempeh Chorizo*

SALAD
Rainbow Slaw with Lime Dressing

MAIN
*Lentil and Walnut Tacos with
Mango Avocado Salsa*

DESSERT
Chocolate Avocado Pie

Recipes for Everyday Celebrations

Creamy Corn Chowder with Tempeh Chorizo

PREPARATION TIME 15 minutes for 6 servings and 30 minutes for 24 servings
COOKING TIME 40 minutes for 6 servings and 50 minutes for 24 servings

If you aren't already in the mood to celebrate, this chowder will change your mind. Hearty, satiating and extraordinarily flavourful, it's a meal that you will happily request seconds of. And visually this chowder is nothing short of gorgeous. It is a conversation starter and ender, and a freezer-friendly dish that people will request again and again. Nutritionally speaking, it is a source of potassium, calcium, and vitamin E, a high source of fibre, iron, free-radical-fighting vitamins A and C, and is packed with probiotics via the fermented tempeh.

Per 1 cup/250 mL serving with tempeh chorizo: 310 calories; 19 g total fat; 30 g total carbs; 6 g fibre; 8 g sugar; 8 g protein; 500 mg sodium.

6 SERVINGS	24 SERVINGS	INGREDIENTS
2 tsp (10 mL)	3 Tbsp (45 mL)	grapeseed oil
1 cup (250 mL)	4 cups (1 L)	diced onions
3 cloves	12 cloves	garlic, minced
1 cup (250 mL)	4 cups (1 L)	diced carrots
2 cups (500 mL)	8 cups (2 L)	diced celery
2 tsp (10 mL)	3 Tbsp (45 mL)	ground cumin
2 tsp (10 mL)	3 Tbsp (45 mL)	paprika
2 cups (500 mL)	8 cups (2 L)	diced white potatoes
1½ cups (375 mL)	6 cups (1.5 L)	diced tomatoes (fresh or canned)
3 cups (750 mL)	12½ cups (3.125 L)	low-sodium vegetable stock or water
1½ cups (375 mL)	6 cups (1.5 L)	corn niblets, fresh or frozen
1 (400 mL) can	3 (400 mL) cans	coconut milk
2 tsp (10 mL)	3 Tbsp (45 mL)	lime zest
2 Tbsp (30 mL) (about ½ lime)	½ cup (125 mL) (about 4 limes)	fresh lime juice
¾ tsp (4 mL)	1 Tbsp (15 mL)	salt
¼ tsp (1 mL)	1 tsp (5 mL)	black pepper
¼ tsp (1 mL)	1 tsp (5 mL)	cayenne (optional)
Garnish		
¼ cup (60 mL)	1 cup (250 mL)	thinly sliced chives
—	—	Tempeh Chorizo (see recipe on page 194)

1. Heat a large stockpot over medium-high heat, then add oil. Once heated, add onions and sauté until translucent, about 3 minutes (7 minutes if making 24 servings).

2. Stir in garlic, carrots and celery and sauté until soft, about 3 to 5 minutes (10 to 12 minutes if making 24 servings).

3. Add cumin and paprika and sauté until fragrant, about 2 to 3 minutes.

4. Stir in potatoes and tomatoes.

5. Pour in vegetable stock (or water) and scrape the bottom of the pot for any stuck pieces. Bring to a simmer, reduce heat to medium and continue to cook until potatoes are soft, about 20 to 25 minutes.

6. Meanwhile, make the tempeh chorizo (see recipe).

7. Add the corn niblets to the chowder and cook for another 2 minutes, or until niblets are tender.

8. Stir in coconut milk, lime zest and juice, salt, pepper and cayenne (if using).

9. Remove from heat and ladle into individual bowls. Top each serving with chives and 1 heaping tablespoon of tempeh chorizo and serve. To freeze, cool completely and store in freezer for up to 3 months.

Tempeh Chorizo

6 SERVINGS	24 SERVINGS	INGREDIENTS
100 g	1 (400 g) block	tempeh, crumbled
1½ tsp (7.5 mL)	2 Tbsp (30 mL)	grapeseed oil
1½ tsp (7.5 mL)	2 Tbsp (30 mL)	tamari
½ tsp (2.5 mL)	2 tsp (10 mL)	smoked paprika
¼ tsp (1 mL)	1 tsp (5 mL)	garlic powder
¼ tsp (1 mL)	1 tsp (5 mL)	onion powder
⅛ tsp (0.6 mL)	¼ tsp (1 mL)	cayenne
⅛ tsp (0.6 mL)	¼ tsp (1 mL)	sea salt
⅛ tsp (0.6 mL)	¼ tsp (1 mL)	black pepper

1. Preheat oven to 350F (180C) and line baking sheet(s) with parchment paper.

2. In a large bowl, thoroughly combine all ingredients until tempeh is completely coated.

3. Spread evenly on prepared baking sheet(s) and bake in oven until fragrant, about 10 to 15 minutes.

Rainbow Slaw with Lime Dressing

Consuming colourful vegetables and fruits is one of the best ways to keep chronic diseases at bay, because they contain the highest amounts of phytonutrients. For those last-minute meals, keep this coleslaw in your fridge, undressed, for a quick and nutrient-dense side. Conveniently, it can also double as a fun and tasty sandwich, taco or burrito topping. So go ahead and eat that rainbow!

Per 1¾ cups/156 g serving: 140 calories; 10 g total fat; 14 g total carbs; 3 g fibre; 8 g sugar; 2 g protein; 125 mg sodium.

6 SERVINGS	24 SERVINGS	INGREDIENTS
¼ large head	1 large head	red cabbage, julienned
¼ large head	1 large head	green cabbage, julienned
1 large	4 large	carrot, grated
¼	1	yellow pepper, julienned
¼	1	orange pepper, julienned
¼	1	red pepper, julienned
Dressing		
¼ cup (60 mL)	1 cup (250 mL)	extra-virgin olive oil
1 tsp (5 mL)	1 Tbsp (15 mL)	lime zest
1 Tbsp (15 mL)	¼ cup (60 mL)	fresh lime juice
(about 1 lime)	(about 4 limes)	
1 clove	4 cloves	garlic, minced
4½ tsp (22 mL)	6 Tbsp (90 mL)	maple syrup
¼ tsp (1 mL)	1 tsp (5 mL)	salt
Garnish		
1	3	green onion, thinly sliced
⅛ bunch	½ bunch	cilantro, leaves removed and stems minced (optional)

1. In a large bowl, toss together all salad ingredients.

2. In a small bowl, whisk together dressing ingredients.

3. Add dressing to salad and toss.

4. When ready to serve, garnish with green onions and cilantro leaves and stems (if using).

Moroccan Quinoa Power Bowl

This multifaceted dish is a beautiful celebration of Moroccan flavours: dried fruits, fresh herbs, juicy pomegranates and fragrant spices like cumin and cinnamon. Separately, each component can stand and be served on its own, which makes for ideal make-ahead meals as you can reinvent the combinations of components all week long! It is also a powerhouse in terms of nutrition, containing health-promoting functional foods like cauliflower, kale, whole grains, legumes, pomegranate seeds, almonds, spices and citrus.

Per 2 cups/467 g serving: 480 calories; 19 g total fat; 67 g total carbs; 13 g fibre; 19 g sugar; 14 g protein; 270 mg sodium.

6 SERVINGS	24 SERVINGS	INGREDIENTS
Quinoa		
1½ cups (375 mL)	6 cups (1.5 L)	uncooked quinoa
1 cup (250 mL)	4 cups (1 L)	water
1½ cups (375 mL)	6 cups (1.5 L)	low-sodium vegetable stock
¼ tsp (1 mL)	1 tsp (5 mL)	ground cinnamon
1½ tsp (7.5 mL)	2 Tbsp (30 mL)	ground turmeric
1½ tsp (7.5 mL)	2 Tbsp (30 mL)	garam masala (or curry powder if unavailable)
¼ bunch	1 bunch	parsley, stemmed and finely chopped, divided
⅛ bunch	½ bunch	mint, stemmed and finely chopped, divided
2 cups (500 mL) (about 1 pomegranate)	8 cups (2 L) (about 4 pomegranates)	pomegranate seeds
¼ cup (60 mL)	1 cup (250 mL)	chopped kale, cut in chiffonade, tightly packed
2 Tbsp (30 mL)	¾ cup (180 mL)	sliced almonds, toasted
1	5	gala apple, cut into small dice
¼ tsp (1 mL)	1 tsp (5 mL)	sea salt
⅛ tsp (0.6 mL)	½ tsp (2.5 mL)	black pepper
Roasted Garlic Chickpeas		
1 (540 mL) can	3 (540 mL) cans	chickpeas, drained and rinsed
1 Tbsp (15 mL)	¼ cup (60 mL)	olive oil
¾ tsp (4 mL)	1 Tbsp (15 mL)	garlic powder
Roasted Spicy Cauliflower		
1 small head	2 large heads	cauliflower, cut into medium to large florets
1 Tbsp (15 mL)	¼ cup (60 mL)	olive oil
¼ tsp (1 mL)	1 tsp (5 mL)	sea salt
1½ tsp (7.5 mL)	3 Tbsp (45 mL)	paprika
½ tsp (2.5 mL)	2 tsp (10 mL)	cayenne (optional)
Fig Dressing		
6	24	dried figs
¼ cup (60 mL)	½ cup (125 mL)	olive oil
⅓ cup (80 mL) (about 1 lemon)	1⅓ cups (350 mL) (about 8 lemons)	fresh lemon juice
6 Tbsp (90 mL)	1½ cups (375 mL)	water

Continued...

Avoid chopping the cauli-flower into florets that are too small as they are more likely to burn.

QUINOA

1. Thoroughly rinse quinoa using a fine-mesh sieve.

2. In a large stockpot over medium-low heat, combine quinoa, water, vegetable stock, cinnamon and turmeric.

3. Bring to a rolling boil then reduce heat to low. Cover and simmer until quinoa is tender and most of the liquid has absorbed, about 15 to 20 minutes (25 minutes for 24 servings).

4. Using a spatula, fold garam masala (or curry powder) into cooked quinoa until well combined. Transfer quinoa to a large bowl or baking sheet and spread out to cool, about 20 minutes.

5. Set aside ¼ cup (60 mL) each parsley and mint (1 cup/250 mL for 24 serv-ings) and ½ cup (125 mL) pomegranate seeds (2 cups/500 mL for 24 servings) for garnish. Gently fold in kale, almonds, apples and the remaining parsley, mint and pomegranate seeds. Set aside until ready to serve.

ROASTED GARLIC CHICKPEAS

1. Preheat oven to 450 F (230 C). Line a baking sheet with parchment paper and set aside.

2. Blot chickpeas dry using a clean towel.

3. In a medium-sized mixing bowl, combine the chickpeas with olive oil and garlic powder.

4. Evenly distribute the chickpeas on prepared baking sheet, ensuring they are in a single layer. (For 24 servings,

depending upon the size of your baking sheet, you may need to use a second one.)

5. Bake for 15 minutes. Mix the chick-peas around and continue to bake for an additional 20 to 25 minutes, or until chickpeas are golden brown and crispy in texture. Set aside to cool.

ROASTED SPICY CAULIFLOWER

1. In a large mixing bowl, toss together cauliflower, olive oil, salt, paprika and cayenne (if using), until cauliflower is coated.

2. Spread florets evenly on a parchment-lined baking sheet (or multiple if making 24 servings). Allow space between the florets to prevent steaming.

3. In the same oven, roast for 25 to 30 minutes, or until golden in colour and tender to the touch. Set aside.

FIG DRESSING

1. In a blender, combine all dressing ingredients and blend until smooth. If a thinner dressing is desired, add addi-tional water ¼ cup (60 mL) at a time, until desired consistency is reached.

2. Strain dressing through a fine-mesh sieve and discard any solids that may remain.

3. To serve, combine 1 cup (250 mL) quinoa with ¾ cup (180 mL) spiced cauliflower in each individual bowl. Garnish with 2 Tbsp (30 mL) roasted chickpeas and 2 Tbsp (30 mL) fig dressing. Sprinkle with reserved pomegranate seeds, mint and parsley.

Pinto Bean and
Sweet Potato Burritos

PREPARATION TIME 20 minutes
COOKING TIME 20 minutes

These beautiful little bundles of beans, brown rice, seasonal vegetables, fresh herbs and crunchy iceberg lettuce, topped with chunky homemade guaca- mole, are a staple in my family's diet. This is our go-to recipe. Each burrito is packed with health- promoting functional foods, contains high fibre and protein, is an excellent source of vitamin A and is a good source of potassium, iron and vitamin E.

Per 1 burrito/406 g serving with guacamole: 440 calories; 15 g total fat; 68 g total carbs; 14 g fibre; 6 g sugar; 11 g protein; 380 mg sodium.

6 SERVINGS	24 SERVINGS	INGREDIENTS
1 Tbsp (15 mL)	¼ cup (60 mL)	grapeseed oil
½ cup (125 mL)	3 small	diced onions
1½ tsp (7.5 mL)	2 Tbsp (30 mL)	minced garlic
2¼ tsp (11 mL)	3 Tbsp (45 mL)	cocoa powder
¾ tsp (4 mL)	1 Tbsp (15 mL)	ground coriander
¾ tsp (4 mL)	1 Tbsp (15 mL)	ground cumin
¾ tsp (4 mL)	1 Tbsp (15 mL)	chili powder
¼ tsp (1 mL)	1½ tsp (7 mL)	cayenne (optional)
1 cup (250 mL)	4 cups (1 L)	water
1 small	4 small	sweet potato, diced
1 (398 mL) can	4 (398 mL) cans	pinto beans, drained and rinsed
½ tsp (2.5 mL)	2 tsp (10 mL)	sea salt
6 (10-inch)	24 (10-inch)	corn or whole wheat tortilla shells

Toppings

6 SERVINGS	24 SERVINGS	INGREDIENTS
2¼ cups	9 cups (2.25 L)	your favourite cooked grain (such as quinoa, brown rice)
1¾ cups (430 mL)	7 cups (1.75 L)	shredded iceberg lettuce
2	9	tomatoes, diced
1 large	4 large	carrot, grated
2	8	green onions, finely sliced
⅛ bunch	½ bunch	cilantro, stemmed
—	—	Your favourite hot sauce (optional)
—	—	Guacamole (see recipe on following page)

Continued ...

1. Heat a sauté pan over medium heat, then add oil. Once heated, add onions and sauté until soft, about 3 to 5 minutes. Add garlic, cocoa powder, coriander, cumin, chili powder and cayenne (if using) and sauté until fragrant, about 2 minutes for 6 servings and 5 minutes for 24 servings.

2. Add water and deglaze the pan by scraping any stuck bits off the bottom. Stir in sweet potatoes, cover and cook until tender, about 10 to 12 minutes.

3. Add pinto beans and sauté for another 5 minutes.

4. Using a fork or masher, slightly mash beans. Stir in salt and remove from heat.

5. Lay out a tortilla shell and spread ½ cup (125 mL) of the bean mixture down the centre.

6. Next, top with:
   - ¼ cup (60 mL) grains
   - ¼ cup (60 mL) lettuce, packed
   - ¼ cup (60 mL) tomatoes, packed
   - ¼ cup (60 mL) carrots, packed
   - 1 Tbsp (15 mL) green onions
   - Pinch of cilantro
   - Dash of hot sauce (if using)
   - 2 Tbsp (30 mL) guacamole

7. Roll up burrito and repeat with remaining ingredients.

Guacamole

6 SERVINGS	24 SERVINGS	INGREDIENTS
¾ tsp (4 mL)	1 Tbsp (15 mL)	grapeseed oil
2 large	6 large	avocados, diced
½ tsp (2.5 mL)	2 tsp (10 mL)	minced garlic
1 small	4 small	tomato, diced
2¼ tsp (11 mL)	3 Tbsp (45 mL)	lime zest
2 Tbsp (30 mL) (about 1 lime)	½ cup (125 mL) (about 3 limes)	fresh lime juice
½ tsp (2.5 mL)	2 tsp (10 mL)	salt
⅛ tsp (0.6 mL)	½ tsp (2.5 mL)	black pepper or cayenne (optional)

TIP

If you save the avocado pits and place them in the bowl of guacamole, it will minimize the oxidation of the avocado.

1. Put all ingredients into a bowl and mix. Use as a burrito topping and/or serve alongside.

Smoky Chipotle Avocado and Cilantro Muffins with Avocado Butter

PREPARATION TIME 20 to 25 minutes

COOKING TIME 30 to 35 minutes

A good side or accompaniment to a dish is something to celebrate as well, and this recipe is certainly worthy. These moist, pillowy whole grain corn muffins loaded with rich avocado butter are a family favourite around our home. They pair perfectly with my creamy corn chowder and are ideal for sopping up every last drop. Or honour them on their own as a savoury breakfast or afternoon treat, because sometimes a simple pleasure like a really good muffin is worth celebrating.

Per 1 muffin/111 g serving with avocado butter:
190 calories; 11 g total fat;
22 g total carbs; 7 g fibre;
3 g sugar; 4 g protein;
160 mg sodium.

6 SERVINGS	24 SERVINGS	INGREDIENTS
½ cup (125 mL)	2 cups (500 mL)	fine-grind cornmeal
¼ cup (60 mL)	1 cup (250 mL)	whole wheat flour
2 Tbsp (30 mL)	½ cup (125 mL)	nutritional yeast
1 Tbsp (15 mL)	¼ cup (60 mL)	ground flaxseed
1 tsp (5 mL)	4 tsp (20 mL)	baking powder
¼ tsp (1 mL)	1 tsp (5 mL)	baking soda
¼ tsp (1 mL)	1 tsp (5 mL)	ground chipotle powder
¼ tsp (1 mL)	1 tsp (5 mL)	smoked paprika
⅛ tsp (0.6 mL)	½ tsp (2.5 mL)	salt
⅓ cup (80 mL) (about ½ small avocado)	1⅓ cups (350 mL) (about 2 small avocados)	mashed ripe avocado
6 Tbsp (90 mL)	1½ cups (375 mL)	light coconut milk
1 Tbsp (15 mL)	¼ cup (60 mL)	coconut oil, melted
2 tsp (10 mL)	2 Tbsp (30 mL)	apple cider vinegar
½ Tbsp (7.5 mL)	2 Tbsp (30 mL)	maple syrup
¾ cup (180 mL)	3 cups (750 mL)	grated carrots
1 Tbsp (15 mL)	¼ cup (60 mL)	chopped cilantro

Garnish

3 Tbsp (45 mL)	¾ cup (180 mL)	frozen corn kernels
½ tsp (2.5 mL)	2 tsp (10 mL)	smoked paprika
—	—	Avocado Butter (see recipe on following page)

1. Preheat oven to 375F (190C) and grease muffin pan(s).

2. In a large bowl, combine all dry ingredients.

3. In a small bowl, whisk together mashed avocado, coconut milk, coconut oil, apple cider vinegar and maple syrup.

4. Add wet mixture to dry ingredients and fully incorporate.

5. Fold in carrots and cilantro.

6. Using a ¼ cup (60 mL) measure, evenly distribute batter into muffin cups. Garnish each muffin with frozen corn and smoked paprika. Bake in the oven for 30 to 35 minutes, or until an inserted toothpick comes out clean.

7. Remove muffins from the tray and allow to cool on a cooling rack. Serve with avocado butter.

Avocado Butter

6 SERVINGS	24 SERVINGS	INGREDIENTS
1½ cups (375 mL) (about 1 large avocado)	6 cups (1.5 L) (about 4 large avocados)	mashed avocado
1 cup (250 mL)	4 cups (1 L)	fresh basil leaves
1 Tbsp (15 mL)	¼ cup (60 mL)	lime zest
2½ Tbsp (37 mL) (about 1–2 limes)	⅔ cup (160 mL) (about 6–8 limes)	fresh lime juice
1 Tbsp (15 mL)	¼ cup (60 mL)	apple cider vinegar
⅛ tsp (0.6 mL)	½ tsp (2.5 mL)	sea salt
⅛ tsp (0.6 mL)	½ tsp (2.5 mL)	cayenne

1. Place all ingredients into a blender or food processor and blend until smooth. If needed, add 1 to 2 Tbsp (15 to 30 mL) water for easier blending. (If making 24 servings, process in batches.)

2. For storage, put into a resealable container, gently pressing plastic wrap on the mixture surface to reduce browning. Refrigerate until ready to eat. Lasts in the fridge for up to 2 days.

Tex-Mex Black Bean Burgers

PREPARATION TIME 20 to 25 minutes

COOKING TIME 45 to 50 minutes

A good two-handed burger slathered with homemade mayo atop a crusty whole grain bun is what summer BBQ gatherings are made of. This plant-based version of a classic burger with a Texas kick uses black beans and rice to provide a meaty texture, along with heaps of spices to give it that crave-worthy BBQ flavour. Each burger contains zero cholesterol and is an excellent source of fibre, protein, iron, and vitamins A and E.

Per 1 burger/240 g serving with bun and mayonnaise: 550 calories; 30 g total fat; 60 g total carbs; 16 g fibre; 5 g sugar; 16 g protein; 480 mg sodium.

6 SERVINGS	24 SERVINGS	INGREDIENTS
1 Tbsp (15 mL)	¼ cup (60 mL)	chia seeds
4½ tsp (22 mL)	6 Tbsp (90 mL)	water
¾ cup (180 mL)	3 cups (750 mL)	diced butternut squash
¼ cup (60 mL)	1 cup (250 mL)	diced carrots
½ cup (125 mL)	2 cups (500 mL)	diced red onions
3 cloves	½ head	garlic, chopped
1 cup (250 mL)	4 cups (1 L)	unsalted cooked black beans, rinsed
½ cup (125 mL)	2 cups (500 mL)	cooked brown rice
¼ cup (60 mL)	1 cup (250 mL)	finely chopped leafy greens (such as Swiss chard, kale, spinach), tightly packed
3 Tbsp (45 mL)	¾ cup (180 mL)	almond flour
1 tsp (5 mL)	1½ Tbsp (22 mL)	chili powder
½ tsp (2.5 mL)	2 tsp (10 mL)	paprika
½ tsp (2.5 mL)	2 tsp (10 mL)	ground cumin
1 tsp (5 mL)	4 tsp (20 mL)	black pepper
½ tsp (2.5 mL)	2 tsp (10 mL)	sea salt
¾ tsp (4 mL)	1 Tbsp (15 mL)	grapeseed oil
—	—	Avocado Sesame Spelt Buns (see recipe on page 210)
—	—	Vegan Mayonnaise (see recipe on page 211)
—	—	Your favourite burger toppings (such as lettuce, tomatoes, onions)

TIP

Substitute spelt or brown rice flour for the almond flour if nuts and nut flours are not an option for you, or if you aren't able to locate the ingredient.

1. Preheat oven to 375F (190C). Line baking sheets with parchment paper.

2. In a small bowl, mix chia seeds and water. Set aside for 5 to 10 minutes, until thick and gelatinous.

3. In a food processor, pulse butternut squash, carrots, red onions and garlic until they form a coarse meal, about 1 minute. If making 24 servings you may need to process in two batches.

4. Add remaining ingredients, except oil, to food processor and pulse until mixture is ground up but still a bit chunky. (If making 24 servings you may need to process the ingredients in batches and combine in a large bowl.)

5. Take 6 Tbsp (90 mL) of the mixture and form into a patty shape, about ½ inch (1.25 cm) thick. Repeat with remaining burger mixture. Arrange on baking sheet(s) an inch apart.

6. Brush the tops of the patties with oil and bake for 45 to 50 minutes, flipping after 35 minutes. Bake until patties are golden brown. Assemble burgers using buns topped with vegan mayo and your favourite burger toppings. To freeze patties, cool completely and freeze individually before transferring to containers or resealable freezer bags. (They can be stored frozen for up to 3 months.)

Avocado Sesame Spelt Buns

6 SERVINGS	24 SERVINGS	INGREDIENTS
2¼ cups (560 mL)	9 cups (2.25 L)	spelt flour
1¼ cups (310 mL)	5 cups (1.25 L)	almond flour
5 tsp (25 mL)	½ cup + 2 Tbsp (155 mL)	ground flaxseed
1½ tsp (7.5 mL)	2 Tbsp (30 mL)	baking powder
¼ tsp (1 mL)	1 tsp (5 mL)	sea salt
1	4	avocado, pitted and skin removed
—	—	Zest and juice of 1 lime
1 Tbsp (15 mL)	¼ cup (60 mL)	maple syrup
¾ cup (180 mL)	3 cups (750 mL)	water
Topping		
1 Tbsp (15 mL)	¼ cup (60 mL)	white and/or black sesame seeds

1. Preheat oven to 375F (190C) and line baking sheet(s) with parchment paper.

2. In a large bowl, combine spelt flour, almond flour, flaxseed, baking powder and sea salt.

3. In a medium bowl, mash avocado pieces with a fork. Mix in lime zest and juice, maple syrup and water until well combined.

4. Add the wet ingredients to the dry ingredients and mix well by hand for 2 to 3 minutes, until a sticky-firm dough is formed. Cover with a damp towel and allow to rest for 30 minutes in a room temperature location.

5. Using ½ cup (125 mL) portions, shape dough into round buns with 5-inch (12.5 cm) diameters. Arrange on prepared baking sheet(s) and lightly press sesame seeds onto tops so they stick.

6. Bake for 30 to 35 minutes, rotating the pans halfway through. Use a toothpick to test buns. If the toothpick comes out clean, they are done.

7. Transfer buns to a cooling rack. Allow to completely cool before slicing open.

Vegan Mayonnaise

24 SERVINGS	INGREDIENTS
1½ cups (375 mL)	unsweetened soy milk
½ bunch	parsley, chopped (including stems)
1½ heads	garlic, roasted and peeled
2 Tbsp (30 mL)	Dijon mustard
2 Tbsp (30 mL)	apple cider vinegar
1 tsp (5 mL)	sea salt
1½ cups (375 mL)	grapeseed oil

1. Place all ingredients except oil in a blender and blend until smooth.

2. Keeping the blender on, slowly add the oil in a thin stream.

3. Continue to blend until it is a spreadable consistency, about 7 minutes.

4. Top your favourite burger with 1 to 2 tablespoons (15 to 30 mL) mayo. Store leftover mayo in the fridge for up to 3 days or freeze for up to 2 weeks.

Lentil and Walnut Tacos with Mango Avocado Salsa

PREPARATION TIME 20 minutes
COOKING TIME 30 minutes

If I had to choose a menu consisting of my last meals on earth, tacos would make the shortlist, particularly this super-simple dish. The substantial texture of lentils and walnuts combined with all the necessary seasonings, topped off with a sweet, tangy and creamy salsa, makes for a perfect taco. Bring this recipe out for all commemorative occasions: a fun, end-of-week celebratory meal with the family, a soccer team victory party or when you receive some good news. You can brag that one taco provides 12 g of fibre, 16 g of protein and 25 percent of your daily iron needs, in addition to the phytonutrients and antioxidants present in every head-tilting bite.

Per 1 taco/194 g serving:
460 calories; 24 g total fat;
51 g total carbs; 12 g fibre;
8 g sugar; 16 g protein;
410 mg sodium.

TIPS

Cashew sour cream, extra sprigs of cilantro, your favourite hot sauce and quick pickled onions are great additional topping options!

Filling can be made ahead and refrigerated, then reheated gently.

6 SERVINGS	24 SERVINGS	INGREDIENTS
Filling		
1½ cups (375 mL)	6 cups (1.5 L)	dry brown lentils, rinsed
1 Tbsp (15 mL)	¼ cup (60 mL)	olive oil
½ cup (125 mL)	2 cups (500 mL)	finely chopped red onions
4 cloves	16 cloves	garlic, minced
¼ cup (60 mL)	1 cup (250 mL)	tomato paste
1 Tbsp (15 mL)	¼ cup (60 mL)	ground cumin
2 tsp (10 mL)	8 tsp (40 mL)	dried oregano
2 tsp (10 mL)	8 tsp (40 mL)	chili powder
1 tsp (5 mL)	4 tsp (20 mL)	paprika
1 tsp (5 mL)	4 tsp (20 mL)	salt
¼ tsp (1 mL)	1 tsp (5 mL)	black pepper
—	—	Cayenne, to taste
1 tsp (5 mL)	4 tsp (20 mL)	red wine vinegar
1 cup (250 mL)	4 cups (1 L)	walnuts, toasted and finely chopped
Mango Avocado Salsa		
1 cup (250 mL)	4 cups (1 L)	diced mango
1 clove	4 cloves	garlic, minced
1	4	avocado, diced
¼ cup (60 mL)	1 cup (250 mL)	finely chopped red onions
1	4	jalapeno, seeded and finely chopped
1 cup (250 mL)	4 cups (1 L)	cilantro, including stems, finely chopped
1 Tbsp (15 mL)	¼ cup (60 mL)	lime zest
3 Tbsp (45 mL)	¼ cup (60 mL)	fresh lime juice
6 (6-inch)	24 (6-inch)	hard tortilla shells

1. Place lentils in a saucepan and cover with cold water. Bring to a boil, reduce heat and simmer until cooked, about 20 minutes (30 minutes for 24 servings). Drain and set aside.

2. Heat a medium frying pan over medium heat, then add oil. Once heated, add onions and sauté until translucent, about 5 minutes. Add garlic and sauté until fragrant, about 30 seconds.

3. Add tomato paste and spices. Stir well to combine, and cook for 1 to 2 minutes for 6 servings and 5 to 6 minutes for 24 servings.

4. Add cooked lentils, vinegar and walnuts and heat through, adding water if necessary to reach desired consistency.

5. In a small bowl, combine all ingredients for the salsa. Cover and refrigerate until needed.

6. To serve, divide filling between tortillas and top with salsa.

Dairy-Free Queso

PREPARATION TIME 30 minutes

COOKING TIME 1 hour

This is the appy to bring to your next shindig. It has all of the qualities needed for a show-stopping dip: it's smooth, spicy, savoury, cheesy and cholesterol-free. Aside from the healthy levels of phytonu-trients present, a ½-cup (125-mL) serving contains 4 g fibre and 44 percent of your daily vitamin A requirement, so dig in and celebrate your health.

Per ½ cup/125 mL serving: 150 calories; 7 g total fat; 19 g total carbs; 4 g fibre; 4 g sugar; 3 g protein; 320 mg sodium.

6 SERVINGS	24 SERVINGS	INGREDIENTS
1 whole	3 whole	jalapeno
½ head	2 heads	garlic, top removed
8 tsp (40 mL)	⅔ cup (160 mL)	extra-virgin olive oil, divided
2 (about 400 g)	8 (about 1.6 kg)	white potatoes, peeled and roughly chopped
4 medium (about 250 g)	16 medium (about 1 kg)	carrots, peeled and roughly chopped
¾ tsp (4 mL)	1 Tbsp (15 mL)	chili powder
¾ tsp (4 mL)	1 Tbsp (15 mL)	ground cumin
½ cup (125 mL)	2 cups (500 mL)	low-sodium vegetable stock
¼ cup (60 mL)	1 cup (250 mL)	nutritional yeast
2 Tbsp (30 mL)	½ cup (125 mL)	fresh lemon juice
¾ tsp (4 mL)	1 Tbsp (15 mL)	salt
⅛ tsp (0.6 mL)	½ tsp (2.5 mL)	black pepper

Garnish

¼ bunch	1 bunch	chives, chopped
1	3	Roma tomato, seeded and diced

1. Preheat oven to 375F (190C). Line a baking sheet with parchment paper.

2. Arrange jalapeno(s) and garlic on the prepared baking sheet and drizzle with one-fifth of the oil until well coated. Roast until jalapenos are slightly charred and garlic is soft, about 30 minutes (45 minutes for 24 servings). Remove from oven and allow to cool slightly. Remove the skins from the garlic and mince the jalapenos. Set aside.

3. Fill a large steamer with water, ensuring that the water does not touch or fill the steam basket. Bring water to a boil over medium-high heat. Add potatoes and carrots and allow to steam until soft, about 15 minutes (25 minutes for 24 servings). Set aside.

4. Heat a small sauté pan over medium heat, then add chili powder and cumin and toast until fragrant, about 2 minutes. Set aside.

5. In a high-powered blender, combine potatoes, carrots, roasted garlic, spices, vegetable stock, the remaining olive oil, nutritional yeast, lemon juice, salt and pepper and blend until smooth, about 8 minutes. Adjust dip's consistency with additional stock or water if necessary. (For best results for 24 servings, blend in batches and combine afterwards.)

6. Transfer to a serving bowl and top with chives and tomatoes. Serve warm with homemade tortilla chips.

7. To store, keep in a resealable container in the refrigerator and heat before serving. The sauce tends to thicken as it cools, so the queso is best served warm. When reheating, adjust with water or stock if needed to meet the desired consistency of a queso.

Protein-Packed
Chickpea Blondies

PREPARATION TIME 15 minutes

COOKING TIME 45 minutes

These are moist, bite-sized pockets of nutrient- and flavour-dense goodness. Each small square is a source of fibre and iron and contains 3 g of protein. They make a great after-school or post-workout treat, or a scrump-tious mid-afternoon pick-me-up!

Per 1 square/39 g serving: 100 calories; 4.5 g total fat; 13 g total carbs; 2 g fibre; 7 g sugar; 3 g protein; 150 mg sodium.

12 SERVINGS	24 SERVINGS	INGREDIENTS
1 (398 mL) can	2 (398 mL) cans	chickpeas, drained and rinsed
⅓ cup (80 mL)	⅔ cup (160 mL)	pure maple syrup
3 Tbsp (45 mL)	6 Tbsp (90 mL)	hemp seeds
1 Tbsp (15 mL)	2 Tbsp (30 mL)	ground flaxseed
4 tsp (20 mL)	8 tsp (40 mL)	vanilla extract
½ tsp (2.5 mL)	1 tsp (5 mL)	salt
¼ tsp (1 mL)	½ tsp (2.5 mL)	baking powder
¼ tsp (1 mL)	½ tsp (2.5 mL)	baking soda
½ cup (125 mL)	1 cup (250 mL)	chopped unsweetened dark chocolate, divided

1. Preheat oven to 375F (190C) and grease an 8 × 8-inch (20 × 20 cm) pan with coconut oil (or two 8 × 8-inch pans if making 24 servings).

2. In a food processor, combine all ingredients except the dark choco-late. Process until batter is smooth, scraping down the sides as needed. Using a spatula, transfer batter from the processor to a large bowl. Fold in half of the chocolate.

3. Spread batter evenly into prepared pan(s). Bake for 10 to 15 minutes or until edges are slightly brown and a toothpick comes out clean. The blondies may look underdone, but you do not want them to dry out.

4. Sprinkle with remaining chocolate and allow to cool in the pan for 30 minutes, on a wire rack.

5. Transfer blondies to the refrigerator for another 45 minutes before attempt-ing to cut.

Chocolate Avocado Pie

Silky, chocolatey and simple to assemble are keystones of a good dessert, and this recipe delivers just that. Avocado is the secret ingredient that makes this dessert so velvety smooth. Fortunately for you, the pie is made with solely plant-based ingredients, so each slice contains almost one-third of your daily fibre intake as well as a cornucopia of phyto-nutrients and antioxidants.

Per 1 slice/140 g serving: 350 calories; 24 g total fat; 33 g total carbs; 9 g fibre; 20 g sugar; 6 g protein; 50 mg sodium.

6 SERVINGS	24 SERVINGS	INGREDIENTS
Chocolate Mousse		
2 large	8 large	ripe avocados, pitted and skin removed
⅓ cup (80 mL)	1⅓ cups (350 mL)	raw cocoa powder
⅓ cup (80 mL)	1⅓ cups (350 mL)	coconut milk
3 Tbsp (45 mL)	¾ cup (180 mL)	maple syrup
1 Tbsp (15 mL)	¼ cup (60 mL)	vanilla extract
2 Tbsp (30 mL)	½ cup (125 mL)	fresh lemon juice
(about ½ lemon)	(about 1 lemon)	
1 Tbsp (15 mL)	¼ cup (60 mL)	agar-agar
Date Crust		
¾ cup (180 mL)	3 cups (750 mL)	walnuts
¾ cup (180 mL)	3 cups (750 mL)	pitted dates
⅛ tsp (0.6 mL)	½ tsp (2.5 mL)	sea salt
Garnish		
2 Tbsp (30 mL)	½ cup (125 mL)	sliced blanched almonds
2 tsp (10 mL)	¼ cup (60 mL)	cocoa nibs
1 cup (250 mL)	4 cups (1 L)	fresh fruit, such as raspberries, cherries or sliced strawberries

TIP

Agar-agar is a thickening agent that is made of seaweed. It can often be found in bulk or health food stores. If agar-agar is difficult to find, omit and serve the pie partially frozen.

1. In a high-powered blender, combine all mousse ingredients. Process until completely smooth, about 5 minutes. (For 24 servings, the filling and crust will have to be processed in batches. Make sure to not overheat the blender or food processor.) Transfer mixture to a medium bowl and place in fridge to firm up to a thick pudding consistency, about 20 minutes (30 minutes for 24 servings).

2. Meanwhile, in a food processor, combine all crust ingredients and process until mealy, about 1 to 2 minutes. If necessary, use a rubber spatula to push down the mixture in the centre of the processor.

Pour into 8-inch (20 cm) pie pan(s), pressing evenly on the bottom and 1 inch (2.5 cm) up the sides.

3. Evenly spread the mousse atop the crust(s). Garnish with almonds, cocoa nibs and fresh fruit. Use parchment paper to cover the mousse, gently applying the paper directly onto the surface. Cover completely with aluminum foil and place in the freezer to firm for at least 2 hours.

4. Remove pie from the freezer 30 minutes before serving and allow to thaw slightly on the counter. Slice (each) pie into 6 slices.

Iced Coconut Lime Green Tea

This is a refreshing and innovative way to incorporate one of the most antioxidant-rich ingredients out there: green tea. Here we take steeped and chilled green tea and team it up with fresh mint leaves, electrolyte-replenishing coconut water and vitamin-C-rich strawberries and limes in order to quench your thirst and fill that fancy drink void. Add more or less sweetener to your taste. Cheers!

Per 1⅓ cups/325 mL serving: 60 calories; 0 g total fat; 15 g total carbs; 1 g fibre; 11 g sugar; 1 g protein; 45 mg sodium.

6 SERVINGS	24 SERVINGS	INGREDIENTS
3 cups (750 mL)	12 cups (3 L)	steeped and chilled green tea
⅛ tsp (0.6 mL)	½ tsp (2.5 mL)	stevia (stir into tea while it's hot) or 1 Tbsp (15 mL) maple syrup (optional)
4 cups (1 L)	16 cups (4 L)	unsweetened coconut water
4 sprigs	16 sprigs	mint, leaves only
2 tsp (10 mL)	8 tsp (40 mL)	lime zest
2 Tbsp (30 mL) (about 1 lime)	½ cup (125 mL) (about 4 limes)	fresh lime juice
2 cups (500 mL)	8 cups (2 L)	frozen strawberries
Garnish		
6	24	lime slices
6	24	mint leaves

1. In a large punch bowl or pitcher(s), combine all tea ingredients. Refrigerate if not serving immediately.

2. When ready to serve, pour tea into fancy glasses filled with ice and garnish with mint leaves and lime slices.

Lavender Lemonade

Break out your fanciest fascinator and picnic attire because the regular old lemonade you know and love has just been upgraded. This is a refined-sugar-free version of the old classic with the addition of the mildly floral flavour of lavender. Serve on a blazing summer's day!

Per 1 cup/250 mL serving: 45 calories; 0.1 g total fat; 12 g total carbs; 0 g fibre; 9 g sugar; 0.3 g protein; 10 mg sodium.

6 SERVINGS	24 SERVINGS	INGREDIENTS
1 cup (250 mL) (about 8 lemons)	4 cups (1 L) (about 32 lemons)	fresh lemon juice
¼ cup (60 mL)	1 cup (250 mL)	maple syrup
10 sprigs	40 sprigs	lavender
4 cups (1 L)	16 cups (4 L)	filtered water of choice, chilled
Garnish		
6	24	lemon slices

1. In a large punch bowl, combine lemon juice, maple syrup and lavender.

2. Stir lemonade base until maple syrup is completely dissolved and allow to rest in the fridge for 10 to 15 minutes.

3. When ready to serve, stir and pour evenly into glasses. Top with water and garnish with a slice of lemon.

Appendix I
Recipe Contributors

A S PART OF the process of this cookbook, Chef Amy incorporated the development of some of the recipes into her Culinary Nutrition students' curriculum. The students were asked to create a health-promoting recipe that includes affordable, minimal, easy-to-find and nutrient-dense ingredients. The selected recipes are mentioned below and in some cases were further developed by Amy and her cookbook team.

The recipes not mentioned in this list are originals and were developed by Chef Amy Symington.

BEAN AND SQUASH SOUP WITH KAMUT DUMPLINGS: Janikka Blair Murray

BLACK AND BLUE CASHEW CHEESECAKE: Alice Hung and Rochelle Goonoo

CARAMELIZED ONION, PEAR AND ARUGULA FOCACCIA: Victoria Seto

CARROT AND GINGER ORANGE JUICE: Maiya Griffith and Cassandra Jackman

COCOA BEAN PIE WITH RASPBERRY STRAWBERRY COULIS: Iafa Cac, adapted by Chef Amy Symington and her cookbook team

CRISP WATERCRESS SALAD WITH TEMPEH AND MANGO: Vica Pelivan, adapted by Chef Amy Symington and her cookbook team

CURRIED CHICKPEA SALAD SANDWICHES WITH TURMERIC GARLIC PARSNIP FRIES: Emily Goncz and Morgan Campbell, adapted by Chef Amy Symington and her cookbook team; Garlic Parsnip Fries by Olga Ni

FALAFEL SLIDERS WITH KALE TABBOULEH, SPICY TAHINI SAUCE AND PAPAYA CHUTNEY: Christine Song and Anna Kania, adapted by Chef Amy Symington and her cookbook team

From left to right: Tamara Saslove, Kelly-Anne Kerrigan, Christine Song, Amy Symington and Bronwyn Cawker.

LEMON, MINT AND GINGER SLUSH: Cristian Maierean

LENTIL AND WALNUT TACOS WITH MANGO AVOCADO SALSA: Anne Hewitt and Bronwyn Cawker

MOROCCAN QUINOA POWER BOWL: Josh Sernal and Leanne Soochan

POT PIES THREE WAYS: CREAM OF CHICKPEA: Daniel Bourdages and Chris Do, adapted by Chef Amy Symington and her cookbook team

RASPBERRY KEY LIME PIE: April Kim and Doris Lee, adapted by Chef Amy Symington and her cookbook team

SPELT AND COCONUT WAFFLES WITH RASPBERRIES AND COCONUT MOUSSE: Solim Lee, adapted by Chef Amy Symington and her cookbook team

SPICED BANANA CAKES WITH ORANGE FROSTING: Kelly-Anne Kerrigan and Rebecca Costa

TEX-MEX BLACK BEAN BURGERS: Jacqueline Zolis and Rebecca Moutoussidis, adapted by Chef Amy Symington and her cookbook team

VEGGIE CANNELLONI WITH CASHEW RICOTTA, BASIL PESTO AND PARMESAN: Tamara Saslove and Maria Sokolowksi

WARM FARRO SALAD WITH SPICY CITRUS DRESSING: Priyanca Patel, adapted by Chef Amy Symington and her cookbook team

WINTER VEGETABLE BORSCHT: Bernadeta Hopek and Natasha Roy, adapted by Chef Amy Symington and her cookbook team

YAM AND COCONUT CURRY SOUP: Julia Hoffe and Cassandra Patterson, adapted by Chef Amy Symington and her cookbook team

Appendix II
Recipe Benefits

RECIPE	GOOD FOR YOUR GUT	EASY TO SWALLOW	GOOD FOR FATIGUE	GLUTEN FREE	GOOD FOR NAUSEA	HIGH PROTEIN	HIGH FIBRE	NUT FREE	SOY FREE
Almond Apricot Blueberry Smoothie	x	x	x	x	x		x		x
Apple, Fennel and Beet Salad with Orange-Ginger Cider Vinaigrette	x		x	x			x		x
Artichoke and Oyster Mushroom Chowder with Sweet Potato	x		x	x	x		x		
Bean and Squash Soup with Kamut Dumplings	x					x	x	x	x
Black and Blue Cashew Cheesecake	x	x	x	x	x	x	x		
Brussels Sprouts with Roasted Apples and Shiitake Bacon	x			x		x	x		
Butterscotch Squash Coffee Cake	x	x	x		x		x		x
Caramelized Fennel, Sweet Potato and Pine Nut Cheese Pizza	x				x	x	x		x
Caramelized Onion, Pear and Arugula Focaccia	x				x		x	x	x
Carrot and Ginger Orange Juice	x	x	x	x	x			x	x
Chocolate Avocado Pie	x	x	x	x	x		x		x
Cinnamon Bun Cookies							x		x
Cocoa Bean Pie with Raspberry Strawberry Coulis	x	x	x	x	x	x	x	x	x

RECIPE	GOOD FOR YOUR GUT	EASY TO SWALLOW	GOOD FOR FATIGUE	GLUTEN FREE	GOOD FOR NAUSEA	HIGH PROTEIN	HIGH FIBRE	NUT FREE	SOY FREE
Creamy Cauliflower and Potato Soup	x	x		x		x	x	x	x
Creamy Corn Chowder with Tempeh Chorizo	x			x		x	x	x	
Creamy Dill and Cannellini Bean Dip	x	x	x	x	x	x	x	x	x
Crisp Watercress Salad with Tempeh and Mango	x		x	x	x	x	x	x	
Cucumber and Lime Gazpacho	x			x			x	x	x
Curried Chickpea Salad Sandwiches with Turmeric Garlic Parsnip Fries	x					x	x	x	
Dairy-Free Queso	x	x		x			x	x	x
Eggplant Moussaka	x			x		x	x		
Falafel Sliders with Kale Tabbouleh, Spicy Tahini Sauce and Papaya Chutney	x				x	x	x	x	x
Fresh Vegan Caesar Salad				x				x	
Iced Coconut Lime Green Tea	x	x	x	x	x			x	x
Kamut Crackers	x	x	x		x		x	x	x
Kung Pao Chickpeas over Sesame-Fried Millet	x					x	x		x
Lavender Lemonade	x	x	x	x	x			x	x
Lemon, Mint and Ginger Slush	x	x	x	x	x			x	x
Lentil and Walnut Tacos with Mango Avocado Salsa	x			x		x	x		x
Mac and Cheese with Coconut Bacon	x					x	x		
Mango Almond Curry	x					x	x		
Mango Turmeric Lassi	x	x	x	x	x		x	x	x
Maple Caramel Sauce with Granny Smith Apples and Toasted Walnuts	x		x	x	x		x		x
Matcha Mint Chocolate Chip Shakes	x	x	x		x	x	x	x	
Moroccan Quinoa Power Bowl	x		x		x	x	x		x
Mushroom and Lentil Shepherd's Pie	x			x		x	x	x	
Okra and Oyster Mushroom Gumbo with Red and White Beans	x			x		x	x	x	x

RECIPE	GOOD FOR YOUR GUT	EASY TO SWALLOW	GOOD FOR FATIGUE	GLUTEN FREE	GOOD FOR NAUSEA	HIGH PROTEIN	HIGH FIBRE	NUT FREE	SOY FREE
Papaya Chutney	x	x	x	x	x		x	x	x
Pasta with Mushroom Walnut Lentil Bites	x		x	x	x	x	x		
Pinto Bean and Sweet Potato Burritos	x		x			x	x	x	x
Pho Noodle Wrap	x		x			x	x	x	
Pot Pies Three Ways: Cream of Chickpea	x				x	x	x	x	
Pot Pies Three Ways: Lentil, Spinach and Onion	x				x	x	x	x	x
Pot Pies Three Ways: Miso, Mushroom and Edamame	x	x			x	x	x	x	
Protein-Packed Chickpea Blondies	x	x	x	x		x	x		x
Rainbow Slaw with Lime Dressing	x			x	x		x	x	x
Raspberry Key Lime Pie	x	x	x	x	x	x	x		x
Raw Carrot Cake Pie with Whipped Cinnamon Orange Cream	x	x	x	x	x	x	x		x
Raw Pad Thai Salad	x		x	x		x	x		
Red Bean and Fennel Sausages with Sweet Onion Mustard and Cultured Veg	x					x	x	x	x
Roasted Tomato and Garlic Soup	x	x	x		x		x	x	x
Smoky Chipotle Avocado and Cilantro Muffins with Avocado Butter	x	x	x		x		x	x	x
Spelt and Coconut Waffles with Raspberries and Coconut Mousse	x		x				x	x	x
Spiced Banana Cakes with Orange Frosting	x	x	x		x		x		
Spicy Chocolate-Dipped Oranges	x		x	x	x	x	x	x	x
Strawberry and Hazelnut Streusel Cake with a Maple Vanilla Glaze	x		x				x		x
Sweet Potato and Tahini Soup	x	x	x	x	x	x	x	x	x
Sweet Potato Pie Parfaits	x	x	x	x	x	x	x		x
Tahini Dill Dressing	x		x	x	x	x	x	x	x
Tex-Mex Black Bean Burgers	x					x	x		

RECIPE	GOOD FOR YOUR GUT	EASY TO SWALLOW	GOOD FOR FATIGUE	GLUTEN FREE	GOOD FOR NAUSEA	HIGH PROTEIN	HIGH FIBRE	NUT FREE	SOY FREE
Thai Noodle Salad with Spicy Roasted Almonds	x		x	x	x	x	x		x
Traditional Greek Salad with Tofu Feta	x			x		x	x	x	
Turmeric Garlic Parsnip Fries	x			x			x	x	x
Turmeric Ginger Latte	x	x	x	x	x				x
Ultimate Chocolate Protein Powder, The	x	x	x	x	x	x	x	x	
Vanilla Chai Chia Seed Pudding	x	x	x	x	x	x	x		x
Veggie Cannelloni with Cashew Ricotta, Basil Pesto and Parmesan	x			x		x	x		x
Waldorf Salad with Pomegranate and Pistachio	x		x	x			x		x
Warm Farro Salad with Spicy Citrus Dressing	x		x			x	x	x	x
Watermelon, Mint, Feta and Arugula Salad	x		x	x	x	x	x	x	
Winter Coleslaw with Orange Vinaigrette	x		x	x			x		x
Winter Vegetable Borscht	x		x	x		x	x	x	x
Yam and Coconut Curry Soup	x	x	x	x	x		x	x	x
Zucchini Noodles with Sunflower Basil Pesto	x			x		x	x		x

Notes

1   World Health Organization (WHO), 2018a. "Obesity and overweight: Key Facts." Retrieved August 17, 2018, from http://www.who.int/news-room/fact-sheets/detail/ obesity-and-overweight.

2   American Dietetic Association and Dietitians of Canada, 2003. "Position of the American Dietetic Association and Dietitians of Canada: Vegetarian Diets." *Journal of the American Dietetic Association* 103, 748–65; Ricker, M.A., and Haas, W.C., 2017. "Anti-Inflammatory Diet in Clinical Practice: A Review." *Nutrition in Clinical Practical* 32(3), 318–25. http//doi. org/10.1177/0884533617700353; Winston, J.C., 2009. "Health Effects of Vegan Diets." *The American Journal of Clinical Nutrition* 89 (suppl.), 1627s–33s.

3   Carter, Patrice; Gray, Laura J.; Troughton, Jacqui; Khunti, Kamlesh, and Davies, Melanie J., 2010. "Fruit and Vegetable Intake and Incidence of Type 2 Diabetes Mellitus: Systematic Review and Meta-analysis." *British Medical Journal* 341; Key, T.J., Davey, Gwyneth K., and Appleby, P.N., 1999. "Health Benefits of a Vegetarian Diet." *Proceedings of the Nutrition Society* 58:2, 271–75; Supric, G., Jagodic, M., and Magic, Z., 2013. "Epigenetics: A New Link Between Nutrition and Cancer." *Nutrition and Cancer* 65(6), 781–92; Tantamango-Bartley, Y., Jaceldo-Siegl, K., Fan J., and Fraser, G., 2013. "Vegetarian Diets and the Incidence of Cancer in a Low-risk Population." *Cancer Epidemiology Biomarkers & Prevention* 22(2): 286–94. doi:10.1158/1055-9965.epi-12-1060; Tonstad, S., Nathan, E., Oda, K., and Fraser, G., 2013. "Vegan Diets and Hypothyroidism." *Nutrients* 5(11), 4642–52. http//doi.org/10.3390/nu5114642.

4   Ricker, M.A., and Haas, W.C., 2017. "Anti-inflammatory Diet in Clinical Practice: A Review." *Nutrition in Clinical Practice* 32(3), 318–25. doi: 10.1177/0884533617700353.

5   Orlich, M.J., Singh, P.N., Sabaté, J., Jaceldo-Siegl, K., Fan, J., Knutsen, S., and Fraser, G.E., 2013. "Vegetarian Dietary Patterns and Mortality in Adventist Health Study 2." *JAMA Internal Medicine* 173(13), 1230–38. http://doi.org/10.1001/jamainternmed.2013.6473; Thorogood, M., Mann, J., Appleby, P., and McPherson, K., 1994. "Risk of Death from Cancer and Ischaemic Heart Disease in Meat and Non-meat Eaters." *British Medical Journal* 308; Wang, A., Han, J., Jiang, Y., and Zhang, D., 2014. "Association of Vitamin A and β-carotene with Risk for Age-related Cataract: A Meta-analysis." *Nutrition* 30(10), 1113–21. http://doi.org/10.1016/j.nut.2014.02.025.

6   Food and Agriculture Organization of the United Nations (FAO), 2013. "Tackling Climate Change Through Livestock: Key Facts and Findings." Retrieved June 2015 from http://www.fao.org/ news/story/en/item/197623/icode/; *National Geographic*. "Thirsty Food: Fueling Agriculture to Fuel Humans." Retrieved June 2019 from https://www.nationalgeographic.com/environ- ment/freshwater/food; *Water Footprint Calculator*. "Food's Big Water Footprint." Retrieved June 2019 from https://www.watercalculator.org/water-use/foods-big-water-footprint; United Nations Environment Program, 2010. "Assessing the Environmental Impacts of Consumption and Production: Priority Products and Materials." *International Panel for Sustainable Resource Management*. Retrieved June 12, 2015, from http://www.unep.fr/shared/publications/pdf/ dtix1262xpa-priorityproductsandmaterials_report.pdf

7   Food and Agriculture Organization of the United Nations (FAO), 2013. "Tackling Climate Change Through Livestock: Key Facts and Findings." Retrieved June 2015 from http://www.fao.org/ news/story/en/item/197623/icode; Goodland, Robert, and Anhang, Jeff, 2009. "Livestock and

climate change." *Worldwatch Institute*, Retrieved June 2015 from http://www.worldwatch.org/files/pdf/Livestock%20and%20Climate%20Change.pdf.

8   World Health Organization (WHO), 2018b. *Noncommunicable Diseases*. Retrieved July 25, 2018, from http://www.who.int/news-room/fact-sheets/detail/noncommunicable-diseases.

9   Patel, S., Winkel, M., Ali, M.K., Venkat Narayan, K.M., Mehta, N.K., 2015. "Cardiovascular Mortality Associated With 5 Leading Risk Factors: National and State Preventable Fractions Estimated From Survey Data." *Annals of Internal Medicine* 163(4), 245-53. http://doi.org/10.7326/M14-1753.

10   Carter, P., Gray, L.J., Troughton, J., Khunti, K., and Davies, M.J., 2010. "Fruit and Vegetable Intake and Incidence of Type 2 Diabetes Mellitus: Systematic Review and Meta-analysis." *British Medical Journal* 341; Key, T.J., Davey, G.K. and Appleby, P.N., 1999. "Health Benefits of a Vegetarian Diet." *Proceedings of the Nutrition Society* 58(2), 271-75; Supic, G., Jagodic, M., and Magic, Z., 2013. "Epigenetics: A New Link Between Nutrition and Cancer." *Nutrition and Cancer*, 65(6), 781-92; Tantamango-Bartley, Y., Jaceldo-Siegl, K., Fan, J., and Fraser, G., 2013. "Vegetarian Diets and the Incidence of Cancer in a Low-risk Population." *Cancer Epidemiology Biomarkers & Prevention* 22(2), 286-94. doi:10.1158/1055-9965.epi-12-1060; Winston, J.C., 2009. "Health Effects of Vegan Diets." *The American Journal of Clinical Nutrition* 89(suppl), 1627S-33S.

11   Huang, T., Yang, B., Zheng, J., Li, G., Wahlqvist, M.L., and Li, D., 2012. "Cardiovascular Disease Mortality and Cancer Incidence in Vegetarians: A Meta-analysis and Systematic Review." *Annals of Nutrition and Metabolism* 60(4), 233-40. doi:10.1159/000337301.

12   Appleby, P.N., Davey, G.K., and Key, T.J., 2002. "Hypertension and Blood Pressure among Meat Eaters, Fish Eaters, Vegetarians and Vegans in EPIC-Oxford." *Public Health Nutrition* 5(5), 645-54. http://doi.org/10.1079/phn2002332; Yokoyama, Y., Nishimura, K., Barnard, N.D., Takegami, M., Watanabe, M., Sekikawa, A.,... Miyamoto, Y., 2014. "Vegetarian Diets and Blood Pressure: A Meta-analysis." *JAMA Internal Medicine* 174(4), 577-87. http://doi.org/10.1001/jamainternmed.2013.14547.

13   Satija, A., Bhupathiraju, S.N., Rimm, E.B., Spiegelman, D., Chiuve, S.E., Borgi, L., Willett, W.C., Manson, J.E., Sun, Q., and Hu, F.B., 2016. "Plant-based Dietary Patterns and Incidence of Type 2 Diabetes in US Men and Women: Results from Three Prospective Cohort Studies." *PLoS Medicine*

13. https://doi.org/10.1371/journal.pmed.1002039.

14   Bradbury, K.E., Crowe, F.L., Appleby, P.N., Schmidt, J.A., Travis, R.C., and Key, T.J., 2014. "Serum Concentrations of Cholesterol, Apolipoprotein A-I, and Apolipoprotein B in a Total of 1694 Meat-eaters, Fish-eaters, Vegetarians and Vegans. *European Journal of Clinical Nutrition* 68(2), 178-83. http://doi.org/10.1038/ejcn.2013.248.

15   Ferdowsian, H.R., and Barnard, N.D., 2009. "Effects of Plant-based Diets on Plasma Lipids." *American Journal of Cardiology* 104, 947-56.

16   Casiglia, E., Tikhonoff, V., Caffi, S., Boschetti, G., Grasselli, C., Saugo, M.,... Palatini, P., 2013. "High Dietary Fiber Intake Prevents Stroke at a Population Level." *Clinical Nutrition* 32(5), 811-18. http://doi.org/10.1016/j.clnu.2012.11.025; Threapleton, D.E., Greenwood, D.C., Evans, C.E., Cleghorn, C.L., Nykjaer, C., Woodhead, C., and Burley, V.J., 2013. "Dietary Fiber Intake and Risk of First Stroke: A Systematic Review and Meta-Analysis." *Stroke* 44(5), 1360-68. http://doi.org/10.1161/strokeaha.111.000151.

17   Asgary, S., Rastqar, A., Keshvari, M., 2018. "Functional Food and Cardiovascular Disease Prevention and Treatment: A Review." *Journal of the American College of Nutrition* 37(5), 429-55. doi: 10.1080/07315724.2017.1410867; Badimon, L., Chagas, P., and Chiva-Blanch, G., 2017. "Diet and Cardiovascular Disease: Effects of Foods and Nutrients in Classical and Emerging Cardiovascular Risk Factors." *Current Medicinal Chemistry* 24. doi: 10.2174/0929867324666617 0428103206; Bitok, E., and Sabaté, J., 2018. "Nuts and Cardiovascular Disease." *Progress in Cardiovascular Disease* 61(1), 33-37. doi: 10.1016/j.pcad.2018.05.003; Blekkenhorst, L.C., Sim, M., Bondonno, C.P., Bondonno, N.P., Ward, N.C., Prince, R.L., Devine, A., Lewis, J.R., and Hodgson, J.M., 2018. "Cardiovascular Health Benefits of Specific Vegetable Types: A Narrative Review." *Nutrients* 10(5), 595. doi: 10.3390/nu10050595.

18   Canadian Cancer Statistics Advisory Committee, 2018. *Canadian Cancer Statistics, 2018*. Toronto, ON: Canadian Cancer Society. Retrieved on August 20, 2018, from cancer.ca/Canadian-Cancer-Statistics-2018-EN.

19   Wiseman, M., 2008. "The Second World Cancer Research Fund/American Institute for Cancer Research Expert Report. Food, Nutrition, Physical Activity, and the Prevention of Cancer: A Global Perspective: Nutrition Society and BAPEN

Medical Symposium on 'Nutrition Support in Cancer Therapy'." *Proceedings of the Nutrition Society* 67(3), 253–56. doi: 10.1017/S002966510800712X.

20   Jones, L.W., and Demark-Wahnefried, W., 2006. "Diet, Exercise, and Complementary Therapies After Primary Treatment for Cancer." *The Lancet Oncology* 7, 1017–26; Rock, C.L., Doyle, C., Demark-Wahnefried, W., . . . Gansler, T., 2012. "Nutrition and Physical Activity Guidelines for Cancer Survivors." *Cancer Journal for Clinicians* 62, 243–74; Schwedhelm, C., Boeing, H., Hoffmann, G., Aleksandrova, K., and Schwingshackl, L., 2016. "Effect of Diet on Mortality and Cancer Recurrence among Cancer Survivors: A Systematic Review and Meta-analysis of Cohort Studies." *Nutrition Review* 74(12), 737–48; World Cancer Research Fund (WCRF) and American Institute for Cancer Research (AICR), 2007. *Food, Nutrition, Physical Activity, and the Prevention of Cancer: A Global Perspective.* Washington, DC: AICR, 2007.

21   World Cancer Research Fund (WCRF) and American Institute for Cancer Research (AICR), 2007. *Food, Nutrition, Physical Activity, and the Prevention of Cancer: A Global Perspective.* Washington, DC: AICR, 2007.

22   Gonzales, J.F., Barnard, N.D., Jenkins, D.J., Lanou, A.J., Davis, B., Saxe, G., and Levin, S., 2014. "Applying the Precautionary Principle to Nutrition and Cancer." *Journal of the American College of Nutrition* 33(3), 239–46. doi:10.1080/07315724.2013. 866527.

23   Supic, G., Jagodic, M., and Magic, Z., 2013. "Epigenetics: A New Link Between Nutrition and Cancer." *Nutrition and Cancer* 65(6), 781–92; Tantamango-Bartley, Y., Jaceldo-Siegl, K., Fan, J., and Fraser, G., 2013. "Vegetarian Diets and the Incidence of Cancer in a Low-risk Population." *Cancer Epidemiology Biomarkers & Prevention* 22(2), 286–94. doi:10.1158/1055-9965.epi-12-1060; Béliveau, R., and Gingras, D., 2006. *Foods that Fight Cancer: Preventing and Treating Cancer Through Diet.* Crows Nest, NSW: Allen & Unwin; Marsh, K., Zeuschner, C., and Saunders, A., 2012. "Health Implications of a Vegetarian Diet: A Review." *American Journal of Lifestyle Medicine* 6(3), 250–67. doi:10.1177/1559827611425762; Gonzales, J.F., Barnard, N.D., Jenkins, D.J., Lanou, A.J., Davis, B., Saxe, G., and Levin, S., 2014. "Applying the Precautionary Principle to Nutrition and Cancer." *Journal of the American College of Nutrition* 33(3), 239–46. doi:10.1080/07315724.2013.866527; World Cancer Research Fund (WCRF) and American Institute for Cancer Research

24   Supic, G., Jagodic, M., and Magic, Z., 2013. "Epigenetics: A New Link Between Nutrition and Cancer." *Nutrition and Cancer* 65(6), 781–92; Tantamango-Bartley, Y., Jaceldo-Siegl, K., Fan, J., and Fraser, G., 2013. "Vegetarian Diets and the Incidence of Cancer in a Low-risk Population." *Cancer Epidemiology Biomarkers & Prevention* 22(2), 286–94. doi:10.1158/1055-9965. epi-12-1060.

25   Huang, T., Yang, B., Zheng, J., Li, G., Wahlqvist, M.L., and Li, D., 2012. "Cardiovascular Disease Mortality and Cancer Incidence in Vegetarians: A Meta-analysis and Systematic Review." *Annals of Nutrition and Metabolism* 60(4), 233–40. doi:10.1159/000337301.

26   Dinu, M., Abbate, R., Gensini, G.F., Casini, A., and Sofi, F., 2016. "Vegetarian, Vegan Diets and Multiple Health Outcomes: A Systematic Review with Meta-analysis of Observational Studies." *Critical Reviews in Food Science and Nutrition* 57(17), 3640–49. http://doi.org/10.1080/10408398.2016.1 138447.

27   Tantamango-Bartley, Y., Jaceldo-Siegl, K., Fan, J., and Fraser, G., 2012. "Vegetarian Diets and the Incidence of Cancer in a Low-risk Population." *Cancer Epidemiology Biomarkers & Prevention,* 22(2), 286–94. doi:10.1158/1055-9965.epi-12-1060.

28   Link, L.B., Canchola, A.J., Bernstein, L., Clarke, C.A., Stram, D.O., Ursin, G., and Horn-Ross, P.L., 2013. "Dietary Patterns and Breast Cancer Risk in the California Teachers Study Cohort." *The American Journal of Clinical Nutrition* 98(6), 1524–32. doi:10.3945/ajcn.113.061184.

29   Tantamango-Bartley, Y., Knutsen, S.F., Knutsen, R., Jacobsen, B.K., Fan, J., Beeson, W.L., Fraser, G., 2016. "Are Strict Vegetarians Protected Against Prostate Cancer?" *The American Journal of Clinical Nutrition* 103(1), 153–60. http://doi.org/10.3945/ajcn.114.106450.

30   Tantamango-Bartley, Y., Knutsen, S.F., Knutsen, R., Jacobsen, B.K., Fan, J., Beeson, W.L., Fraser, G., 2016. "Are Strict Vegetarians Protected Against Prostate Cancer?" *The American Journal of Clinical Nutrition* 103(1), 153–60. http://doi.org/10.3945/ajcn.114.106450.

31   Donaldson, M.S., 2004. "Nutrition and Cancer: A Review of the Evidence for an Anti-cancer Diet." *Nutrition Journal* 3(19). https://doi.org/10.1186/1475-2891-3-19.

32   Donaldson, M.S., 2004. "Nutrition and Cancer: A Review of the Evidence for an Anti-cancer Diet." *Nutrition Journal* 3(19).

https://doi.org/10.1186/1475-2891-3-19.; World Cancer Research Fund (WCRF) and American Institute for Cancer Research (AICR), 2007. *Food, Nutrition, Physical Activity, and the Prevention of Cancer: A Global Perspective*. Washington, DC: AICR, 2007.

33 Simopoulos, A.P., 2008. "The Importance of the Omega-6/Omega-3 Fatty Acid Ratio in Cardiovascular Disease and Other Chronic Diseases." *Experimental Biology and Medicine* 233(6), 674–88. doi: 10.3181/0711-MR-311.

34 Donaldson, M.S., 2004. "Nutrition and Cancer: A Review of the Evidence for an Anti-cancer Diet." *Nutrition Journal* 3(19). https://doi.org/10.1186/1475-2891-3-19; World Cancer Research Fund (WCRF) and American Institute for Cancer Research (AICR), 2007. *Food, Nutrition, Physical Activity, and the Prevention of Cancer: A Global Perspective*. Washington, DC: AICR, 2007.

35 Donaldson, M.S., 2004. "Nutrition and Cancer: A Review of the Evidence for an Anti-cancer Diet." *Nutrition Journal* 3(19). https://doi.org/10.1186/1475-2891-3-19; World Cancer Research Fund (WCRF) and American Institute for Cancer Research (AICR), 2007. *Food, Nutrition, Physical Activity, and the Prevention of Cancer: A Global Perspective*. Washington, DC: AICR, 2007.

36 Jones, L.W., and Demark-Wahnefried, W., 2006. "Diet, Exercise, and Complementary Therapies After Primary Treatment for Cancer." *The Lancet Oncology* 7, 1017–26; Rock, C.L., Doyle, C., Demark-Wahnefried, W., . . . Gansler, T., 2012. "Nutrition and Physical Activity Guidelines for Cancer Survivors." *Cancer Journal for Clinicians* 62, 243–74; Schwedhelm, C., Boeing, H., Hoffmann, G., Aleksandrova, K., and Schwingshackl, L., 2016. "Effect of Diet on Mortality and Cancer Recurrence Among Cancer Survivors: A Systematic Review and Meta-analysis of Cohort Studies." *Nutrition Review* 74(12), 737–48.

37 Schwedhelm, C., Boeing, H., Hoffmann, G., Aleksandrova, K., and Schwingshackl, L., 2016. "Effect of Diet on Mortality and Cancer Recurrence Among Cancer Survivors: A Systematic Review and Meta-analysis of Cohort Studies." *Nutrition Review* 74(12), 737–48.

38 Schwedhelm, C., Boeing, H., Hoffmann, G., Aleksandrova, K., and Schwingshackl, L., 2016. "Effect of Diet on Mortality and Cancer Recurrence Among Cancer Survivors: A Systematic Review and Meta-analysis of Cohort Studies." *Nutrition Review* 74(12), 737–48.

39 World Health Organization (WHO), 2016. *Global Report on Diabetes*. Retrieved August 15, 2018, from http://apps.who.int/iris/bitstream/handle/10665/204871/9789241565257_eng.pdf;jsessionid=BF89DB7186AB-851D57A341669616444B?sequence=1.

40 World Health Organization (WHO), 2016. *Global Report on Diabetes*. Retrieved August 15, 2018, from http://apps.who.int/iris/bitstream/handle/10665/204871/9789241565257_eng.pdf;jsessionid=BF89DB7186AB-851D57A341669616444B?sequence=1.

41 Tonstad, S., Butler, T., Yan, R., and Fraser, G.E., 2009. "Type of Vegetarian Diet, Body Weight, and Prevalence of Type 2 Diabetes." *Diabetes Care* 32(5), 791–96. http://doi.org/10.2337/dc08-1886; World Health Organization (WHO), 2016. *Global Report on Diabetes*. Retrieved August 15, 2018, from http://apps.who.int/iris/bitstream/handle/10665/204871/9789241565257_eng.pdf;jsessionid=BF89DB7186AB-851D57A341669616444B?sequence=1.

42 Diabetes Canada, 2018. *Are You at Risk?* Retrieved on August 16, 2018, from https://www.diabetes.ca/DiabetesCanadaWebsite/media/Managing-My-Diabetes/Tools%20and%20Resources/are-you-at-risk.pdf?ext=.pdf

43 Barnard, N.D., Cohen, J., Jenkins, D.J., Turner-McGrievy, G., Gloede, L., Green, A., and Ferdowsian, H., 2009. "A Low-fat Vegan Diet and a Conventional Diabetes Diet in the Treatment of Type 2 Diabetes: A Randomized, Controlled, 74-wk Clinical trial." *The American Journal of Clinical Nutrition* 89(5), 1588S–96S. http://doi.org/10.3945/ajcn.2009.26736H; Tonstad, S., Butler, T., Yan, R., and Fraser, G.E., 2009. "Type of Vegetarian Diet, Body Weight, and Prevalence of Type 2 Diabetes." *Diabetes Care* 32(5), 791–96. http://doi.org/10.2337/dc08-1886.

44 Tonstad, S., Butler, T., Yan, R., and Fraser, G.E., 2009. "Type of Vegetarian Diet, Body Weight, and Prevalence of Type 2 Diabetes." *Diabetes Care* 32(5), 791–96. http://doi.org/10.2337/dc08-1886.

45 Satija, A., Bhupathiraju, S.N., Rimm, E.B., Spiegelman, D, Chiuve, S.E., Borgi, L., Willett, W.C., Manson, J.E., Sun, Q., and Hu, F.B., 2016. "Plant-based Dietary Patterns and Incidence of Type 2 Diabetes in US Men and Women: Results from Three Prospective Cohort Studies." *Public Library of Science Medicine* 13 (e1002039).

46 Chen, Z., Zuurmond, M.G., Van der Schaft, N., Nano, J., Wijnhoven, H.A.H., Ikram, M.A., Franco, O.H., and Voortman, T., 2018. "Plant Versus Animal Based Diets and Insulin Resistance, Prediabetes and

Type 2 Diabetes: The Rotterdam Study."
European Journal of Epidemiology 33(9),
883–93. doi:10.1007/s10654-018-0414-8.

47 Satija, A., Bhupathiraju, S.N., Rimm, E.B.,
Spiegelman, D., Chiuve, S.E., Borgi, L.,
Willett, W.C., Manson, J.E., Sun, Q., and
Hu, F.B., 2016. "Plant-Based Dietary
Patterns and Incidence of Type 2 Diabetes
in US Men and Women: Results from Three
Prospective Cohort Studies." *PLoS Medicine*
13. https://doi.org/10.1371/journal.
pmed.1002039.

48 Tonstad, S., Butler, T., Yan, R., and Fraser,
G.E., 2009. "Type of Vegetarian Diet,
Body Weight, and Prevalence of Type 2
Diabetes." *Diabetes Care* 32(5), 791–96.
http://doi.org/10.2337/dc08-1886.

49 Chen, Z., Zuurmond, M.G., Van der Schaft,
N., Nano, J., Wijnhoven H.A.H., Ikram,
M.A., Franco, O.H., and Voortman, T.,
2018. "Plant Versus Animal Based Diets
and Insulin Resistance, Prediabetes and
Type 2 Diabetes: The Rotterdam Study."
European Journal of Epidemiology 33(9),
883–93. doi:10.1007/s10654-018-0414-8.

50 Satija, A., Bhupathiraju, S.N., Rimm, E.B.,
Spiegelman, D., Chiuve, S.E., Borgi, L.,
Willett, W.C., Manson, J.E., Sun, Q., and
Hu, F.B., 2016. "Plant-Based Dietary
Patterns and Incidence of Type 2 Diabetes
in US Men and Women: Results from Three
Prospective Cohort Studies." *PLoS Medicine*
13. https://doi.org/10.1371/journal.
pmed.1002039.

51 World Health Organization (WHO),
2016. *Global Report on Diabetes.*
Retrieved August 15, 2018, from
http://apps.who.int/iris/bitstream/
handle/10665/204871/9789241565
257_eng.pdf;jsessionid=BF89DB7186AB-
851D57A341669616444B?sequence=1.

52 Afshin, A., Micha, R., Khatibzadeh, S., and
Mozaffarian, D., 2014. "Consumption of
Nuts and Legumes and Risk of Incident
Ischemic Heart Disease, Stroke, and
Diabetes: A Systematic Review and
Meta-analysis." *American Journal of
Clinical Nutrition* 100, 278–88. http://doi.
org/10.3945/ajcn.113.076901; Boeing,
H., Bechthold, A., Bub, A., Ellinger, S.,
Haller, D., Kroke, A., Leschik-Bonnet, E.,
Müller, M.J., Oberritter, H., Schulze, M.,
Stehle, P., and Watzl, B., 2012. "Critical
Review: Vegetables and Fruit in the
Prevention of Chronic Diseases." *European
Journal of Nutrition* 51, 637–63; Diabetes
Canada, 2018. *Are You at Risk?* Retrieved
on August 16, 2018, from https://www.
diabetes.ca/DiabetesCanadaWebsite/
media/Managing-My-Diabetes/
Tools%20and%20Resources/are-you-
at-risk.pdf?ext=.pdf; Feskens, E.J., Sluik,
D., and van Woudenbergh, G.J., 2013.

"Meat Consumption, Diabetes, and Its
Complications." *Current Diabetes Reports*
13, 298–306; Jannasch, F., Kröger, J., and
Schulze, M.B., 2017. "Dietary Patterns and
Type 2 Diabetes: A Systematic Literature
Review and Meta-analysis of Prospective
Studies." *The Journal of Nutrition* 147(6),
1174–82. https://doi.org/10.3945/
jn.116.242552.

53 World Health Organization (WHO), 2018a.
Obesity and Overweight: Key Facts. Retrieved
August 17, 2018, from http://www.who.
int/news-room/fact-sheets/detail/
obesity-and-overweight.

54 World Health Organization (WHO), 2018a.
Obesity and Overweight: Key Facts. Retrieved
August 17, 2018, from http://www.who.
int/news-room/fact-sheets/detail/
obesity-and-overweight.

55 Farmer, B., Larson, B.T., Fulgoni, V.L.,
Rainville, A.J., and Liepa, G.U., 2011. "A
Vegetarian Dietary Pattern as a Nutrient-
dense Approach to Weight Management:
An Analysis of the National Health and
Nutrition Examination Survey 1999–2004."
Journal of the American Dietetic Association
111(6), 819–27. http://doi.org/10.1016/j.
jada.2011.03.012; Rizzo, N.S., Jaceldo-
Siegl, K., Sabaté, J., and Fraser, G.E.,
2013. "Nutrient Profiles of Vegetarian and
Nonvegetarian Dietary Patterns." *Journal
of the Academy of Nutrition and Dietetics*
113(12), 1610–19. http://doi.org/10.1016/j.
jand.2013.06.349; Sabaté, J., and Wien, M.,
2010. "Vegetarian Diets and Childhood
Obesity Prevention." *The American Journal
of Clinical Nutrition* 91(5). http://doi.
org/10.3945/ajcn.2010.28701f.

56 Sabaté, J., and Wien, M., 2010. "Vegetarian
Diets and Childhood Obesity Prevention."
*The American Journal of Clinical
Nutrition* 91(5). http://doi.org/10.3945/
ajcn.2010.28701f.

57 Rosell, M., Appleby, P., Spencer, E., and
Key, T., 2006. "Weight Gain Over 5
years in 21966 Meat-eating, Fish-eating,
Vegetarian, and Vegan Men and Women
in EPIC–Oxford." *International Journal
of Obesity* 30(9), 1389–96. http://doi.
org/10.1038/sj.ijo.0803305; Turner-
McGrievy, G.M., Davidson, C.R., Wingard,
E.E., Wilcox, S., and Frongillo, E.A., 2015.
"Comparative Effectiveness of Plant-based
Diets for Weight Loss: A Randomized
Controlled Trial of Five Different Diets."
Nutrition 31(2), 350–58. http://doi.
org/10.1016/j.nut.2014.09.002.

58 Sabaté, J., and Wien, M., 2010.
"Vegetarian Diets and Childhood Obesity
Prevention." *The American Journal
of Clinical Nutrition* 91(5). http://doi.
org/10.3945/ajcn.2010.28701f.

59 T.H. Chan School of Public Health, Harvard, 2018. "Obesity Prevention Source: Health Weight Checklist." Retrieved on August 17, 2018, from https://www.hsph.harvard.edu/obesity-prevention-source/diet-lifestyle-to-prevent-obesity/.

60 Cespedes, E.M., and Hu, F.B., 2015. "Nutrition: Dietary Prevention of Obesity and Cardiometabolic Disease." *Nature Reviews Endocrinology* 11(8), 448–49. doi: 10.1038/nrendo.2015.88.

61 House, J.S., Landis, K.R., Umberson, D., 1988. "Social Relationships and Health." *Science* 241(4865), 540–45; Uchino, B.N., 2006. "Social Support and Health: A Review of Physiological Processes Potentially Underlying Links to Disease Outcomes." *Journal of Behavioral Medicine* Aug. 29 (4): 377–87.

62 Barth, J., Schneider, S., and von Känel, R., 2010. "Lack of Social Support in the Etiology and the Prognosis of Coronary Heart Disease: A Systematic Review and Meta-analysis." *Psychosomatic Medicine* 72(3), 229–38.

63 Bassuk, S.S., Glass, T.A., and Berkman, L.F., 1999. "Social Disengagement and Incident Cognitive Decline in Community-dwelling Elderly Persons." *Annals of Internal Medicine* 131(3), 165–73.

64 Grant, N., Hamer, M., and Steptoe, A., 2009. "Social Isolation and Stress-related Cardiovascular, Lipid, and Cortisol Responses." *Annals of Behaviour Medicine* 37(1), 29–37.

65 Holt-Lunstad, J., Smith, T.B., and Layton, J.B., 2010. "Social Relationships and Mortality Risk: A Meta-analytic Review." *PLoS Medicine* 7(7), e1000316.

66 Steptoe, A., Shankar, A., Demakakos, P., and Wardle, J., 2013. "Social Isolation, Loneliness, and All-cause Mortality in Older Men and Women." *Proceedings of the National Academy of Sciences of the USA* 110(15), 5797–5801.

67 Monteiro, C.A., Cannon, G., Moubarac, J.C., Martins, A.P., Martins, C.A., Garzillo, J., Canella, D.S., Baraldi, L.G., Barciotte, M., Louzada, M.L., Levy, R.B., Claro, R.M., and Jaime, P.C., 2015. "Dietary Guidelines to Nourish Humanity and the Planet in the Twenty-first Century A Blueprint from Brazil." *Public Health Nutrition* 18(13), 2311–22. doi: 10.1017/S1368980015002165.

68 Gisslen, W., 2007. *Professional Cooking for Canadian Chefs: Sixth Edition*. Hoboken, NJ: John Wiley & Sons, Inc.; BC Ministry of Advanced Education, *FoodSafe Level One Student Workbook: Fourth Edition*, Victoria, BC: BC FoodSafe Secretariat, 2006.

69 Gisslen, W., 2007. *Professional Cooking for Canadian Chefs: Sixth Edition*. Hoboken, NJ: John Wiley & Sons, Inc., p. 30.

70 Gisslen, W., 2007. *Professional Cooking for Canadian Chefs: Sixth Edition*. Hoboken, NJ: John Wiley & Sons, Inc.

71 Health Canada, 2018. *Nutrition Facts Tables*. Retrieved on August 20, 2018, from https://www.canada.ca/en/health-canada/services/understanding-food-labels/nutrition-facts-tables.html.

Selected References

American Dietetic Association, 2003. "Position of the American Dietetic Association and Dietitians of Canada: Vegetarian Diets." *Journal of the American Dietetic Association*, 103(6): 748-65

Campbell, Thomas M., and T. Collin Campbell, 2012. "The Breadth of Evidence Favoring a Whole Foods, Plant-based Diet." Retrieved on August 20, 2018 from https://www.reliasmedia.com/articles/77085-the-breadth-of-evidence-favoring-a-whole-foods-plant-based-diet

Gonzales, J.F., N.D. Barnard, D.J. Jenkins, A.J. Lanou, B. Davis, G. Saxe and S. Levin, 2014. "Applying the Precautionary Principle to Nutrition and Cancer. *Journal of the American College of Nutrition*, 33(3), 239-246. doi: 10.1080/07315724.2013.866527

Mariotti, François, ed., 2017. *Vegetarian and Plant-Based Diets in Health and Disease Prevention*. London: Elsevier Inc. https://www.medicosadventistas.org/wp-content/uploads/2018/09/Fran%C3%A7ois-Mariotti-Eds.-Vegetarian-and-Plant-Based-Diets-in-Health-and-Disease-Prevention-Academic-Press-2017.pdf

Rinaldi, Sylvia, Emily E. Campbell, John Fournier, Colleen O'Connor and Janet Madill, 2016. "A Comprehensive Review of the Literature Supporting Recommendations from the Canadian Diabetes Association for the Use of a Plant-Based Diet for Management of Type 2 Diabetes." *Canadian Journal of Diabetes*, 40(5), 471-77

Satija, A., and F.B. Hu, 2018. "Plant-based Diets and Cardiovascular Health." *Trends in Cardiovascular Medicine*, 28(7), 437-41

Slavin, Joanne, 2013. "Fiber and Prebiotics: Mechanisms and Health Benefits." *Nutrients*, 5(4), 1417-35. http://doi.org/10.3390/nu5041417

Supic, G., M. Jagodic and Z. Magic, 2013. "Epigenetics: A New Link between Nutrition and Cancer." *Nutrition and Cancer*, 65(6), 781-92

Tuso, Philip, Mohamed H. Ismail, Benjamin P. Ha and Carole Bartolotto, 2013. "Nutritional Update for Physician: Plant-based Diets." *The Permanente Journal*, 17(2), 61-66. https://www.ncbi.nlm.nih.gov/pmc/articles/PMC3662288/

World Cancer Research Fund / American Institute for Cancer Research, 2018. "Diet, Nutrition, Physical Activity and Cancer: A Global Perspective." https://www.wcrf.org/dietandcancer

World Cancer Research Fund / American Institute for Cancer Research, 2018. "Wholegrains, Vegetables and Fruit and the Risk of Cancer." https://www.wcrf.org/sites/default/files/Wholegrains-veg-and-fruit.pdf

Acknowledgements

WOULD LIKE TO thank the following contributors and reviewers whose expertise made this book possible:

Thank you to my unstoppable team and book family, whose talents made this project come to life: Jaime Slavin, RD, Christine Song, Kelly-Anne Kerrigan, Bronwyn Cawker, Tamara Saslove, photographer Darren Kemper and assistant Will Putz, food stylists Nancy Midwicki and Heather Shaw, and prop stylist Franny Alder from Geary House Props. Thank you also to our non-stop supporters and contributors: Chef Lynn Crawford, Dr. David Jenkins, Tushar Mehta, Alison Fryer, Jillian Hillier, Vica Pelivan, Yinghua Liang, all the Culinary Management Nutrition (CMN) students who contributed their time and recipes, Gilda's Club Greater Toronto's members, board, staff and tireless volunteers, George Brown College, the Office of Research and Innovation and the CMN department, and the Social Sciences and Humanities Research Council (SSHRC) and its granting body, as well as my publicist, Corina Eberle, and the amazing team of editors and designers at Douglas & McIntyre. And finally, and most importantly, thank you to my irreplaceable family, chosen and provided, particularly the lady who has inspired my life's work to date: my mom, Sharon Helps-Symington.

Index

Page numbers in **bold** refer to photos.

About the Author

AMY SYMINGTON is a nutrition professor, research associate and plant-based chef at George Brown College. She is also the culinary nutrition program coordinator at Gilda's Club Greater Toronto, a not-for-profit that provides social support for those who have been touched by cancer, where she will be donating all royalties from the sales of this book.